DISCOVERING DENVER PARKS

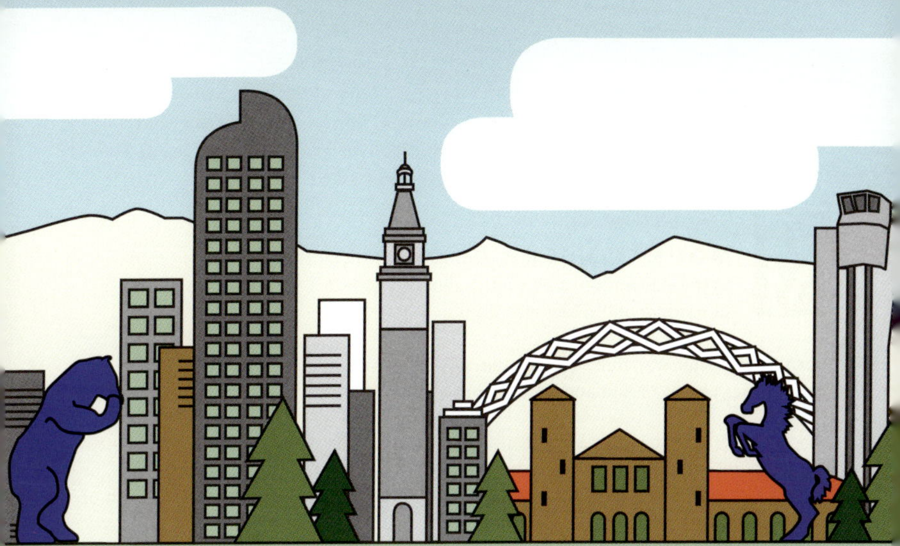

DISCOVERING DENVER PARKS

A LOCAL'S GUIDE

CHRIS ENGLERT

MOUNTAINEERS BOOKS is dedicated to the exploration, preservation, and enjoyment of outdoor and wilderness areas.

1001 SW Klickitat Way, Suite 201, Seattle, WA 98134
800-553-4453, www.mountaineersbooks.org

Printed in Korea
Distributed in the United Kingdom by Cordee, www.cordee.co.uk
First edition, 2020

Copyeditor: Diane Durrett
Design: Jen Grable
Layout and illustrations: McKenzie Long
Cartographer: Lohnes+Wright
All photographs by the author unless credited otherwise

Library of Congress Cataloging-in-Publication data is on file for this title.

Printed on FSC®-certified materials

ISBN (paperback): 978-1-68051-248-9
ISBN (ebook): 978-1-68051-249-6

An independent nonprofit publisher since 1960

Contents

NORTHWEST PARKS

EAST PARKS

NORTHEAST PARKS

SOUTHWEST PARKS

Denver Area

Denver Area
Broomfield
25
36
Thornton
76
Denver International Airport
93
Westminster
Arvada
Golden
70
see Northwest Denver map
70
see Northeast Denver map
70
DENVER
Idaho Springs
6
70
Lakewood
see East Denver map
Aurora
103
see Mountain Parks map
74
see Southwest Denver map
25
225
30
Morrison
Englewood
Littleton
Centennial
285
470
Highlands Ranch
85
Daniels Park
see Mountain Parks map
25
N
285
0   5   10 Miles

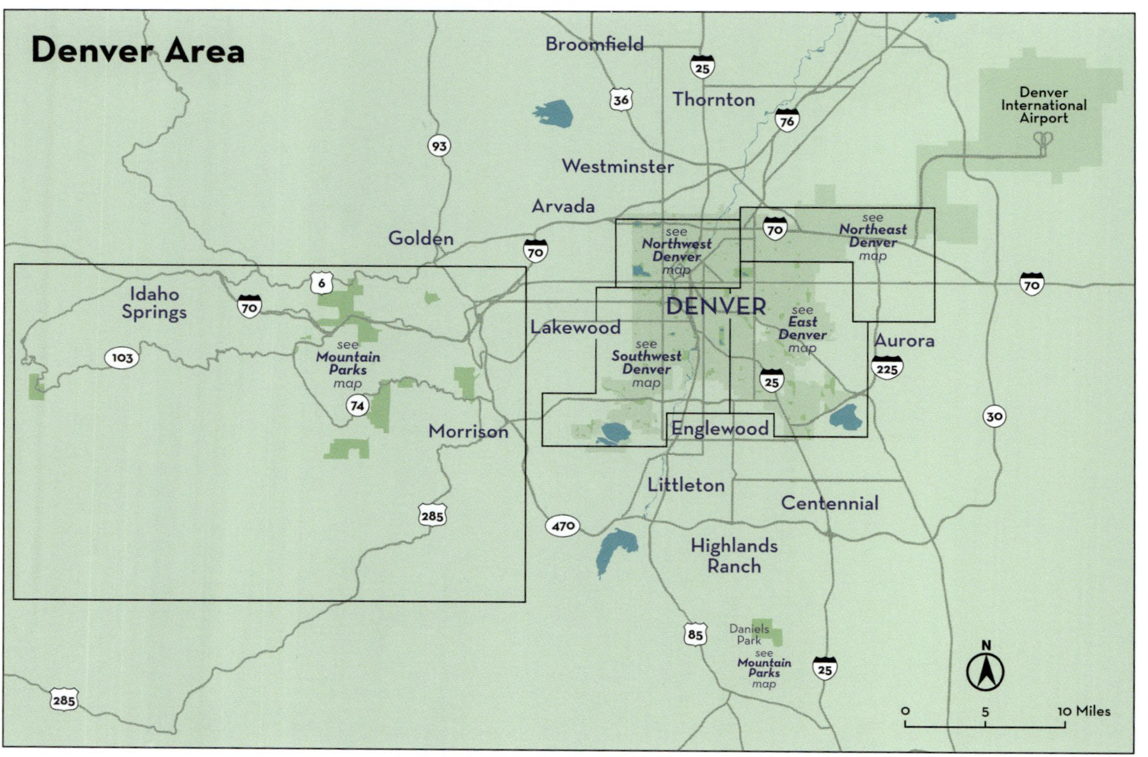

Introduction

In 2017 I set out to walk all of Denver's neighborhoods. A rowdy bunch of nine strangers joined me, and together we ten women walked seventy-eight loops of about 3 miles through each Denver neighborhood. Getting to know Denver on a pedestrian level with natives and newcomers alike changed my view of this fabulous, mile-high city.

We always started at a neighborhood park. Prior to each walk, I'd research a bit about the park and its neighborhood. Along the way, I began to learn about Denver's history. Some parks had no printed history, while others gushed volumes. Denver's founding leaders, forgotten civil rights advocates, and historic places came alive as I pieced together the mosaic of Denver's story.

I combined my new love for the parks with my existing love of walking the Denver Regional Trail System. People came to view me as an expert in trails and parks, and they began to ask me where they could take their kids, escape the noise of the city, and get a bit of exercise. The idea for this book came from these requests.

This book is for natives, locals, and newcomers alike. Whether you're a family of seven or of one, you'll find that Denver's parks have something for everyone. Grab your favorite ball, strap on your walking shoes, skates, or skis—or mount your bike, horse, hoverboard, or tricycle—and make your way outside. I've combined my love of history, the outdoors, and the joy of play in a way that I hope will make you want to get out and explore your neighborhood park, then the one next to that, and then every single one in Denver.

After visiting hundreds of parks, I realized that writing about every park in Denver would be a giant undertaking. Besides, some of the parks just weren't that inviting; they need a little freshening up. The focus of this book is on the most interesting parks within the city and county of Denver, a few regional parks that abut Denver's boundaries, and the best of Denver's Mountain Parks. Although not all of Denver's parks are included in this book, each park has value and is intriguing in its own way.

OPPOSITE: *Some of Denver's parks can satisfy just about everyone; visit Barnum Park for a fun day for the whole family.*

How to Use This Book

The city and county of Denver form a crazy polygon shape. Breaking the city into logical quadrants is awkward, although there are some obvious ways to regionalize the city around Interstates 25, 70, and 225, and Colorado Boulevard and Colfax Avenue. Even so, there is no one commonly agreed upon way to organize Denver into geographic sections. Thus, this book uses approximate boundaries to describe each region.

PARKS BY REGION

The parks in this book are organized into five distinct regions: Northwest, East, Northeast, Southwest, and Mountain Parks.

Parks in the Northwest are located west of Interstate 25 and north of 6th Avenue, east of I-25 to Downing Street and/or Colorado Boulevard, and north of I-70 to west of Colorado Boulevard. Parks in this region include: Inspiration Point, Sloan's Lake, and Globeville Landing. Some of the oldest parks in Denver are in the Northwest.

Parks in the East are located east of Downing Street, south of 26th Avenue, and north of Belleview Avenue. Parks in this region include: City Park, Cheesman Park, and Cherry Creek State Park. Here you'll find some of Denver's more well-known parks.

Parks in the Northeast are located north of 26th Avenue at Colorado Boulevard, east of Quebec Street all the way to the eastern county line in Green Valley Ranch and down to E. Mississippi Avenue. Parks in this region include: Green Valley Ranch East and West, Crescent, and Great Lawn. Here you'll find some of Denver's newer parks.

Parks in the Southwest are located south of 6th Avenue, west of Colorado Boulevard, south to the county line at Berry Avenue, and west to the county line at Kipling Street. Parks in this region include: Barnum, Ruby Hill, and Washington. Here you'll find many parks oriented around water.

OPPOSITE: *The city of Denver has Sister City relationships with more than a dozen cities throughout the world and expresses those relationships in corresponding parks; at City of Kunming Park you can learn about the Himalayas!*

Playing outside is a great way to engage all your senses for children and adults alike.

The Mountain Parks are city holdings in the Rocky Mountain Front Range in Jefferson County and Douglas County. Parks in this region include: Daniels, Genesee, and Lookout Mountain. Here you'll find parks with higher elevations and mountain trails.

Although most of the parks in the book are managed by the City of Denver, a few state parks are included due to their proximity to Denver.

FOLLOWING THE TRAILS

To understand the Denver park system, it's important to understand Denver Park and Recreation's ongoing strategy to connect the parks through its regional trail system. Throughout the book, there is reference to the Denver Regional Trail System. The four major trails within the system are the Sand Creek Greenway, the High Line Canal Trail, the Cherry Creek Trail, and the South Platte River Trail. Although there are other trails, these are the major bike and pedestrian thoroughfares of the system within Denver. You can access many of the parks via the trail system.

The Sand Creek Greenway runs northwest to southeast from the confluence of the Sand Creek and the South Platte River in Commerce City to the Aurora Soccer Fields in Aurora. It runs about 14 miles and somewhat parallels I-70.

The High Line Canal Trail is a 71-mile trail running from Green Valley Ranch in the northeast to Waterton Canyon in the southwest. It roughly parallels I-225 and then cuts west under I-25 to the foothills.

The Cherry Creek Trail is a 40-mile trail that runs from the confluence of the South Platte River Trail in downtown Denver to the southeast below the Cherry Creek Reservoir, where it ends at Franktown. It roughly follows Speer Boulevard to Parker Road.

The South Platte River Trail has many names depending on where in the trail it is. Within Denver, it's the South Platte River Trail. North of Denver it's the Front Range Trail, and south of Denver it's the Mary Carter Trail. The Denver portion of the trail is 18 miles long and roughly parallels I-25.

MAPS OF LARGE PARKS

In a few cases, this book features maps of the larger parks in order to give you an overview of the park's major features. Sometimes, several parks make up one large public area, and so a few of the smaller contingent parks are combined into one large map. For the most up-to-date information on Denver parks, you can find park maps at Denver Park and Recreation's website (denvergov.org/maps/map/parks) and the Colorado State Park website (cpw.state.co.us/placestogo/parks/pages/parkmap.aspx).

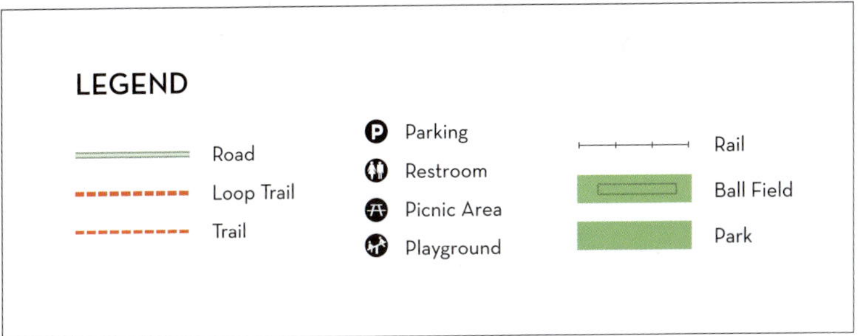

ABOUT THE PARK ENTRIES

To help you plan your outing and get the most from each visit, each entry contains at-a-glance icons, location information, acreage details, notes about amenities, advice for getting there, and a helpful description.

Icons Each park has something different to offer. The icons note key features found at a particular park. For more details, see "What the Icons Mean" below.

Location The street address of the park.

Acreage Approximate size of the park. In some cases, where several small parks make up one large public area, the acreages are summed.

Amenities The major amenities of the park. Note that Denver Parks and Recreation often updates the amenities in a park without notice.

Getting There Whether traveling by car, public transit, bike, or on foot, you can access the parks via these directions. Please note that it's always best to use GPS when traveling to a park, as construction and road or trail closures can modify these directions.

By Car Directions to the parks are offered via the main intersections if they are easily available. When exiting an interstate, the cardinal direction is given to start you in the correct direction to the park.

By Transit When available, public transit directions are offered. Always double check your transit information via Denver's Regional Transportation District website (www.rtd-denver.com).

By Bike Directions to the parks are offered from the perspective of the four major regional trails when possible, starting from the downtown area.

WHAT THE ICONS MEAN

Each park is amazing in its own way. The icons in each entry call out a few relevant key features.

♿	Accessible		Unpaved trails
👪	Kid-friendly		Paved paths
🦴	Dog-friendly		Lakefront
👓	Views		Riverfront
🏠	Historic significance		Spray park/wading pool
&	Public art		Horseback riding
🌼	Gardens	❄	Winter sports

Throughout Denver and especially on many of the trails that connect the parks, public art displays, like this one in Creekfront Park, brighten up walls.

Accessible Folks with assistive devices will find appropriate ramps and rails to approach and use the park and its facilities.

Kid-Friendly These parks have a playground, skate park, or other attractions that kids will like.

Dog-Friendly Outside of the designated dog parks, most Denver parks are dog friendly. After all, shelter and rescue dogs and cats are the official state pets of Colorado. Be sure dogs are leashed and that you pick up after them.

Views With the Rocky Mountains looming to the west, most Denver parks have great views. This icon is for when the views are beyond spectacular.

Historic Significance Most all of the parks have historical stories to tell. This icon is for the parks whose history is the bedrock of Denver.

Public Art Denver has a robust art program, and when the park has significant or relevant art on view, this icon is used.

Gardens If a manicured or seasonal garden appears in a park, you'll find this icon.

Unpaved Trails For parks with significant trail systems, an approximate total trail mileage is listed. Otherwise, most trails are under a mile and create a loop.

Paved Paths On these concrete paths, be sure to follow yielding rules. Bikes yield to everyone, pedestrians stay to the right, and horses always have the right-of-way. Skaters follow biking rules. Downhill yields to uphill.

Lakefront Parks that include or abut a lake.

Riverfront Parks that include or abut a river.

Spray Park/Wading Pool Designed with summer in mind, these areas squirt water or spray mist to entertain kids and adults alike.

Horseback Riding Horses are generally not allowed in Denver parks. But if horseback riding is allowed in a park, you'll find this icon.

Winter Sports When it snows, Denver plays. This icon denotes an ideal place for sledding, tubing, cross-country skiing, or ice skating (take note of thin ice warnings).

KEEP IN TOUCH

As parks and trails change, you can keep up with new information by visiting my website DenverByFoot.com and following me on social media at @DenverByFoot. I post suggestions daily for what parks to visit, what hikes to take in Denver, and how to enjoy Denver's bounty. You'll even find links there to my two-minute videos for every park in this book.

REFERENCES TO CHILDREN

Sprinkled in the park descriptions are references to "littles," "middles," and "bigs." These terms describe the approximate age and/or size of kids. Littles are toddlers and preschoolers, middles are elementary to middle schoolers, and bigs are middle schoolers to older kids.

Dog parks such as Willow Bark Park in Stapleton, grace all corners of the Denver park system.

Note: The information in this book was accurate at the time of printing. Denver Parks and Recreation is constantly changing the resources at parks, updating old equipment, and adding new features. Please take time to review the Denver Parks and Recreation website for updates and changes to ensure accuracy on park hours, permit requirements, access points, rules, and regulations. The publisher and the author are not responsible for any adverse effects or consequences resulting from the use of any of the suggestions presented in this book.

10 FUN FACTS
ABOUT DENVER PARKS

1 The city's founding mayors, including Robert Speer, wanted Denver to look like Paris, so they built a park system and parkways designed to allow Denverites to move through the city while surrounded by parks.

2 The Mountain Parks provide a place for Denverites to get out of the heat of the city during the summer. The Colorado Supreme Court legislation that allowed a city to own land outside of its contiguous boundaries was groundbreaking.

3 Curtis Park is Denver's oldest park and the first one to legally allow cuddling.

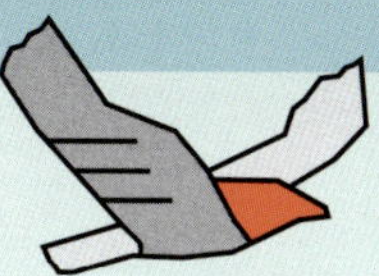

4 Several of Denver's parks, including Central Park and Heron Park, include remnants of the old Stapleton Airport runway.

5 City Park is Denver's biggest park within the city.

6 There are eleven Sister City Parks and thirteen Denver Sister Cities.

7 The City of Denver owns over sixty bison that reside within its parks, and they are descendants of the seven bison brought here from Yellowstone National Park in 1914.

8 As long as you have the proper fishing license, you can fish in most of the lakes or creeks within Denver parks.

9 Denver's Skate Park consistently ranks in the world's top ten list because of its variety of apparatuses and because it's free.

10 Denver has one of the world's only free snowboard obstacle courses in the world.

CHAMBERLIN OBSERVATORY

A Brief History of Denver's Parks

To understand why Denver's bounty of gorgeous parks, trails, and boulevards exist, you must think back to the frontier days. Denver led the charge for western expansion, growing from a mere 5,000 residents in 1875 to over 213,000 in 1910. A gold rush had fueled wild imaginations, wanderlusters, and adventurers to come West. With them came interesting morals, mismatched urban growth, and lots of quick money. By the time Robert Walter Speer was elected Denver's mayor in 1904, the city needed a strong personality with vision to clean it up, organize it, and transform it from a frontier village into a respectable city. Speer had big tasks, big visions, and big designs.

Over two terms marked by vice, politics, and frustration, Speer visited Europe and the World's Fair in Chicago. His ego grew as Denver grew, and his big plans for beautiful places in Denver that would rival Paris and Düsseldorf took shape. Under Speer's direction, Denver improved. Speer gets leadership credit for the banking of Cherry Creek, a doubling of the park system, citywide playgrounds, open-air swimming at Lincoln Park, the bathhouse at Washington Park, Berkeley Park's golf course, a boulevard system with ornamental lighting, Sunken Gardens, skating ponds, the Denver Museum of Nature and Science, the Denver Public Library, the Cheesman Memorial, Inspiration Point Park, the Pioneer Monument, the now-gone Mizpah Arch at Union Station, the McLellan Gateway at City Park, the City Park Esplanade, the electric fountain on Ferril Lake at City Park, the tradition of free concerts in parks, the distribution of 111,000 saplings for residents to plant citywide, the *Wynken, Blynken, and Nod* statue in Washington Park, the Thatcher Memorial Fountain in City Park, and more.

But his leadership wasn't confined to the city limits of Denver. To the west of Denver rise the giant Rocky Mountains. Their colors, from majestic purples to vibrant greens, set the tone of each day , and winter brings changing tops of white that reflect pink during sunrise. In the summers, the Rockies welcome city folk to cooler breezes, lush forests, and views that Kathrine Lee Bates chorused

OPPOSITE: *Although it's no longer an active research facility, Observatory Park's namesake still hosts nighttime sky watching.*

Several Denver parks reflect upon Native American history; Aztlan Park includes Mayan artwork as a theme throughout the park.

in "America the Beautiful." So with inspiration such as this, it was no wonder Denver's leadership wanted to provide a way for its citizens to enjoy their mountains.

Credit goes to Mayor Speer and John Brisben Walker (Red Rocks Park) way back in the early twentieth century for imagining what has become a system of open spaces. Walker fashioned the idea for the Mountain Parks as a way to bring tourism into the mountains. But his vision would require good planning, road building, and clout. Speer, together with a joint committee of commercial bodies, delivered those items and pitched the idea to Denver's citizens. Denverites loved the idea and passed a mill levy to pay for the vision. In 1912, Frederick Law Olmsted Jr., the designer of New York's Central Park, appeared on the scene to execute the vision with beauty.

You'll find many of Olmsted's trademark shelters and well stations (where people could draw water for their vehicles) throughout the Mountain Parks and park system. Together with J. J. Benedict and later with the help of the Civilian Conservation Corps, these designers and builders fashioned solutions from local granite and quartz. In addition, the road system built to access the Mountain Parks, known as the Bear Creek Canyon Scenic Mountain Drive and the Lariat Trail Scenic Mountain Drive, provides sweeping views of Denver and the Continental Divide with artistic flair.

In 1913, Denver had 30 parks for a total of 1,238 acres (not including the Mountain Parks). In 1971 the holdings had grown to 147 parks of 3,490 acres. Today, Denver Parks and Recreation has over 320 parks, dozens of recreation centers, hundreds of miles of trails, and a mountain park system that rivals the national parks. In fact, the Denver Mountain Park system features twenty-two accessible parks and twenty-four conservation areas. The Denver Mountain Parks, administered by Denver Parks and Recreation, features some 14,000 acres. It is described as being one of the most expansive park systems in the West.

It's worth noting that despite being listed on the National Register of Historic Places, the Mountain Parks need help. Although they once had dedicated funding from the city, they are now part of Denver Parks and Recreation's total budget. The advocacy group Denver Mountain Parks Foundation formed in order to rally for the preservation and funding of this local and national treasure. Learn more at www.mountainparksfoundation.org.

Denver citizens have always supported its parks, passing mill levies to pay for park growth and improvements. In 2018 the citizens passed the GO Bond, which once again funds new parks, better trails, and even the daylighting of lost waterways along Montclair Creek. In the next decade you'll see new parks in the Stapleton and Green Valley Ranch areas, open spaces appearing downtown, and greenway connections from Globeville Landing to Montclair. What will be your new favorite?

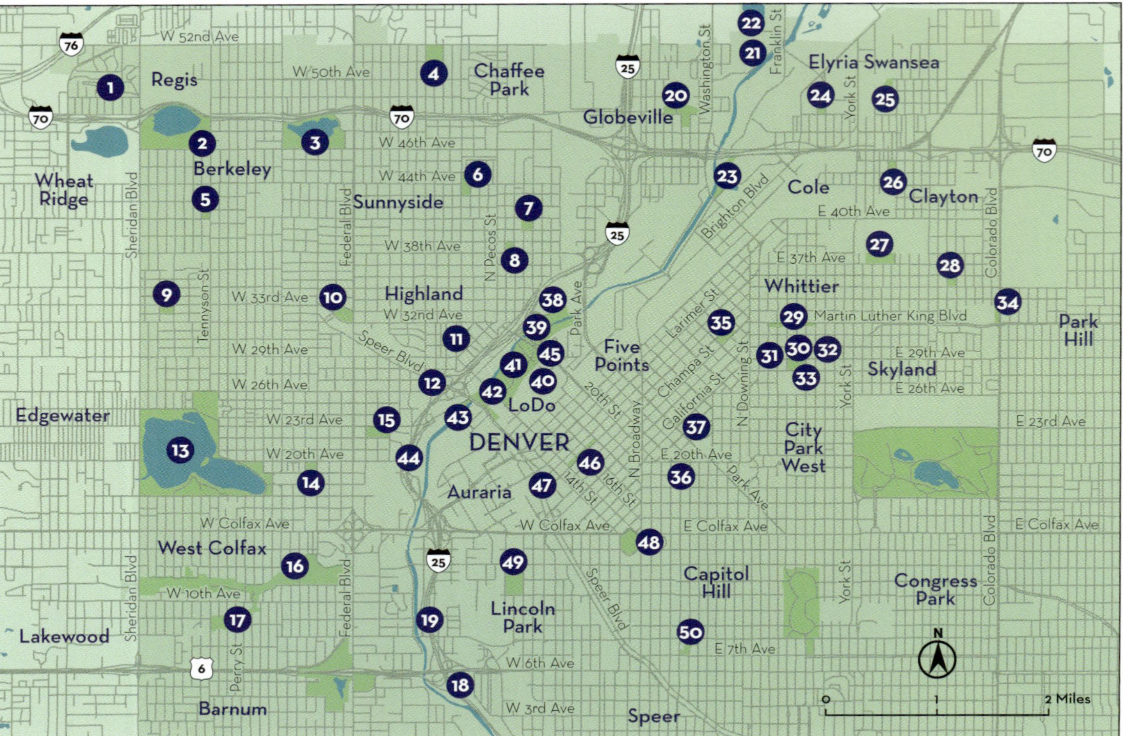

76
70
W 52nd Ave
Regis
W 50th Ave
Chaffee Park
1
25
70
Globeville
Washington St
22
21
Franklin St
Elyria Swansea
20
24
York St
25
Wheat Ridge
Sheridan Blvd
2
Berkeley
3
W 46th Ave
5
W 44th Ave
6
Sunnyside
Federal Blvd
7
23
Brighton Blvd
Cole
26
Clayton
E 40th Ave
70
Colorado Blvd
N Pecos St
8
25
27
E 37th Ave
28
W 38th Ave
9
W 33rd Ave
10
Highland
W 32nd Ave
Tennyson St
Speer Blvd
11
38
Park Ave
Whittier
34
Park Hill
35
Larimer St
29
Martin Luther King Blvd
39
45
31
30
32
E 29th Ave
Skyland
Five Points
Champa St
33
41
40
California St
N Downing St
E 26th Ave
12
42
LoDo
W 29th Ave
W 26th Ave
W 23rd Ave
Edgewater
15
43
37
City Park West
E 23rd Ave
13
DENVER
20th St
N Broadway
44
E 20th Ave
36
14
Auraria
47
46
14th St
16th St
Park Ave
York St
W 20th Ave
W Colfax Ave
W Colfax Ave
E Colfax Ave
48
E Colfax Ave
West Colfax
16
49
Capitol Hill
Congress Park
Colorado Blvd
W 10th Ave
Lincoln Park
17
Speer Blvd
York St
50
19
E 7th Ave
Lakewood
Sheridan Blvd
Perry St
6
Federal Blvd
18
N
W 6th Ave
Barnum
W 3rd Ave
Speer
0   1   2 Miles

NORTHWEST PARKS

1   INSPIRATION POINT PARK

360-degree views of Denver

Location: 4901 N. Sheridan Blvd., Denver
Acreage: 25.5
Amenities: Picnic tables, benches, bike/pedestrian path, flower beds, natural areas, scenic overlook

GETTING THERE

BY CAR Exit Sheridan Blvd. off I-70 and head north. Park is on the west side of the street just north of W. 49th Ave. **BY TRANSIT** Buses 44 and 52 stop near the east entrance. **BY BIKE** Take the Clear Creek Trail to Harlan St. to W. 49th Ave., or the Platte River Trail to Inca St. to W. 46th Ave. to Sheridan Blvd.

In 1906, Charles Mulford Robinson envisioned a vista point to see all of Denver and its Front Range. A few years later, this 25-acre park, designed by Henry Wright, opened. Western views up and down the Clear Creek Valley mean you can see from Pikes Peak in the south to Longs Peak in the north and everywhere in between. Look to the southeast and you'll have a full view of downtown Denver, to the east you'll overlook Willis Case Golf Course, and to the north you'll glimpse Boulder and maybe even Fort Collins. In the past, Inspiration Point was the go-to for late night trysts, but now it's popular in the daytime for families.

Inspiration Point draws you in with its gorgeous gardens.

As you enter the park and go up its eastern hillside, vibrant flower beds greet you in the spring and summer. At the top of the hill, you'll find picnic tables under linden, silver maples, honey locust, and hackberry, which sit next to an open area of ponderosa pines. Under the pines, knee-high native grasses invite you to roam and find nature. In the winter, sled down the banks.

Take the short 0.3-mile trail or meander through the pine trees and meadows to the west until you reach the edge of the bluff that overlooks the valley. As you work your way back east to the picnic tables, be sure to read the plaque on the north side of the park denoting where Louis Ralston found gold in 1850, spurring Colorado's gold rush.

EXTEND YOUR VISIT

Head south along Sheridan Boulevard just four blocks to **Berkeley Lake Park**, where you'll find a dog park, a lake, and across the street, Denver's oldest amusement park, Lakeside.

2   BERKELEY LAKE PARK

Fun with dogs and kids

Location: 4601 W. 46th Ave., Denver
Acreage: 81
Amenities: Dog park, lake, flower beds, drinking fountain, picnic shelter, picnic tables, playground, recreation center, outdoor pool, basketball court, tennis court, bike/pedestrian path, soccer field, baseball/softball field, restroom, benches, picnic area

GETTING THERE

BY CAR Take I-70 to Sheridan Blvd. Go south to W. 46th Ave. Go east to the parking lot on the north side of the street. **BY TRANSIT** Buses 38, 44, and 52 stop near the entrance. **BY BIKE** Take the Clear Creek Trail to Harlan to W. 49th Ave. to Sheridan Blvd., or the Platte River Trail to Inca to 46th Ave. to Sheridan Blvd.

This park has something for everyone and is easily accessible. It also sits across from Denver's oldest amusement park, Lakeside. Berkeley Lake has always attracted the neighborhood's residents. John Walker, an early Denver farmer, originally used the lake to irrigate alfalfa, and eventually a racetrack was built around it. By 1906 the city purchased the property, adding it to George Kessler's Denver Park and Parkway System. From there, the city's first public golf course appeared, cobblestone restrooms and a bathhouse were added, and the William H. Smiley branch of Denver Public Library opened. In 1927 the park got a bit of a face-lift and S. R. DeBoer rerouted the roads to limit commuter traffic through the park. Cedar, oak, pine, birch, and cottonwood provided shade for lake goers. Interstate 70 settled the northern boundary of the park. Soon afterward, residents petitioned for the park to enter the National Register of Historic Places.

Thanks to its recreation center, eight tennis courts, dog park, 1 mile of concrete paths, and dirt trails around the lake, you'll always find folks out enjoying the park.

EXTEND YOUR VISIT

About a mile to the east is Berkeley's sister park, **Rocky Mountain Lake Park**. It has similar facilities, although it's a bit smaller. You can access Rocky Mountain Park by walking east along 46th Avenue. Along the way, you'll see how the area grew into a modern Denver suburb.

3   ROCKY MOUNTAIN LAKE PARK

See the Rockies!

Location: 3301 W. 46th Ave., Denver
Acreage: 55.5
Amenities: Drinking fountain, restroom, baseball/softball field, bike/pedestrian path, football field, horseshoe pits, lake, flower beds, tennis court, playground, benches, picnic tables, picnic area

A giant frog welcomes kids to leap around at Rocky Mountain Lake Park.

GETTING THERE

BY CAR Take I-70 to Sheridan Blvd. Go south to W. 46th Ave. Go east to the parking lot on the north side of the street. **BY TRANSIT** Buses 44 and 52 stop near the entrance. **BY BIKE** Take the Clear Creek Trail to Harlan St. to W. 49th Ave. to Sheridan Blvd. or the Platte River Trail to Inca St. to 46th Ave.

With the Rockies beaming to the west, Rocky Mountain Lake Park, not to be confused with Rocky Mountain National Park, is the sister park to Berkeley Lake Park, just a mile away. Like its sister, Rocky Mountain Lake Park has a lake for fishing, and a 1-mile walking trail loops around the lake. Ball fields and horseshoe pits provide opportunities for some family play or a chance to watch the neighborhood games. A playground with a large frog attracts younger kids, while picnic tables and plenty of shade around the lake welcome lollygaggers and relaxers. For a bit more action, head to the two tennis courts here.

EXTEND YOUR VISIT

If you have your dog with you, head west on 46th Avenue to **Berkeley Lake Park** and its fun dog park.

4   51ST & ZUNI

Fields of view

Location: 5100 N. Zuni St., Denver
Acreage: 12.75
Amenities: Benches, picnic tables, playground, baseball/softball field, basketball court, picnic shelter, drinking fountain, bike/pedestrian path, picnic area, fitness zone

GETTING THERE

BY CAR From I-70, take the N. Pecos St. exit to the north. Take a left on W. 52nd Ave. The park will be on your left. **BY TRANSIT** Buses 19 and 52 stop nearby. **BY BIKE** Take the South Platte River Trail to E. 47th Ave. Go north on Broadway then west on 48th Ave. Take a right on Vallejo St. The park will be on your left.

This unnamed park has a lot of open fields to play in, plus a 3.5-mile wellness track to get your heartrate up.

You have excellent views into downtown Denver from this unnamed park at 51st and Zuni. Be sure to bring your Frisbee because there are acres and acres of open fields to toss a ball, throw a horseshoe, or swing a bat. And you'll find plenty of room to roam. Come in the evening and catch a local pick-up game of baseball at the ball field, sit on the benches and enjoy the view, or do a workout session in the free-standing gym. A kids' playground of swings, teeter-totters, and climbing walls sits next to the outdoor fitness center, so the entire family can enjoy playtime at the same time. Plenty of parking can be had on the streets alongside the park.

When Denver has a good snowfall, this park attracts all the neighborhood kids for fun downhill sledding. Adults strap on their cross-country skis and do laps. You might even find colonies of snowpeople standing guard.

EXTEND YOUR VISIT

A well-marked, 3.5-mile Wellness Trail connects pedestrians and cyclists of the **Chaffee Park** neighborhood with the Regis neighborhood to its west. This loop features several points of interest, including the **Clear Creek Trail**, **Rocky Mountain Lake Park**, and the **Sister Gardens at Aria**. Just to the west along West 52nd Avenue is **Regis University**. You can enjoy a nice walk on its campus to view some beautiful public art. On the north side of the campus, locate the statue of James Joyce. Regis

University commissioned the piece, rejected the original due to some unwanted quotes from Joyce's *Ulysses*, and after alterations were made on a second piece, installed the current version. The original was returned to Dublin.

5   CÉSAR E. CHÁVEZ PARK

Inspiring—and there's ping-pong!

Location: 4131 N. Tennyson St., Denver
Acreage: 2.5
Amenities: Picnic tables, benches, playground, basketball court, baseball/softball field, picnic area, bocce ball court, ping-pong table

GETTING THERE

BY CAR Take I-70 to Tennyson St. Head south; the park will be on your right. **BY TRANSIT** Buses 38 and 44 stop nearby. **BY BIKE** Take the South Platte River Trail to E. 47th Ave. Go north on Broadway then west on 48th Ave. Take a left on Zuni St., a right on W. 46th Ave., a left on Tennyson St.

Square in the center of the fast-flipping Berkeley neighborhood sits the socially conscious César E. Chávez Park. Originally named Alcott Park, the park's name was changed in 2005 to César E. Chávez Park. Named after the American labor leader and civil rights activist who helped organize migrant farm workers, the park oozes with thoughts about workers' rights. You'll find vibrant murals along the outer perimeter of the park and stamped concrete with sayings such as, "The fight is never about grapes or lettuce . . ." You'll even find a bust of Chávez overlooking Tennyson Street.

Chávez, together with Rodolfo "Corky" Gonzales and other Chicano leaders, made their mark on Denver in the 1970s. (See Columbus, Paco Sanchez, and Aztlan Parks.)

This small but mighty park has basketball and bocce ball courts,

César Chávez had a giant impact on Denver, and several of his sayings are embedded in this park's concrete.

soccer fields, plus ping-pong tables and a great playground for kids. It attracts latte-sipping moms hanging around in the late afternoon and teens in the evening.

EXTEND YOUR VISIT

Tennyson Street bursts with restaurants, bars, and chic shops. You'll even find stroller parking and water bowls for pets up and down this trendy shopping area.

MUSIC IN THE PARK

The Sunnyside Music Festival started in 2000 as the Sunnyside Bluegrass Festival. A local couple would invite their friends over to listen to two bands, drink two kegs of beer, and hang out. In 2004 the couple moved away, and the growing festival went defunct. But in 2007 local Sunnysiders organized to get the proper permits and a grant or two to underwrite the festival. It revived, and now locals look forward to this public event that occurs the second Saturday in September.

6   JEROME B. CHAFFEE PARK

The neighborhood parties here

Location: 1901 W. 43rd Ave., Denver
Acreage: 5
Amenities: Benches, drinking fountain, picnic tables, playground, restroom, basketball court, baseball/softball field

GETTING THERE

BY CAR From I-70, take N. Pecos St. exit to the south. Take a right on W. 46th Ave., then a left on Tejon St. **BY TRANSIT** Buses 44 and 52 stop nearby. **BY BIKE** Take the South Platte River Trail to E. 47th Ave. to Broadway and take a right. Take a left on W. 48th Ave. to N. Pecos St. Take a right to W. Elk Place then a left on Quivas St. Take a right on W. 46th Ave. then a left on Tejon St.

Square in the middle of the Sunnyside neighborhood sits Chaffee Park, not to be confused with the neighborhood called Chaffee Park. This community park, punctuated by Mark Lansdon's lively steel flower sculpture, *Garden of Flowers*, is the heartbeat of the neighborhood and where the community organizes its annual Sunnyside Music Festival in September.

Bright metal flowers tower as public art in Chaffee Park.

Even if it's not time for the music festival, you can still enjoy a game of pick-up basketball, toss a ball on the ball fields, or let your kids scale the climbing wall, twist on the bridge, and drive a tractor!

In 1892 the city purchased the land for the park from Ezra Humphreys for $10,000. Ezra lived with her brother, Ed Brinkley, who died tragically when his horse darted in front of a moving train operated by Burlington Railroad.

EXTEND YOUR VISIT

Elsewhere in the neighborhood at 3825 Shoshone Street is the **Troy Chavez Memorial Peace Garden**. After gang violence many years ago, parents in the community organized to provide a safe place for kids to reflect, garden, and meditate. Enjoy this peaceful area with your family.

7   AZTLAN PARK

A little Aztecan art history in the city

Location: 4435 N. Navajo St., Denver
Acreage: 3.6
Amenities: Recreation center, benches, picnic tables, playground, outdoor pool, basketball court, baseball/softball field, soccer field

GETTING THERE

BY CAR From I-70, take the N. Pecos St. exit. Head south to W. 46th Ave., take a left then take a right on Navajo St. The park is on the corner of Navajo and 44th. **BY TRANSIT** Buses 19 and 52 stop nearby. **BY BIKE** Take the South Platte River Trail through the City of Cuernavaca Park to Inca St. to W. 44th Ave.

Aztlan Park sits on the corner of a very busy community. The small park invites children to play on the swings, slides, and climbers, and it even has a stand-up sand pit for making messy hands. Embedded in the concrete are mythical Aztecan creatures and their names, while larger Aztecan art pieces crown the center of the park.

The term "Aztlan" refers to the southwestern United States and is considered the mythical homeland of Chicanos from where the Chichimecas—forefathers of the Aztecs—migrated south.

Next to the park is the Aztlan Recreation Center with pool, ball fields, indoor gym equipment, basketball gym, and ping-pong tables. The interior and the exterior of the gym have murals reflecting Aztecan culture, including a scene of an eagle rising upon someone's life transition.

Across from the recreation center is the Quigg Newton Community Center and down the street is Denver Health. If you have appointments at any of these nearby facilities, this little corner playground is a great place for the kids to have a break before or after. If they have a MY Denver Card, they can enjoy the recreation center as well. Children living in Denver can get a MY Denver Card from any Denver recreation center, which they can use to get free access to the facilities of all the recreation centers in the city.

EXTEND YOUR VISIT

Visit **Columbus Park** just down the street to continue your exploration of the Chicano influence on this area.

8　COLUMBUS PARK

Otherwise known as La Raza Park

Location: 1501 W. 38th Ave., Denver
Acreage: 2.3
Amenities: Picnic tables, playground, plaza, basketball court, benches, flower beds

GETTING THERE

BY CAR From I-25, exit W. 38th/Fox St. to the west. Park is between Navajo and Osage. **BY TRANSIT** Buses 19 and 35 stop nearby. **BY BIKE** From the South Platte River Trail, exit Jason St. Jason turns into W. 36th Ave. Turn right on Navajo and left on W. 38th Ave.

Columbus Park, called Navajo Park until it got a name change in the 1970s, was at the center of political struggle between the Italian-American and Chicano communities in Denver. It once held a swimming pool and was the social hub of the neighborhood. Struggles between these two communities persisted for years, but harmony now reigns.

"El Viaje" tells a powerful story in Columbus Park, which is also known as La Raza Park.

I AM JOAQUIN

The late 1960s and early 1970s in Denver saw the rise of the Chicano movement. Migrant farm workers wanted to unionize to create better working conditions. Together with the voices and leadership of César Chávez and Corky Gonzales, they organized boycotts of grapes and Coors beer, arranged student sit-ins and walkouts, and gathered their power into a rallying cry for the Hispanic populations. At the same time, Gonzales published a poem entitled "Yo Soy Joaquin" that eloquently identified and named Chicanos. Together with the radio personality of Paco Sanchez, the Chicano population in Denver amplified its voice. Various parks in Northwest and West Denver acknowledge this history, including Aztlan, Columbus, Paco Sanchez, and César E. Chávez Parks.

Rodolfo "Corky" Gonzales started the La Raza movement here, giving voice to the community. In 1990 a kiosk in the style of an Aztec pyramid was built in this park, and artist David Ocelotl Garcia painted beautiful murals on its tiered ceilings that celebrate the rise of the Chicano movement within Denver. Now much quieter, you can sit in this historic park and reflect on how areas change and how people express themselves. Spring flower beds run through the center of the park, and a playground sits in its northeast corner.

EXTEND YOUR VISIT

Nearby, you'll find **Aztlan**, **Paco Sanchez**, and **César E. Chávez Parks**, which continue the story of Chicano influence in Denver.

9 PFERDESTELLER PARK

Play hide-and-seek in a tree

Location: 4815 W. Moncrieff Pl., Denver
Acreage: 3
Amenities: Drinking fountain, benches, picnic tables, playground, restroom, basketball court, soccer field, picnic area

GETTING THERE

BY CAR From I-70, take Sheridan Blvd. south. Take a left on W. Moncrieff Pl. **BY TRANSIT** Buses 32 and 38 stop nearby. **BY BIKE** Take the South Platte River Trail to

15th St. Turn left on W. 29th Ave. Turn right on Tennyson St. Turn left on W. Moncrieff Pl.

This small neighborhood park is named after the president of the local typesetters union, Fred Pferdesteller, who did double duty as deputy district attorney. He was kidnapped in 1945; his abductor, who was captured and brought to justice, escaped the Colorado State Penitentiary in 1947—only to be captured again.

Tree trunk or mastodon? Either way, it's fun for kids at Pferdesteller Park.

Young kids may not care about the history, but they'll love the park's gear that's focused on tots, and they'll have fun playing hide-and-seek with you in the re-created tree trunk with secret spots to explore. You can also shoot some hoops or kick a soccer ball around on the grassy field. This might even be the perfect park to count clouds.

EXTEND YOUR VISIT

If you have older kids, head just to the east to **Highland Park** where the equipment draws bigger kids.

10 HIGHLAND PARK

A place for play where once only the wealthiest could walk

Location: 3265 N. Federal Blvd., Denver
Acreage: 7
Amenities: Picnic tables, playground, basketball court, benches, library, bike/pedestrian path

GETTING THERE

BY CAR Take I-25 to Speer. Go north to Federal Blvd. Take a left on 32nd Ave. **BY TRANSIT** Buses 32 and 38 stop nearby. **BY BIKE** Take the South Platte River Trail to 15th St. Go west to W. 29th Ave. Take a right on Zuni St. Take a left on W. Dunkeld Pl., which turns into Clay St. Take a left on W. 32nd Ave. to the park.

Sitting in the shadows of the old Potter Highlands mansions, this park echoes with the sounds of neighborhood kids at play. With a playground full of kids from tots to teens, caregivers gather in the late morning to chat while the kids romp. South of the playground sits a large grassy field just waiting for kickballs to be booted. Next to the grassy field is the historic Woodbury branch of the Denver Public Library. Although Federal Boulevard edges the eastern border of the park, quiet and relaxation can happen on the western and southern edges.

Be sure to admire the historic homes that ring the park, and drop in to the library if you need water or restrooms. The city purchased the park land from Charles Hallack (see Hallack Park) for $18,000 on May 27, 1899. This area historically was the place where the richer folks settled, as opposed to the smoggy, dirty area of "The Bottoms" along the South Platte River (see Commons Park). Not only did they want cleaner air, they wanted a more moral and upright way of life, which they couldn't find elsewhere in the rough-and-tumble frontier town of Denver.

EXTEND YOUR VISIT

If you have younger kids, head west along 32nd Avenue to **Pferdesteller Park**. A bit smaller and quieter, this park features a playground that is just right for younger kids. Look for a re-created tree trunk that gives them a chance to play hide-and-seek.

11 HIRSHORN PARK

Heartbeat of the Highland neighborhood

Location: 3000 N. Tejon St., Denver
Acreage: 2
Amenities: Benches, picnic tables, drinking fountain, playground, baseball/softball field, bleachers, basketball court

GETTING THERE

BY CAR Take I-25 to the 20th St. exit. Take a right and then a left on Central. Take a right on 16th St., which merges into Tejon St. **BY TRANSIT** Buses 32 and 44 stop nearby. **BY BIKE** Take the South Platte River Trail to the Highland Bridge. Turn left on Central, right on 16th St., then right on Tejon St.

Squeezed onto a rhombus shape in the middle of Highland neighborhood sits the very active Hirshorn Park. Locals will secretly tell you the baseball field, surrounded by a fence, is an unofficial dog park. Next to it is a lovely little playground for the younger kids that squeezes in next to a basketball court. Many of the folks enjoying Hirshorn grab an ice cream at Little Man Ice Cream across the street and amble into the park to sit and people-watch. Make the park your starting point for a walking date, then venture afield into a bevy of good neighborhood places to eat. Parking can be tough, so arriving by foot or bike is your best bet.

EXTEND YOUR VISIT

Grab your ice cream and meander through the **Highland neighborhood**. Originally made up of over thirty-five subdivisions including Highlands, Potter Highlands, and Scottish Highlands, the neighborhood features giant mansions, quaint cottages, and every type of housing flip you can imagine.

12   DIAMOND HILL PROMENADE

A minute diamond in the rough!

Location: 2600 N. Zuni St., Denver
Acreage: 1.9
Amenities: Bike/pedestrian path, benches

GETTING THERE

BY CAR Take I-25 to Speer. Go west. At the intersection of Speer and Zuni, it's on the left. **BY TRANSIT** Bus 28 stops nearby. **BY BIKE** Take the South Platte River Trail to Speer Blvd. Go west to intersection of Speer and Zuni.

This linear park allows Highland residents and those on Diamond Hill to access the South Platte River Trail and downtown. The small green space at the intersection of Zuni and Speer offers two surprises: the great view right into downtown across I-25 and the red adobe tiles set into the large monuments on either side of Speer Boulevard. In the tiles, you can

Diamond Hill Promenade unravels the mystery of why Denver has such cattywampus intersections.

see a re-creation of Denver's street grid in relation to the South Platte River, illustrating how the two grid systems come together on the diagonal, making a series of diamonds.

EXTEND YOUR VISIT

Jump on the connector trail down to the **South Platte River** and enjoy a day along the river, biking or walking its banks.

13 SLOAN'S LAKE PARK

"The Leaky Sloan"

Location: 1700 N. Sheridan Blvd., Denver
Acreage: 284
Amenities: Drinking fountain, picnic tables, picnic shelter, playground, restroom, basketball court, bike/pedestrian path, football field, soccer field, baseball/softball field, tennis court, lake, boating, flower beds, picnic area

GETTING THERE

BY CAR Take I-70 to Sheridan Blvd. Go south to the lake. **BY TRANSIT** Buses 16 and 51 stop nearby. **BY BIKE** Take the South Platte River Trail to W. 17th Ave./Dick Connor Ave. Turn right on Sheridan to the park.

Let's start with how the neighborhood got its official name. Actually, we have to go back to before the official naming. In 1861, Thomas M. Sloan decided he needed some water for his farm. So he drilled a well and supposedly punched a hole into the unknown aquifer below. It sprang a leak, and twenty-four hours later, a lake was born. It has been called Sloan's Leak, Sloan Lake, and Sloan's Lake. For decades, the names interchanged.

In the early 1990s the local residents gathered signatures on a petition to officially name the neighborhood Sloan's Lake. The City of Denver then changed all the names designating the neighborhood as Sloan's Lake. But someone forgot to tell the city's copywriter, and thus, the city officially calls the neighborhood Sloan Lake although the residents call it Sloan's Lake.

Regardless of its official name, Sloan's Lake has invited Denverites to its shores for over a century. Pleasure boats once cruised the lake (and ultimately sank), and historic Manhattan Beach, an amusement park, once housed circus acts, ostrich-drawn Cinderella sleds, elephants, and even human cannonballs. Today, the lake

Sloan's Lake with its 3-mile circumference started as an accidental leak, or did it?

has sailboats, paddleboats, and if it ever gets cold enough again for the lake to freeze for consecutive days, ice skating.

Walking around the lake on the paved or unpaved paths, you'll clock about 3 miles. Elsewhere in the park, you'll find shorter trails connecting and weaving through the lake's loop trail. You'll also pass the marina, outdoor art, playgrounds, memorial gardens, tennis courts, ball fields, picnic tables and shelters, picnic areas, and restrooms. The best way to enjoy the lake is to just park in one of the many lots around the lake and get out.

Many festivals happen on the lake including the Lake Art and Music Festival and the Colorado Dragon Boat Festival in the summer. You'll often find 5K and 10K running contests, and you might even happen across the funky, free Glow-in-the-Dark Dance Walk put on by the organization Walk2Connect.

EXTEND YOUR VISIT

You can spend an entire day at this park, but if you get hungry, check out the many local places to eat along **Sheridan Boulevard**.

14   HALLACK PARK

From lumberyard to muddy field to neighborhood park

Location: 1900 N. Julian St., Denver
Acreage: 3
Amenities: Picnic tables, playground, soccer field, benches

GETTING THERE

BY CAR Take I-25 to exit 211 toward 23rd/20th Ave. Follow 20th to Irving. **BY TRANSIT** Buses 1, 16, 20, and the light rail W line stop nearby. **BY BIKE** Take the South Platte River Trail to W. 17th Ave./W. Dick Connor Ave. Go west to Irving St. Take a right on Irving St. to 19th Ave.

This park was once the location of the Hallack & Howard lumberyard, and freight cars were once built here. After a fire destroyed this commercial area, the land eventually became a muddy parking lot for the nearby Mile High Stadium. For years, the only thing to do here was to make mud pies. But thanks to the efforts of local citizens, this is now a wonderful neighborhood park. With two playgrounds that have an insect and butterfly theme, Hallack Park provides plenty of fun for kids from smalls to talls. There's also plenty of room to romp and roll on the grass where soccer fields are lined in chalk and soccer goals await positioning. The paved perimeter path offers about a half-mile loop.

EXTEND YOUR VISIT

About eight blocks to the west is the large **Sloan's Lake Park**, a mecca for great walks, picnics, and outdoor leisure.

15   JEFFERSON PARK

Arguably, Denver's first suburban park

Location: 2201 N. Clay St., Denver
Acreage: 6.6
Amenities: Benches, picnic shelter, picnic tables, playground, restroom, drinking fountain, basketball court, picnic area

GETTING THERE

BY CAR Take I-25 to exit 211. Continue on W. 23rd Ave. to Clay St. **BY TRANSIT** Buses 10 and 28 stop nearby. **BY BIKE** Take the South Platte River Trail to Water St. Go west to W. 23rd and Clay. Turn left to the park.

Jefferson Park, which came about through a series of annexations and maneuvers within the Highland neighborhoods, could be considered Denver's first suburban park. This determination is debatable, and one that many Highlanders will arm wrestle you over.

Denver's first suburban park, Jefferson Park, offers a playground with a view.

The city purchased the park on May 11, 1889, from Marcia Chipman, society editor for the Delta Gamma sorority, for $10,000. Despite its glamorous origin, Jefferson Park has always needed love and attention from its neighbors. It's an area many folks have had other plans for, causing the neighborhood to rally often. At one time, when the area had become undesirable and homes fell into disrepair, developers had many ideas and plans for the land, including turning it into an amphitheater. But the neighbors fended off those schemes, and others like it, to protect their space and defend it from development.

Now it's a wonderful neighborhood park sitting in the middle of the Jefferson Park neighborhood. It overlooks the valley, Mile High Stadium, and downtown Denver. Showing a love for the local NFL football team, the Broncos, the two playground areas are painted in Bronco's blue and orange. As in most neighborhood parks, there are open fields, picnic tables, and a covered picnic area.

EXTEND YOUR VISIT

Jefferson Park's sidewalks invite a good stroll through this historic neighborhood of homes from the 1880s to the present.

16   PACO SANCHEZ PARK

One park, two characters

Location: 1290 N. Knox Ct., Denver
Acreage: 29
Amenities: Playground, basketball court, bike/pedestrian path, Lakewood Gulch Trail, baseball/softball field, benches, picnic tables

GETTING THERE

BY CAR Take I-25 to Colfax. Go west to N. Knox Ct. Take a left to the park. **BY TRANSIT** Bus 1 and the light rail W line stop nearby. **BY BIKE** Take the South Platte River Trail to Lakewood Gulch Trail. Go west to the park.

This large park, split in the middle by the light rail that runs through the historic location of the old Interurban Shortline Railway, has two very different parts. On the south side, the park opens up to wide space where Lakewood Gulch runs through. You can follow the gulch and its trail to the west for 3 to 4 miles to Lakewood, or you can go east for 1 to 2 miles to downtown Denver. All along the gulch are footbridges, and the gulch meanders with mostly quiet banks for fun amphibian hunting. On the south side, you'll also find a basketball court.

On the north side, the entire theme of the park echoes that of its namesake, Francisco "Paco" Sanchez. Paco arrived in Denver in 1948 as the front man for a Latin music group. He quickly learned that Denver had no radio stations to promote his music. He bought time on local stations to play Hispanic music and community notes, earning the trust

Recently renovated, Sanchez Park includes a giant microphone that contains trampolines, slides, and just plain fun for kids to enjoy.

of Denver's Hispanic community throughout the 1950s and onward. He later started Denver's first Spanish-language radio station, KFSC-AM, and founded what became the Good Americans Organization (GAO). The GAO helped Hispanics find and fund housing. As a community leader who was heavily involved in the Hispanic community, Paco was later elected to Colorado's House of Representatives.

As the Hispanic community found its voice on Denver's radio, it also began to find its identity in the Chicano movement that rose up in the late 1960s and early 1970s. (See Aztlan, Columbus, Joseph P. Martinez, and César E. Chávez Parks.)

Park visitors are greeted by the bright orange PACO sign that doubles as a climbable photo opportunity. Just to the north of the sign is Denver's newest play structure, which was inspired by feedback from the community and Paco's history. This structure resembles a large "mic" that stands many stories tall, and inside you can find ropes, trampolines, slides, bars, and twisty turns that kids of all ages will enjoy. The park's new focus is to have the entire family play together, so additional play things are scattered around the mic, including a fitness center and hoops for crawling through.

EXTEND YOUR VISIT

The **Rodolfo "Corky" Gonzales** branch of the **Denver Public Library** is a few blocks away, on the corner of Irving and Colfax. This library highlights the history of this leader and writer who coined the term "Chicano" in his poem "Yo Soy Joaquin."

17   JOSEPH P. MARTINEZ PARK

Another two-for-one park deal!

Location: 900 N. Raleigh St., Denver
Acreage: 12
Amenities: Picnic tables, playground, basketball court, baseball/softball field, bike/pedestrian path, Lakewood Gulch Trail

GETTING THERE

BY CAR Take I-25 to exit 210A. Turn west on Colfax. Turn left on Perry St., right on W. 10th Ave., left on Raleigh. **BY TRANSIT** Bus 9 and the light rail W line stop nearby. **BY BIKE** Take the South Platte River Trail to the Lakewood Gulch Trail.

Named after the first Hispanic-American and Coloradan to receive the Medal of Honor for his efforts during World War II, this park sits along the Lakewood Gulch.

A multi-colored tile mosaic decorates the playground near Martinez Park.

The gulch runs along the southern edge of the park, inviting fun-seeking and curious crawfish hunters and salamander finders for about three-quarters of a mile. A small playground for little kids sits on the north side of the gulch. The Lakewood Gulch Trail runs alongside the gulch and makes its way to the W train line, about a mile away.

If you have larger kids or want to try a more modern playground, walk about a third of a mile east along the Lakewood Gulch Trail to the second playground at the corner of Osceola St. and W. 10th Ave. Although there's no name on this park, it's a hub of activity. This newer park has two play areas. It invites folks to shoot hoops, play on the more modern equipment, or watch all the commuters moving through the park along its trails to the W line. The park celebrates Hispanic history in its Aztec-influenced play sculptures, the artwork embedded in the cement, and through its freestanding murals.

EXTEND YOUR VISIT

To understand why the park has an Aztec-influenced theme, head to the **Rodolfo "Corky" Gonzales** branch of the **Denver Public Library** and read "Yo Soy Joaquin," a poem about Chicano culture. Corky lived nearby. (See Columbus Park.)

18   PHIL MILSTEIN PARK

The Platte's best fishing hole in Denver?

Location: 6th Ave. and South Platte River, Denver
Acreage: 6.5
Amenities: Picnic tables, bike/pedestrian path, South Platte River Trail

GETTING THERE

BY CAR Take I-25 to exit 209C. Go west to Zuni. Take that south to W. 8th Ave. Cross 8th and park at the trailhead. Walk through Frog Hollow Park to Phil Milstein Park. **BY TRANSIT** Buses 9, 15, and 30/36 stop nearby. **BY BIKE** Take the South Platte River Trail to W. 6th Ave.

Only accessible by foot, bike, or kayak, Phil Milstein Park is rumored to offer Denver's best fishing hole on the South Platte River. To find the fishing hole, walk in from the north end of the park. You'll see an eddy on the northwest side of the railroad trestle. It's said this is the spot to catch rainbow trout, brown trout, smallmouth bass, and big carp. Or, if this is really a fish tale and you'd like to spend your time wandering, you can walk a bit farther south and enjoy views of the art deco Denver Wastewater Management building and its fine modern art sculpture and bridge over the Platte.

The Denver Wastewater Building was built in 1993. Although not actually historic, it harkens to the great public works projects constructed throughout the

Does the public art across from Phil Milstein Park mark the best fishing hole on the Platte River?

nation during the 1930s, which were influenced by the iconic art deco–style architecture of the period and includes buildings such as the Rockefeller Center and the Empire State Building in New York City. Denverites sometimes call it the Batman Building. On the bridge crossing over to the building from the South Platte River Trail, you'll find the interesting Bridge of Recycling Fountains, by Laura Audrey Steel, which is part of a sculpture series made to reflect water and light.

The park's namesake, Phil Milstein, is considered the visionary behind Denver's 16th Street Mall and the Auraria Higher Education Campus (see La Alma/Lincoln Park). He also garnered support to create the South Platte Greenway and Cherry Creek Greenway and trails.

EXTEND YOUR VISIT

You'll be on the **South Platte River**. Head up or down the river for miles and miles of river meandering.

19   FROG HOLLOW PARK

A skinny escape for a lunchtime break

Location: 2350 W. 8th Ave., Denver
Acreage: 5.6
Amenities: Drinking fountain, picnic tables, bike/pedestrian path, South Platte River Trail

GETTING THERE

BY CAR Take I-25 to exit 209C. Go west to Zuni. Take that south to W. 8th Ave. Cross 8th and park at trailhead. **BY TRANSIT** Buses 9, 15, and 30/36 stop nearby. **BY BIKE** Take the South Platte River Trail to W. 8th Ave.

This small linear park has a great name, but you may not find any frogs here. It is, however, a great place to take a break from your ride along the Platte or just sit and enjoy a sandwich. Once a dumping ground for the highway maintenance teams of the past, it was the original home to Lake Archer. The lake, named after James Archer, who founded the Denver City Water Company in 1870, was one of the original water sources for the city of Denver. Perhaps that's where the frogs were!

EXTEND YOUR VISIT

Continue south along the South Platte River Trail to **Phil Milstein Park**, where you may be able to catch yourself a fish.

20 ARGO PARK

A company town's park

Location: 4700 N. Logan St., Denver
Acreage: 12
Amenities: Picnic tables, picnic shelter, playground, outdoor pool, basketball court, football field, soccer field, baseball/softball field

GETTING THERE

BY CAR Take I-70 to Washington St. Go north. Take a left on E. 47th Ave. Turn right on Logan. **BY TRANSIT** Buses 12 and 48 stop nearby. **BY BIKE** Take the South Platte River Trail to E. 47th Ave. Turn right on Logan.

One of Denver's older parks, Argo Park was intended for the residents of the town of Argo (later annexed to Denver). These residents worked mostly for the Argo Smelting Works of the Boston and Colorado Smelting Company, which began operations in 1879. Many folks who moved to Argo, named after the mythical ship sailed by Jason in search of the Golden Fleece, were following Colorado's gold rush. At the time, Nathaniel Hill discovered a way to extract valuable minerals from ore in a process that became known as smelting. Smelters started appearing

Playground equipment is a big draw at Argo Park, but it has even more to offer.

throughout Colorado, and people who hadn't struck it rich through panning gold needed jobs. The smelters fulfilled those needs.

In the town of Argo, folks would gather nightly to dance, play, and sing under the stars after a hard day's work. At one time, Argo contained a theater, dance pavilion, bowling alley, and a small zoo.

Argo was annexed to Denver in 1902, and as part of the deal, Denver offered to add a swimming pool, changing rooms, and baseball fields to Argo Park. Over time, the park's boundaries shrank, but the neighborhood continued to use the park as a gathering place. Today, with lighted baseball and softball fields, a basketball court, playgrounds for littles and bigs, and picnic tables, the park is still a big draw. The pool underwent $1 million in renovations in 2005, a "sprayground" was added in 2007, and a half-mile walking path appeared in 2014.

EXTEND YOUR VISIT

North of the park is a famous Denver landmark, **Hammond's Candies**, located at 5735 Washington Street. Stop by for a tour and get a candy cane.

21 CARPIO SANGUINETTE PARK

An inspirational park with a new name and intriguing history

Location: 1400 53rd Ave., Denver
Acreage: 14
Amenities: Bike/pedestrian path, soccer field, drinking fountain, South Platte River Trail

GETTING THERE

BY CAR Take I-70 to Washington St. Go north to E. 51st, take a right to the park. **BY TRANSIT** Buses 12 and 48 stop nearby. **BY BIKE** Take the South Platte River Trail to the park.

Located on land that once housed a wastewater treatment plant for metro Denver, this park received a Merit Award in Design from the American Society of Landscape Architects in 2001 for its innovative approach to a former industrial landscape. After working with the neighborhood to decide what to do with the area once the treatment plant moved north, designers fashioned an open space that incorporated some of the original infrastructure from the plant.

Located along the Platte River, Carpio Sanguinette Park has received many awards for its creative use of old stormwater pipes and infrastructure.

Now, those large geometric shapes of concrete supply a backdrop to the undulating hills and paths through the park and its trees. Street murals decorate sections of the park, and kids can climb and play on the concrete structures or enjoy the open grassy spaces. Embedded in the concrete paths throughout the park are sayings, dreams, and wishes from the community. They are designed to inspire and encourage you to walk the entire park while looking for additional cemented comments.

In 2018, the park received a new name, Carpio Sanguinette. It is named after two families, the Carpios and the Sanguinettes. Sal Carpio, a professor at Metropolitan State University in the 1960s, took a seat on the Denver City Council in 1975. He improved communication between the city and its minority populations, eventually leading to the creation of the Denver Housing Authority where he brought additional low-income housing options to the area.

Louis and his brother, William Sanguinette, farmed this land in the 1870s. They grew tired of dirty water runoff from the nearby pig slaughter, and they pestered the city enough to successfully outlaw the dumping of carcasses and animal waste into the Platte River.

EXTEND YOUR VISIT

Head up or down the South Platte River Trail, which borders the park, for a nice walk or bike ride along the **South Platte River.**

22 HERON POND/HELLER OPEN SPACE

Unexpected natural area near a recycling center

Location: 5275 Franklin St., Denver
Acreage: 42
Amenities: Lake, open space, natural areas

GETTING THERE

BY CAR Take I-70 to Brighton. Go north to Race St. Take a right. Take a right on Race Ct. Take a right on Franklin. Turn left on 53rd Ave. The park entrance is located at the cul-de-sac just past the National Guard armory parking. **BY TRANSIT** Buses 42 and 45 stop nearby. **BY BIKE** Take the South Platte River Trail to Franklin St. Go north. Take a left on 53rd Ave.

Hiding in an area most people don't visit is the undeveloped Heron Pond Natural Area, which in 2018 received approval for an overhaul. On the west side of the park is Denver's recycling center, and on the east side is a National Guard armory. But sitting between the two is a quiet restored oasis that attracts heron, killdeer, magpies, and other Colorado birds to a lake covering several acres. An unmaintained trail travels along the lakeshore for a couple of miles, but you'll probably best enjoy your time at Heron Pond at the mosaic wall on the south side of the lake. The wall is made out of sections of old runway from the long gone Stapleton International Airport and pays tribute to Amelia Earhart. Come and stay for a while on the benches to bird watch or just relax away from the nearby hubbub.

EXTEND YOUR VISIT

South of the National Guard armory are the remains of a city wastewater treatment plant that became Northside Park, now **Carpio Sanguinette Park**. Children were asked what the park should be, and their quotes are memorialized in the concrete paths in the park. Go have a read and feel inspired. (See Carpio Sanguinette Park.)

23   GLOBEVILLE LANDING PARK

Discover a daylighted creek and a chance to explore and picnic

Location: 3901 Arkins Ct., Denver
Acreage: 8
Amenities: Picnic tables, picnic shelter, bike/pedestrian path, South Platte River Trail, drinking fountain, disc golf course

GETTING THERE

BY CAR Take I-70 to Washington St. Go south to Arkins Ct. Take a left to the park. **BY TRANSIT** Buses 12, 48, and the light rail A line stop nearby. **BY BIKE** Take South Platte River Trail to the park.

Globeville Landing Park sits at the confluence of Montclair Creek and the South Platte River. Historically, Montclair Creek was tunneled and channeled underground, and only just recently was it daylighted. Now, Globeville Landing Park mitigates runoff from Northeast Denver into a filtration system of native grasses that cleans the water before it enters the Platte. As you walk through the park on the soft surface and hard surface trails, you'll see how the creek emerges into the park.

To get the best view of the wetlands, ascend the giant climbing wall at the north end of the park. With multiple routes to the top, providing access for all sizes, you and the family can climb all day long. When you're finished, consider cooking up a nice barbeque in the new pits that overlook the South Platte River as you watch the sunset.

Globeville, the neighborhood next door, together with Elyria and Swansea to the east, have long fought to remain a tight-knit community. Both I-25 and I-70 run through the heart of Globeville. This intersection was once known as the Mousetrap due to its crazy configuration of on-ramps and off-ramps. Despite what's happening on the roads above the neighborhood, the residents below have always gathered to keep its neighborhood as a community. Together, they have dealt with toxic waste, Superfund sites, and rail and car infrastructure changes. It's a neighborhood worth exploring and supporting. (See Elyria and Swansea Parks.)

EXTEND YOUR VISIT

Head into Globeville and grab a bite to eat at the **Comal Heritage Food Incubator** (3455 Ringsby Court #105), where you can find Syrian mothers cooking dishes from their homeland and Hispanic grandmothers churning out tamales.

24 ELYRIA PARK

Ramps and rails!

Location: 4809 N. Race St., Denver
Acreage: 2.5
Amenities: Recreation center, drinking fountain, picnic tables, playground, basketball court, baseball/softball field, sand volleyball court, benches, skate park

GETTING THERE

BY CAR Take I-70 to Brighton Blvd. Turn north. Turn right on 48th Ave., left on Race St. **BY TRANSIT** Bus 48 stops nearby. **BY BIKE** Take Sand Creek Greenway to Brighton Blvd. Turn north. Turn right on 48th Ave., left on Race St.

Although Elyria is a small park and a little bit out of the way, it actually has quite a few fun amenities for tweens and teens to enjoy. They can skate the ramps and rails in the skate park, volley a ball on the sand court, or shoot hoops at the basketball court. A small recreation center sits on the property, as well as a baseball field good for younger athletes to call out, "Batter up!"

EXTEND YOUR VISIT

If you're looking for some organic produce and a farm stand with lots of variety, be sure to stop by **The GrowHaus**, a nonprofit indoor farm located at 4751 York Street, for fresh veggies or even a quick snack.

This secret skateboarding park in Elyria Park has just enough for the skater in the family.

THREE COMMUNITIES AT A CROSSROADS

Swansea might be Denver's most dynamic neighborhood; its history has been difficult, but it is tight-knit and determined. Named after a port in Wales and established soon after the Kansas Pacific and Union Pacific Railroads were completed in the 1880s, the district was originally settled by immigrant populations who worked at the local smelter. Over the years, Swansea locals have formed alliances with residents of the nearby Globeville and Elyria neighborhoods, uniting in vision and community.

The three communities at the intersection of I-70 and I-25 have long fought environmental and social battles together. These neighbors have rallied to clean up toxic waste, brawled with transportation officials to keep their communities from splitting, and built a tight-knit group of longtime residents who refuse to give in. Now, these citizens will see their neighborhoods change yet again, as I-70 gets put underground and a new park appears over top of it, offering the neighborhood new opportunities to celebrate itself. (See Swansea Park, Globeville Landing Park, and Elyria Park.)

25 SWANSEA PARK

Fitness for everyone

Location: 2650 E. 49th Ave., Denver
Acreage: 10.7
Amenities: Recreation center, picnic tables, playground, outdoor pool, futsal court, football field, baseball/softball field, bike/pedestrian path, fitness zone, horseshoe pits

GETTING THERE

BY CAR Take I-70 to E. 45th Ave. Take exit 275C. Follow E. 45th Ave. to Clayton St. Go north. Turn left on E. 49th Ave. **BY TRANSIT** Bus 48 stops nearby. **BY BIKE** From the South Platte River Trail, turn left onto Arkins Ct. Take a slight right onto McFarland Dr. Take a slight left to stay on McFarland Dr. Turn left onto 44th St./ E. 46th Ave. Turn left onto Columbine St. Turn right onto E. 47th Ave. Turn left onto Thompson Ct.

In what might be Denver's most transformed neighborhood—one that sits on a pile of history that includes smelters, railroads, Superfund sites, and reclamation—this tight-knit community loves its neighborhood and its park. Named after a port in Wales and established once the Kansas Pacific and Union Pacific Railroads were completed, the community of hard workers has kept itself together despite many external pressures to break it apart.

Swansea Park, together with its attached recreation center, keeps the locals moving. With an outdoor fitness track, a walking path that circles half a mile, a playground, a futsal court, and multiuse fields, all ages can engage in outdoor activities here. Don't forget to bring your horseshoes for a rousing game in the pits.

EXTEND YOUR VISIT

Head on over to the **National Western Complex** and see what events are going on, be it a car show, a stock show, or maybe even a rodeo!

26   LEE DUNHAM PARK

A well-appointed play-ground is a good spot to meet the neighbors

Location: 4401 N. Clayton St., Denver
Acreage: 2.4
Amenities: Benches, picnic tables, playground, basketball court, baseball/softball field

GETTING THERE

BY CAR Take I-70 to Vasquez. Turn south to E. 45th Ave. Take a left and left again on Clayton to the park. **BY TRANSIT** Buses 40 and 48 stop nearby. **BY BIKE** Take the South Platte River Trail to 38th St. Turn right. Turn left on Blake St./E. 40th Ave. Turn left on Clayton to the park.

A nice little neighborhood park with a well-appointed playground, this community gathering place is great for people-watching. The playground accommodates kids from ages five to twelve, with three slides of different heights and fun circles to wiggle in and out of. A basketball court invites a game of H-O-R-S-E, and a mixed-use field welcomes Frisbees and soccer balls alike.

The city purchased the park from F. P. Ernest, who was president of American National Bank, in April of 1892, for $13,500. Lee Dunham, the park's namesake, was a Union Pacific switchman who died while saving a child from being hit by a train.

EXTEND YOUR VISIT

Would you like to enjoy a good Mexican ice cream shop? Walk on over to **Bandoleros Neveria** at the corner of 46th and Josephine.

27 MARTIN J. SCHAFER PARK

Lots of open space!

Location: 3724 N. Columbine St., Denver
Acreage: 8.9
Amenities: Playground, baseball/softball field, basketball court, football field, tennis court, picnic tables, bike/pedestrian path

GETTING THERE

BY CAR Take I-70 to the Vasquez exit. Go south to E. 37th. Take a left to the park. **BY TRANSIT** Buses 24, 34, and 43 stop nearby. **BY BIKE** Take the South Platte River Trail to 38th St. Turn right. Turn left on Blake St./E. 40th Ave. Turn right on York. Turn left on 37th Ave. to the park.

Although it's not fancy, there's plenty of open space to run, kick a ball, or even geocache here. The park is named after Martin Schafer, who was first a gardener, then foreman, and eventually superintendent for the park. A large backstop grabs a corner of the park, and on the opposite side you'll find brand-new tennis courts next to three basketball hoops. A pleasant picnic table area under a shelter invites families or groups to hang out, and a small playground beckons children to come climb and laugh.

EXTEND YOUR VISIT

An old-school Mexican diner, **Lucero's**, sits near the southeast corner of the park. Be sure to stop in for some home-style cooking.

28 CITY OF NAIROBI PARK

An adventurous Sister City Park

Location: 3500 N. Cook St., Denver
Acreage: 2.2
Amenities: Benches, picnic tables, playground, drinking fountain, baseball/softball field

GETTING THERE

BY CAR Take I-70 to Colorado Blvd. Go south to Bruce Randolph Ave. and turn left. Take a right on Cook St. to the park. **BY TRANSIT** : Buses 24, 40, and 43 stop nearby. **BY BIKE** Take the South Platte River Trail to 38th St. Turn right. Turn left on Blake St./E. 40th Ave. Turn right on Cook St. The park is on the left.

Jambo! That's how you say "hello" in Nairobi, Kenya. As part of its Sister Cities International program, the city of Denver changed the name of this park to City of Nairobi Park in 1975. Nairobi, the capital of Kenya, has a similar elevation as Denver, sits on a high plateau, and Mounts Kilimanjaro and Kenya are nearby. Surrounded by giraffes, big game, and wildlife, Nairobi makes a great destination for Denverites to visit, and they will find a City of Denver Park there.

Tall as it is, the giraffe at City of Nairobi Park is still small for its age!

Closer to home, throughout the City of Nairobi Park, educational opportunities abound. You can learn about Denver's historic African-American history, geographical information about Nairobi, and even how to say a few things in Swahili. And you can take a break from your studies to climb on the giraffe that stands nearby or kick a soccer ball in the open field.

Purchased by the city in 1912, and originally called the North Capitol Hill Playground, the City of Nairobi Park is just a block away from the socially significant intersection of Cook Street and Bruce Randolph Avenue: John Cook Jr. developed a streetcar line in 1885 that ran along what would become Cook Street. And Bruce Randolph Avenue is named after "Daddy" Bruce who, in the 1960s, gave away thousands of meals at his barbecue restaurant located to the west in the Five Points area.

EXTEND YOUR VISIT

If this park is too small for you, head about eight blocks to the south to enjoy the giant **City Park** and all of its amenities.

29   GEORGE MORRISON SR. PARK

Go ahead; toot your horn!

Location: 1400 E. Martin Luther King Blvd., Denver
Acreage: 3.75
Amenities: Benches, picnic tables, bike/pedestrian path

GETTING THERE

BY CAR Take Martin Luther King Blvd. to N. Lafayette St. **BY TRANSIT** Buses 43 and 88 stop nearby. **BY BIKE** Take Martin Luther King Blvd. to N. Lafayette St.

Named after the acclaimed violinist and musician George Morrison Sr., this park tells the story of African-Americans and their impact on jazz in Denver's Five Points and Whittier areas. Morrison grew up in Boulder and attended the Columbia Conservatory of Music in Chicago. His touring group included Cuthbert Byrd, Desdemona and Leo Davis, Hattie McDaniel, Eugene Montgomery, Theodore Morris, Jimmie Lunceford, and Andy Kirk. When not touring, he gave free music lessons to neighborhood kids at Whittier Elementary School, Cole Junior High, and Manual

Stopping by Morrison Park is a nice surprise for music lovers.

High School. He resided on Gilpin Street despite attempts by the Ku Klux Klan to persuade him to live elsewhere. His home became the stopover point for many famous musicians, including Count Basie, Jelly Roll Morton, Nat King Cole, and others.

Enjoy the monument to Morrison in the center of this linear park while taking a nice stroll or a break under the shady trees. You'll notice the large cello sculpture along the walkway. Be sure to read more about Morrison and his impacts on the music industry on the park's signage as you travel along the meandering path under the shady tree canopy.

EXTEND YOUR VISIT

There are several parks in the Whittier area that are full of African-American history, including **Frederick Douglass**, **Dr. Daniel Hale Williams**, and **Madame C. J. Walker Parks**. Venture south of George Morrison Sr. Park to visit them.

30   FREDERICK DOUGLASS PARK

Vote!

Location: 3000 N. Franklin St., Denver
Acreage: 0.5
Amenities: Picnic tables, playground, benches

GETTING THERE

BY CAR Take Martin Luther King Blvd. to Franklin St. Turn south to the park. **BY TRANSIT** Buses 28, 34, and 43 stop nearby. **BY BIKE** Take Martin Luther King Blvd. to Franklin St. Turn south to the park.

Many people know of Frederick Douglass, the slave-turned-abolitionist from Maryland who moved voting rights forward for African-Americans. But most don't know that his sons made quite an impact on Denver. Lewis and Frederick Jr. served in the first black regiment during the Civil War and then migrated to Denver in 1886. They created Denver's first black school, opened a restaurant on California Street, started the Douglass Undertaking Company located at 2745 Welton Street, and refused to support Colorado for statehood until all blacks could vote.

In this small park, which celebrates the city's connection to Douglass, you'll find a few benches and a small playground for younger kids. Although the amenities are few here, the park offers a refreshingly cool stand of pine trees, and it's

Enjoy the playground equipment and learn a bit about Frederick Douglass's family when you visit Douglass Park.

a great starting point for a longer exploration of the neighborhood and its parks. Folks gather here in the summer evenings to enjoy the stories of the neighborhood.

EXTEND YOUR VISIT

Explore other nearby parks in Whittier for more African-American history, including **George Morrison Sr.**, **Dr. Daniel Hale Williams**, and **Madame C. J. Walker Parks**. Venture around the neighborhood to visit them.

31   DR. DANIEL HALE WILLIAMS PARK

Open heart park

Location: 3000 N. Lafayette St., Denver
Acreage: 0.5
Amenities: Playground, basketball court, benches, picnic tables

GETTING THERE

BY CAR Take Martin Luther King Blvd. to N. Lafayette St. Turn south to the park. **BY TRANSIT** Buses 12, 28, and 43 stop nearby. **BY BIKE** Take Martin Luther King Blvd. to N. Lafayette St. Turn south to the park.

This tiny pocket park has a big heart—actually, it has a big open heart! The park is named after Dr. Daniel Hale Williams, who was one of the first doctors to successfully perform open-heart surgery all the way back in 1893! As an African-American, he often could not get privileges in hospitals, so he started his own in Chicago—the Provident Hospital and Training School for Nurses. Eventually, Dr. Williams cofounded the National Medical Association and became a charter member of the American College of Surgeons in 1913. Although he has no connection to Denver, he's an inspiration for many people.

At this park, younger kids will enjoy the playground and swings, while moms and dads will enjoy the shade under the pines. This is the largest of the series of parks here in the Whittier neighborhood; it includes two slides, a rope climb, some twirly poles to slide down, and a couple of swings.

EXTEND YOUR VISIT

Take an educational stroll around Whittier to visit the other parks in Whittier that celebrate African-American history, including **George Morrison Sr.**, **Frederick Douglass**, and **Madame C. J. Walker Parks**.

32 MADAME C. J. WALKER PARK

Work hard. Live free.

Location: 1900 E. 30th Ave., Denver
Acreage: 1
Amenities: Picnic tables, playground, benches

GETTING THERE

BY CAR Take Martin Luther King Blvd. to York St. Go south. Turn right on E. 30th Ave. to the park. **BY TRANSIT** Buses 34 and 40 stop nearby. **BY BIKE** Take Martin Luther King Blvd. to York St. Go south. Turn right on E. 30th Ave. to the park.

Another great pocket park in the Whittier neighborhood with the theme of African-American history, this park tells the story of Madame C. J. Walker. As the first self-made, female millionaire in the United States, she made her money selling a hair tonic and brush system throughout the Americas. She lived briefly in Denver where she learned her sales skills, but then continued most of her career in Pittsburgh, ultimately passing away in New York in 1919. Her "can-do" attitude is celebrated throughout the park via its signs about Walker's life and the sayings imprinted in the concrete around the park.

The park sits in a cul-de-sac with artwork painted on the asphalt and handprints along the sidewalk. Explore the various educational signs around the park while the kids play in the playground with its swings and animal house. This playground is the most modern of the ones in the Whittier chain, and kids have two chances to climb walls.

EXTEND YOUR VISIT

Explore the nearby parks in the Whittier neighborhood that offer a bit of African-American history, including **George Morrison Sr.**, **Frederick Douglass**, and **Dr. Daniel Hale Williams Parks**.

33 FULLER PARK

A spot for Spot to have some fun

Location: 2801 N. Williams St., Denver
Acreage: 5.8
Amenities: Dog park, picnic tables, picnic shelter, playground, basketball court, benches, drinking fountain, picnic area

GETTING THERE

BY CAR Take Martin Luther King Blvd. to N. Williams St. Turn south. The park is on the right. **BY TRANSIT** Buses 34, 43, and 88 stop nearby. **BY BIKE** Take Martin Luther King Blvd. to N. Williams St. Turn south. The park is on the right.

Sitting in the shadows of Manual High School, Fuller Park is more about dogs than people. A nice-sized dog park flanks the western boundary, holding room for both big and small dogs. There are plenty of places to sit in the sun or shade to keep an eye on your pups as they play.

To the east is a small, underwhelming playground with one or two items for kids to play on, but odds are they'll quickly abandon it to watch the dogs chase Frisbees or play with the pine cones. A gazebo in the middle of the park allows you to watch both kids and dogs frolic.

The park is named after Horace Fuller, who responded to a plea from Mayor Joseph E. Bates in the 1860s. Fuller donated land to the city in hopes that other leaders would do the same to grow the park system. Fuller Park was Denver's second official park.

EXTEND YOUR VISIT

Venture to one or more of the other parks in the vicinity to engage in some great African-American history.

AN OLD SCHOOL REBORN

One of the oldest schools in Denver, and among the first to educate African-Americans, Manual High School fell on hard times when Denver Public Schools ended mandatory busing in 2005. Test scores plummeted and gang violence increased. The district decided to close the school, causing the students to protest, unsuccessfully. After reorganizing the curriculum and hiring new leadership, the district reopened the school in 2007 to great success. Many famous Denverites have attended or graduated from Manual, including National Public Radio correspondent Scott Horsley; writer Ted Conover; folk singer and musician Walt Conley; boxer, poet, and activist Rodolfo "Corky" Gonzales; Denver mayors Michael B. Hancock and Wellington Webb; Seattle's first black mayor, Norm Rice; and the first female manager of an American symphony orchestra, Helen Marie Black.

34   J. LANGSTON BOYD PARK

This park promises music to your ears!

Location: 3101 Colorado Blvd., Denver
Acreage: 4.8
Amenities: Benches, bike/pedestrian path, flower beds

GETTING THERE

BY CAR Take I-70 to Colorado Blvd. Turn south. Cross Martin Luther King Blvd. The park is on the left. There is no parking along Colorado Blvd. You'll need to park on one of the side streets. **BY TRANSIT** Buses 34, 40, and 43 stop nearby. **BY BIKE** Take Martin Luther King Blvd. to Colorado Blvd. Turn south. The park is on the left.

This park is named after J. Langston Boyd, a third-generation minister of Shorter Community African Methodist Episcopal Church. Boyd celebrated life and influenced the African-American community and beyond. He co-chaired state campaigns for Democrats, including the Rev. Jesse Jackson, Gary Hart, and Michael Dukakis. He served as director of the Southern Christian Leadership Conference and project director of Operation Breadbasket. He chaired the board of directors of Denver-Metro PUSH and the Rainbow Coalition, and served on the Colorado Parks and Wildlife Commission. Mayor John Hickenlooper even proclaimed June 24, 2004, as J. Langston Boyd day. Boyd helped win a $300 million agreement

Hidden off Colorado Boulevard in Boyd Park, you'll find a magic door full of music.

with Coors Brewing Company to promote contracts with minorities. He fought racism until the day he died.

The park itself is a small linear park along Colorado Boulevard. When walking along the boulevard, it's nice to weave into the park and away from traffic. Toward the southern end of the park, you'll find two Catalpa logs that form a sculpture called *Sound Totem*. Approach the logs and you'll see a small door with a silver knob. Open the door and enjoy the music by a local neighborhood artist. The music rotates frequently to allow surprises for listeners while giving exposure to the music of local artists.

EXTEND YOUR VISIT

If you're looking for more things to do, the very large and engaging **City Park** is just a few blocks to the south.

35   MESTIZO-CURTIS PARK

Denver's oldest park offers plenty of old beauty and new adventure

Location: 3000 Curtis St., Denver
Acreage: 8.5
Amenities: Picnic tables, benches, playground, outdoor pool, picnic shelter, basketball court, tennis court, bike/pedestrian path, picnic area, fitness zone

GETTING THERE

BY CAR Take I-70 to Washington St. Turn right on Walnut. Left on N. Downing St. Right on Arapahoe St. Left on 31st St. to the park. **BY TRANSIT** Buses 43 and 88 stop nearby. **BY BIKE** Take the South Platte River Trail to Market St. on to Walnut. Turn right on 26th St. and then left on Curtis to the park.

On April 7, 1868, Denver Mayor Francis Case and Frederick Ebert, a developer, wanted to make a new development more attractive to home buyers, so they donated 2.88 acres of land within their plat to the city and named it Curtis Park, after Samuel S. Curtis, a Denver founding father. The donation started what would become today's Denver Parks and Recreation.

This park, which ultimately grew to nearly three times its original size, has waxed and waned in favor and condition. Over the years, it grew, equipment changed, and through-streets closed in order to create one open space. Ultimately, Denver's first park made the National Register of Historic Places in 1975. In the 1980s the fabulous *Eyes on the Park*, a mural by Emanuel Martinez, appeared on the pool building walls and the community added "Mestizo" to the name to reflect the many cultures of the local neighborhoods. Unfortunately, the park once again fell into disrepair shortly after.

Geraldolyn Horton-Harris, whose family had lived near the park for more than fifty-seven years, couldn't stand the deterioration of the park. In 2013 she led a partnership with other neighborhood members and the Trust for Public Land to upgrade and save the park with its aged red sandstone paths, Olmstead-decorated lines of trees, and rich history.

Now, the neighborhood park thrives with activity. The playground is a dream come true, with a giant custom play tower that looks like a tree house and bears the name Rossonian after Five Points' famous jazz lounge, which played host to distinguished black musicians such as Duke Ellington, Count Basie, Nat King Cole, Billie Holiday, and Ella Fitzgerald. A smaller playground stretches the imagination of younger kids who aren't quite ready for the giant slide, with caves to crawl around in and lower bridges to giggle across. A fitness zone is filled with locals getting their morning and evening workouts in, and the mixed-use area is where geocachers, tai chi'ers, yogis, sunbathers, and picnickers can enjoy the open space.

With great murals, centrally located Mestizo-Curtis Park is also Denver's first park.

EXTEND YOUR VISIT

You could easily spend the whole day in this park, and if you do then you might get hungry. Stop into the **Curtis Park Creamery** for take-out. Don't let the name fool you. Named after the dairy shop that replaced the meat processor and taxidermy shop that used the building in the early 1950s, this amazing tiny place with its homemade green and red chile pushes out some of the best Mexican food in town. Get the tamales! Then head south to the actual Five Points intersection. Check out the renovation of the **Rossonian**, grab a cuppa at Coffee at the Point, and read about Five Points history on the murals across from the Rossonian.

36 BENEDICT FOUNTAIN PARK

A busy park with a beautiful fountain

Location: 401 E. 20th Ave., Denver
Acreage: 2.9
Amenities: Benches, picnic tables, fountain, passive open space

GETTING THERE

BY CAR Take Colfax to Logan St. Turn north to E. 20th Ave. to the park. **BY TRANSIT** Buses 20, 28, 43, and 48 stop nearby. **BY BIKE** Take the South Platte River Trail to the Cherry Creek Trail. Slight right onto Market St. Turn right onto 14th St. Turn left onto Glenarm Pl. Glenarm Pl. turns slightly right and becomes E. 19th Ave. Turn left onto Logan St. Turn left onto E. 20th Ave.

This active park is at the transition zone between the North Capitol Hill and Five Points neighborhoods, and provides a stage for the change and hubbub of this popular area. Older kids who like to swing and hang out will love the brand-new playground equipment. But the centerpiece of the park is the Benedict Fountain.

Named after the prolific and controversial Denver architect J. B. Benedict, who donated the fountain, the beaux arts fountain features four regal lions. Sculpted by Maurice Bardin and made of terra cotta, it was originally designed for a home in the Belmar neighborhood. But the fountain fell into disrepair, was razed, and rebuilt in Italy with travertine marble. A duplicate of this fountain can be found in Hungarian Freedom Park. Benedict designed over eighty buildings around Colorado including Washington Park Boathouse, Chief Hosa Lodge (see Genesee Park), and Echo Lake Lodge.

EXTEND YOUR VISIT

The **Colorado State Capitol** is not far away. Head over to the capitol and enjoy the building and its views, including the one from the thirteenth step that demarks the elevation of 5280 feet, Denver's official elevation!

37   SONNY LAWSON PARK

Don't let the size fool you; Sonny Lawson is jam-packed with fun

Location: 2301 Welton St., Denver
Acreage: 2.4
Amenities: Drinking fountain, playground, restroom, basketball court, baseball/softball field, benches, ping-pong table, fitness zone, dog park, plaza

GETTING THERE

BY CAR From Martin Luther King Blvd., turn left on Champa, left on 25th St., right on California St. to the park. **BY TRANSIT** Buses 43 and 88 stop nearby. **BY BIKE** From Martin Luther King Blvd., turn left on Champa, left on 25th St., right on California St. to the park.

You'll find many things to do here in this tiny space squeezed onto a small lot,. This historic park hosted a Sunday afternoon baseball game for many years, and anyone who showed up could play. Just ask Jack Kerouac or Neal Cassady who wrote about this ball field in *On the Road* and *The First Third*, respectively. Kerouac often came to Denver to visit Cassady, his friend and a city native.

Sonny Lawson, the park's namesake, was Five Point's first druggist. He ran the Radio Pharmacy just down the street on Welton, and he became quite the leader among Denver's Democrats. From 1924 until 1963, rising and already-risen stars would stop by Sonny's for a political chat or to fill a script.

Over the years, the park has found and lost the city's attention, often becoming an area where Denverites experiencing homelessness would go. Today, you will find all sorts in the park. They play ping-pong, work at fitness, and pitch baseball. A nicely appointed playground with a double slide for racing completes the many things to do in this small space.

EXTEND YOUR VISIT

Right next door to the park is the award-winning **Blair-Caldwell African American Research Library**, which maintains a fantastic archive of African-American history in Denver and the West.

38   CITY OF CUERNAVACA PARK

Denver's Mexican Sister City offers history, art, and places to lounge

Location: 3500 Rockmont Dr., Denver
Acreage: 24
Amenities: Drinking fountain, picnic tables, picnic shelter, public art, baseball/softball field, natural areas, bike/pedestrian path, South Platte River Trail, picnic area

GETTING THERE

BY CAR Take I-25 and exit 20th St. Go east to a right on Little Raven St. Turn right on 19th St. Turn right on Rockmont Dr. to the park. **BY TRANSIT** Buses 19, 52, and the A train stop nearby. **BY BIKE** Take the South Platte River Trail to the park.

Before baseball and football fields, the Pride of the Rockies—flour—was manufactured here. This area was home to one of the many flour mills owned by various wheat farmers and conglomerates, including John K. Mullen, who relentlessly promoted Denver as the agricultural gateway to the West. Eventually, other Denver mills competitively forced the closing of other mills, but the Pride of the Rockies' flour mill building remained and was placed on the National Register of Historic Places. Dana Crawford, who also developed Larimer Square and Union Station, turned the mill into housing, which now overlooks the park and its wonderful artwork.

Spanning both sides of the South Platte River, this park continues to tell stories. Jack Kerouac and Neal Cassady used to walk through here on their way to Denargo Market to work for their daily wages. Between the mills and Kerouac tales falls the amazing baseball and football history of Denver. This region was home to the original Bears Stadium, which started as a baseball field for the Denver Bears. It then gave way to the Broncos' first football field. Baseball returned to the area when the Colorado Rockies moved into their new ballpark, called Coors Stadium. The major league ballpark is located southeast of the City of Cuernavaca Park.

In 1983, Denver and Cuernavaca, Mexico, became sister cities. Cuernavaca, which means "surrounded by trees," sits at the same elevation as Denver and, like Denver, enjoys a huge tourist draw for its beauty.

Within the park itself, which was originally named Rockmont Park, you'll see four pieces of an art installation called *Elements* by the artist Nancy Lovendahl. Fire, ice, water, and earth are each fashioned from various types of Colorado stone, which can be found on both sides of the river. A loop path that's about a mile around takes you

Nancy Lovendahl's "Elements" forms a focal point in City of Cuernavaca Park.

to the artwork. The park's wide-open fields and undulating hills along both banks of the South Platte River provide a place for sunbathers, sledders, yogis, and dog walkers.

EXTEND YOUR VISIT

Walk south along the South Platte River Trail to the **Denver Skate Park**. There you can watch local and world-class skateboarders ply their tricks.

39 DENVER SKATE PARK

Also known as DPark, this internationally acclaimed park is free!

Location: 2205 19th St., Denver
Acreage: 1.9
Amenities: Benches, skate park, picnic shelter, picnic tables, drinking fountain

GETTING THERE

BY CAR Take I-25 to 20th St. exit to the east. Turn right on Little Raven to the park.
BY TRANSIT The A train and many other light rail and bus lines stop at Union Station, near the park. **BY BIKE** Take the South Platte River Trail to the park.

In the mid-1990s, Denver's teen set wanted something to do. The city had begun to outlaw skateboarding along its downtown avenues, and teens cried out from boredom. They rallied together, finally convincing the city to build a skate park. The

Internationally famous, Denver Skate Park might encourage you to try out your own skateboard on its many hubbas.

city responded reluctantly at first, but when sixty youths and thirty adults organized to complete the vision, the city was all in. It ultimately built the largest free skate park in the United States at 60,000 square feet. Tony Hawk even stopped by on his world tour.

Denver Skate Park is noted on many top ranking national and international lists, including the rank of third in the United States by the skateboard company Board Blazers and first by *Complex* magazine. As such, this skate park attracts boarders, bikers, skaters, and onlookers. It features bowls for every level of experience, including a snake that runs down the middle of the park and an extensive street course with ledges, hubbas, banks, and hips. Best of all, the park is free. It's open every day from 7:00 AM to 11:00 PM. There are even lights so you can get a quick skate in after work or school.

EXTEND YOUR VISIT

Continue on your wheels south to **Commons Park** where you can read about the history of the area. Before leaving the park, see if you can find "Skate Mom," a lady who sells snacks and drinks from her cart to thirsty park users.

40   RAILYARD DOG PARK

A great little spot for dogs to meet and greet

Location: 2111 19th St., Denver
Acreage: 0.76
Amenities: Dog park, benches, picnic tables, shade structure, drinking fountain

GETTING THERE

BY CAR Take I-25 to 20th St. Go east to Little Raven St. Take a left on 19th St. to the park. **BY TRANSIT** Buses 40, 120x, and the A train stop nearby. **BY BIKE** Take the South Platte River Trail to 20th St. Go east to Little Raven St. Take a left on 19th St. to the park.

Tucked into a little corner up against the railroad tracks, you'll find this triangle-shaped dog park. Just big enough for big dogs and just small enough for small dogs, there's just enough space for your urban pup to catch a ball or sniff a mate.

EXTEND YOUR VISIT

Head toward the Platte River to the west to the **Denver Skate Park** to watch all the action.

41   COMMONS PARK

A park suited to all moods, conveniently located near Union Station

Location: 2101 15th St., Denver
Acreage: 17.6
Amenities: Benches, restroom, drinking fountain, bike/pedestrian path, South Platte River Trail, walking/jogging paths, natural areas

GETTING THERE

BY CAR Take I-25 to 20th St. Turn east to Little Raven St. Take a left to the park. **BY TRANSIT** The A train and many other light rail and bus lines stop at Union Station, near the park. **BY BIKE** Take the South Platte River Trail to the park.

Bernar Venet's 222.5º Arc x 5 is just one of the thought-provoking sculptures found at Commons Park.

With dozens of things to do in Commons Park, including 5 miles of winding trails, you could spend an entire day here just enjoying the outdoors. Meander along the many soft surface trails, bike along the South Platte River Trail, or just lollygag your way through the artwork, undulating landscape, and various interpretive and historical pieces embedded throughout the park. From grassy knolls to private places, there's a spot for every mood you may feel to express.

Denver, and its central park, waxed and waned with the times (see "LoDo Ho!" sidebar), and in 2000 Mayor Wellington Webb rededicated this area as Commons Park, giving it new life, though many still call it LoDo Park. Millennium Bridge and the South Platte River Bridge were built to connect Commons Park to Union Station and Highland. The art piece *Common Ground* by Barbara Grygutis was erected to honor the many people who have lived on this strip of land. The north wall of this grand art piece echoes the Front Range, and cutouts give vistas to the landscape. Additionally, a circular sculpture by Bernar Venet was donated to the community. The Colorado AIDS Memorial sits on the southeast corner of the park, creating a quiet reflective grove to remember those who passed from AIDS.

You can make several loops in the park. If you come to the park from Union Station, you'll cross the Millennium Bridge. You'll pass by visual artist John McEnroe's thought-provoking sculpture *National Velvet*, and descend into the common areas of Commons Park. From the bridge, you can make a slight loop to the south to go through the Colorado AIDS Memorial (also known as *The Grove*). Be sure to swing your way north to visit *Common Ground* and walk up through the art piece to view the Platte both up and down river. You can finish a nice loop by heading east toward the Venet's circular sculpture, ending along the path that you can take to the south and back to your start.

EXTEND YOUR VISIT

Take the **South Platte River Bridge** over the river into Highland and grab a bite to eat at any of the many cafés and bars scattered throughout the neighborhood.

LODO HO!

Welcome to the Bottoms, where bison once migrated, gold was struck, and Denver was founded. The name has changed many times over the years, from Riverfront Park, to the Bottoms, then to LoDo. Today this area is known as Commons Park. Oh, what a story it tells!

Here at the center of all things Denver, you'll find where the Indian Wars began in the mid-1800s. Cheyenne and Arapahoe banked here along the Platte, but ultimately feuds erupted with frontiersmen and gold diggers. Despite Chief Little Raven's best efforts for peace, treaties moved the Native Americans eastward, culminating with the tragic Sand Creek Massacre east of La Junta, Colorado.

The trains came in the late 1800s, and with them came agriculture, coal, and population. Competing train stations popped up and closed, with Union Station winning the battle for rail lines and customers. The city grew, and western "law" allowed for duels, whiskey, madams, and gambling. Circus acts arrived, horse races ran, and Riverfront Park attracted locals for entertainment. The area was raucous and loud, causing the more elite to move upland to the west in the Highland area where "morals and virtues" could once again be found.

The Dust Bowl transported the transients in and out of Denver, while mid-century literature brought Neal Cassady and Jack Kerouac on the road through Denver. Like elsewhere in the country in the 1970s and 1980s, downtowns and their once-beautiful parks crashed as populations fled to the suburbs and urban residences deteriorated. But in the 1990s, under the leadership of Mayor Wellington Webb, what was then Riverfront Park received some modern-day attention.

42 CONFLUENCE PARK

There's plenty to keep you occupied where Denver began

Location: 2250 15th St., Denver
Acreage: 2.8
Amenities: Bike/pedestrian path, South Platte River Trail, Cherry Creek Trail, kayak course, benches, flower beds, Shoemaker Plaza

GETTING THERE

BY CAR Take I-25 to 20th St. Turn east to Little Raven. Turn right to the park. **BY TRANSIT** The A train, several light rail lines, and many bus lines stop at Union Station, near the park. **BY BIKE** Take the South Platte River Trail to the park.

It may be small, but Confluence Park is a crown jewel of the South Platte River parks and the center of Denver's history. It was here, somewhere south of the southeast corner of the confluence of the South Platte River and Cherry Creek in 1858, that a party from Lawrence, Kansas, found gold and established Montana City (see Grant Frontier Park). Shortly afterward, Montana City was abandoned as folks began to populate the town of Auraria (named after the gold-mining town of Auraria, Georgia), just east of this confluence.

From either side of the river, you can find put-in points to launch your kayak into whitewater chutes on the watery kayak trail. In the summer, you can join in on the largest tube float in Colorado. If getting in the water is not your style, hang on the sandy beach on the northeast corner of the confluence, or get a bird's eye view from the grassy hill on the southeast corner of the park. You'll be able to watch kayaks, canoes, and tubers in the water, cyclists making the turn from the South Platte River Trail to the Cherry Creek Trail, or walkers appreciating the art program on the walls of the river banks. Regardless of what you do, it's easy to enjoy many hours of activity here at the confluence of Cherry Creek and the South Platte River.

EXTEND YOUR VISIT

Pick a direction at the confluence and explore. Go south to Denver's hidden garden, **Centennial Gardens**, or **REI**. Go east toward **Cherry Creek Reservoir**, or go north up through **Commons Park** all the way to Thornton via the extensive trail system.

43   CENTENNIAL GARDENS

Discover the City of Denver's secret garden

Location: 1301 Elitch Cir., Denver
Acreage: 5.5
Amenities: Benches, fountain, bike/pedestrian path, South Platte River Trail, flower beds, natural areas, restroom, drinking fountain

A RIVER AND A CREEK RUN THROUGH IT

Were it not for the determination of General William Larimer Jr., modern Denver might never have been. The Pennsylvania native traveled to Colorado in 1858 as part of the gold rush, and soon set about convincing those on both sides of the South Platte River and Cherry Creek confluence to join forces and name the area Denver after then Kansas territorial governor James Denver, who had migrated from Manchester, Virginia. With Denver on one side of the river and Auraria on the other, Larimer then encouraged further unification to build what became "The Queen City of the Plains." Folklore says that a deal was made over a shot of whiskey, and Auraria merged with Denver City, both ultimately becoming Denver. Thus, the city and her streets joined. If you've ever wondered why Denver's streets get cattywampus, with many five-pointed intersections, it's because Denver's streets were laid relative to the South Platte River and Auraria's to Cherry Creek. They come together in diamond shapes due to the northwest and southeast flows of the two rivers. (See Diamond Hill Promenade.)

Over time, the rivers became polluted. Floods took out bridges and rearranged the river's banks. Despite earlier warnings from the Arapahoe and Cheyenne of persistent flooding, people continued to live too close to the water. In 1965, disaster struck. A storm that dumped fourteen inches of rain caused a flood that ravaged Denver, killing two people and ruining all but one bridge and most buildings for miles.

After cleaning up the damage, the city reviewed its flood control system, and ultimately turned to the Army Corps of Engineers to get Chatfield Dam built. In addition, State Senator Joe Shoemaker, through savvy legislation and fundraising, took on the task of cleaning up the river and removing its abundant pollution. Now, the Greenway Foundation, headed by the retired senator, lobbies and leads the vision of the South Platte River's growth and recreation, resulting in new parks up and down the Platte throughout the city. (See Confluence Park, Pasquinel's Landing, and Grant Frontier Park.)

On the west bank of the juncture of the river and the creek, you'll find a new outdoor theater and stadium. When the City of Denver built up this area in 2017, it came across sludge and oily mud possibly left over from the 1965 flood or from the old tramway depot, which is now home to REI. After much money and a year's delay, the city reopened Confluence Park.

GETTING THERE

BY CAR Take I-25 to Speer Blvd. Exit south to Elitch Circle. Turn right to the gardens.
BY TRANSIT Bus 43, 44, and the A train stop nearby. **BY BIKE** Take the South Platte River Trail to the park.

Tucked away just south of Confluence Park and just north of the previous Elitch Gardens site, you'll find the smells of spring! This garden, managed by Denver Botanic Gardens, offers free access to these formal gardens featuring drought-tolerant plants. Patterned after the gardens at the Palace of Versailles in France, local master gardeners have engineered rows and plots of native fernbush and mountain mahogany mixed in with 40,000 bulbs of tulips, crocus, and irises to give your senses a delight in springtime. In the fall, the Rockies supply a nice back-drop to the turning trees. Centennial Gardens sits next to the South Platte River, offering an inviting respite for anyone strolling along its watery banks. Although hard to find, Centennial Gardens is worth a visit.

EXTEND YOUR VISIT

Walk north along the South Platte River Trail to **Confluence Park** and catch the hubbub of activity at the confluence of the South Platte River and Cherry Creek.

44   GATES CRESCENT PARK

Gateway to kid fun

Location: 2100 Children's Museum Dr., Denver
Acreage: 10.8
Amenities: Picnic tables, bike/pedestrian path, South Platte River Trail, sand volleyball court, natural areas, playground, drinking fountain

GETTING THERE

BY CAR Take I-25 to 23rd Ave./20th Ave. Turn left on 23rd Ave. Turn right onto Children's Museum Dr. to the park. **BY TRANSIT** Bus 10 and the A train stop nearby. **BY BIKE** Take the South Platte River Trail to the park.

The gateway to all things kids, this park on the western bank of the South Platte River could actually be torture for you and your kids! Because this park sits next to the vibrant and energetic Children's Museum of Denver, your kids may yearn to skip the park and instead experience the bigger venues.

But if you stay in the park, kids can run up and down the undulating grassy hills, watch the trains go by, or play a game of volleyball in the sand courts. For unstructured time, the park is the obvious choice; plan for super happy, super worn out, or super sad kids after visiting this park.

This park sits on the former Denver Public Works facility. Together in partnership with the Greenway Foundation, the Platte River Development Committee, Denver Parks and Recreation, the Urban Drainage and Flood Control District, plus a large grant from a foundation operated by the Gates Corporation, this park finally opened in the mid-1980s.

EXTEND YOUR VISIT

For adults, this park makes for a nice trailhead for accessing the South Platte River Trail. With kids, you can have the best of both worlds and head over to the **Children's Museum of Denver** after exhausting the park's attractions—or at least visit the museum's playground, located just north of the building along the South Platte River Trail.

45   DOWNTOWN PLAYGROUND

A downtown park that kids will love

Location: 1800 N. Speer Blvd., Denver
Acreage: 0.8
Amenities: Playground, benches, picnic shelter, picnic tables

GETTING THERE

BY CAR Take I-25 to Speer Blvd. to the park. **BY TRANSIT** Bus 44 stops nearby. **BY BIKE** Take the Cherry Creek Trail to the park between Wynkoop and Wewatta.

To find the park locate the bright pinwheel-like structure popping up twenty feet into the air from the park's southwest corner. You can access the park from Cherry Creek Trail, you can park on the other side of Speer Boulevard and cross it, or you can enter from Wynkoop Street via the railroad trestle over the creek that was built by the Philadelphia steel company in 1907.

Nestled between Wynkoop and Wewatta, and snug up between Speer Boulevard and Cherry Creek is this gem of a children's park. Although small, it's packed with fun and goodness. Two playful and colorful play structures sit on the banks

Nestled along Cherry Creek, the Downtown Playground is especially appealing to the urbanites who live nearby.

of Cherry Creek and the trail. A two-story-tall slide tops a bright blue climbing wall, and a three-sided triangle rope course towers next to it. From the top of the slide, players can look up Cherry Creek and spy approaching pirates! Kids will also love the hand-operated water feature, which brings a calming effect to the scene.

EXTEND YOUR VISIT

Walk two blocks northwesterly on the Cherry Creek Trail to catch all the action at **Confluence Park** or the sandy beach along the South Platte River.

46   SKYLINE PARK

Time marches on, but the old clock tower remains; see what else you can find at Skyline Park!

Location: 1701 Arapahoe St., Denver
Acreage: 2.5
Amenities: Plaza, fountain, picnic tables, restroom, benches, drinking fountain

GETTING THERE

BY CAR Take I-25 to the 20th St. exit. Go east to Arapahoe St. to the park. **BY TRANSIT** Take any one of the many transit options to Union Station, then take the 16th St. MallRide bus to Arapahoe. **BY BIKE** Take South Platte River Trail to 20th St. Go east to Arapahoe St. to the park.

Built in the early 1970s as a way to entertain and bring folks downtown, this park has always had a "play" feel to it. Designed by landscape architect Lawrence Halprin, who also designed Ghirardelli Square in San Francisco, the park includes

A rare interlude of quiet at dynamic Skyline Park

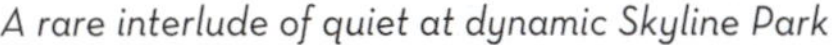

three water features as well as an ice rink in the winter and a mini-golf course in the summer. Although not free to use when skates and golf balls are involved, the park always welcomes people to engage or watch what's happening within it. Throughout the year, other temporary exhibits, such as the Christkindl Market during the holiday season, thrive in the park and on both sides of the street. In the off seasons, you can make use of some of the planters for a bit of hide-and-seek.

The park spans the 16th Street Mall. There is a cop shop on the southern side where you can seek help, if necessary, not to mention nice, clean restrooms. This park was once home to the Daniels & Fisher department store, but only its clock tower remains. Note the brick outline on the west side of the tower where the original department store attached to the tower. (See Daniels Park.)

EXTEND YOUR VISIT

Walk up and down the **16th Street Mall**, enjoying the freestanding pianos, artwork, and gardens along the way. If you like people-watching, this is probably the best place in Denver to gaze and gawk.

47 CREEKFRONT PARK

A must-visit park for hard-core newshounds

Location: 1300 Larimer St., Denver
Acreage: 0.76
Amenities: Bike/pedestrian path, Cherry Creek Trail, fountain, benches

GETTING THERE

BY CAR Take I-25 to Speer Blvd. Go south to Lawrence. Turn left. Turn left on Speer. Turn left on Larimer to the park. **BY TRANSIT** Buses 43, 48, and the A train stop nearby. **BY BIKE** Take the Cherry Creek Trail to the park.

As the gateway from Larimer Square to the Cherry Creek Trail, Creekfront Park also marks the location where the offices of the *Rocky Mountain News* settled until 1887 after moving from its original location at 13th and Market. Founded in 1859 by William Byers, the *Rocky* survived for almost 150 years as a Denver institution. It was a go-to for all things Denver, winning several Pulitzer Prizes along the way, until it ultimately merged operations with the *Denver Post* and stopped publishing in 2009.

The park has two levels. On top you'll find the *Rocky* monument. Take the stairs below to the Cherry Creek Trail. There you can find a brightly colored 3-D mural and fountain along the wall.

EXTEND YOUR VISIT

Take a walk up and down the Cherry Creek Trail, perhaps visiting **Confluence Park** to the northwest.

WHERE WERE THE HORSES?

When the first parks opened, horses were required for keeping up with the parks, grading the streets, and maintaining the grounds. Two large draft horses did much of the work in City Park. In 1893 they were kept just south of the superintendent's house at 2080 York Street. The stables were the headquarters where all park employees met each morning before heading out to do their jobs. Eventually, the park's team outgrew this location. A larger barn, a tool shed, and eventually two more barns were built just north of the zoo on 23rd Avenue. Every morning, the horses, with fanciful plumes in their manes and their drivers atop red wagons with gold lettering, would leave the barns to a daily audience of admirers. The last of the horse teams were put out to pasture in 1973.

48 CIVIC CENTER PARK

Head to the park to check out the statues, festivals, flowers, civic action, and more

Location: 101 W. 14th Avenue Pkwy., Denver
Acreage: 10.6
Amenities: Voorhies Memorial, Greek amphitheater, benches, drinking fountain, fountain, flower beds, public art

GETTING THERE

BY CAR Take I-25 to Speer Blvd. Turn left on W. 14th Ave. to the park. **BY TRANSIT** Buses 0 and 15 stop nearby. **BY BIKE** Take the Cherry Creek Trail to Galapago St. Turn left, then take a right on W. 14th Ave. to the park.

It almost didn't happen. This giant park in the middle of the city had opposition—lots of it—but the Colorado Supreme Court eventually ruled in favor of the city, clearing the way for the park. In the early 1900s, the story goes, Mayor Speer envisioned a grand park in the center of the city that would anchor the new library (near what is now the Daniels & Fisher clock tower) and the Denver Civic Center. (See Skyline Park.) Between the two landmarks were houses.

At the time, the city was split into four park districts, and each district held responsibility for building and paying for its own parks. Mayor Speer's plan required the residents of the East Park District to approve and fund his grand scheme. They protested, but the mayor's office ruled that less than 25 percent of the citizens had protested, so the city would move ahead with modified plans. As the city began condemnation proceedings on the homes, no one could agree to the value of the homes. The residents filed suit—and up to the Colorado Supreme Court the case went. The city won, and now we have Civic Center Park.

Many visionaries and authors had designs for the park, including Edward H. Bennett, Frederick Law Olmsted Jr., Reinhard Schuetze, and S. R. DeBoer. The ultimate layout resulted after many drafts and discussions about the positioning of the park within the city's grid system so it would feature the appropriate buildings. On one end of the park you'll find the Colorado State Capitol building rising above the area once known as Brown's Ridge, and at the other end you'll find city and county buildings. In between, Denverites gather for festivals, concerts, protests, and rallies.

At the Capitol steps, are two wayfinders. Each marks the official 5280 feet of elevation of the City—thus, the Mile High City—can you guess which of the two is the accurate marker? As you work your way down the steps and across to the city and county buildings, you'll pass many monuments honoring soldiers, veterans, weaponry, and victory.

At the intersection of Broadway and Colfax, take some time to explore the Pioneer Monument Fountain, created by Frederick MacMonnies. With Kit Carson leading the way (instead of a Sioux chief as originally designed by MacMonnies), this monument marks the end of the Smoky Hill Trail and commemorates the many pioneers who traveled West. It's thought-provoking and detailed.

Continuing westerly, you'll find a set of statues, including the controversial Columbus statue created by William F. Joseph, a long-time professor of the arts at Denver's Loretto Heights College. Look also for the pair of statues entitled *On the War Trail* and *Bronco Buster*, both fashioned by Alexander Phimister Proctor in the early 1920s. The model for the male figures was actually four men. They were Jackson Sundown (Nez Perce); Gray Eagle (Blackfoot); and Eddie Beaver of Browning,

In the center of everything, Civic Center Park has everything you need to enjoy a day out in downtown Denver and is a great place to join in special holiday events.

Montana. The fourth model, used to finish *Bronco Buster*, was Slim Ridings, whom the sculptor bailed out of jail so he could finish his work.

On the south end of the park, you'll find the Greek Theater. The focal point and gathering spot for many protests, marches, and parades, the Greek Theater balances out the north side of the park, where the John H. P. Voorhies Plaza. Voorhies is located, a pioneer who invested in mining and Denver politics, bequeathed to the City of Denver $125,000 for a memorial to him and his wife to be erected here. Notice the fun seals in the water inviting kids to splash.

Throughout the park, formal flower beds bloom in the summer and lush tree canopies provide good shade for relaxing. People from everywhere gather on the grassy areas, and occasionally the city closes areas of the park so the grass and tree roots have a break. In the summer, lunchtime food trucks rally several times a week. For most holidays, you'll find special lighting and firework celebrations.

EXTEND YOUR VISIT

You can spend many hours exploring the monuments and people-watching. But don't forget to visit the **Capitol building** itself. On the east lawn behind the Capitol is a bronze statue of a bison and an Indian by sculptor John Preston Powers. Called *Closing Era*, it is one of the most emotional pieces of sculpture downtown. This statue first displayed at the Chicago World's Fair of 1893. The poet John Greenleaf

Whittier gave the statue its name. Powers, one-time dean of University of Denver's art department, was commissioned by the Fortnightly Club under the leadership of Mrs. E. M. Ashley and Eliza Routt to create this statue. Powers and Whittier were friends, and Whittier wrote this poem as he engaged with the statue:

The mountain eagle from his snow-locked peaks
For the wild hunter and the bison seeks,
In the chang'd world below; and find alone
Their graven semblance, in the eternal stone.

49   LA ALMA/LINCOLN PARK

The vibrant heart and soul of the neighborhood

Location: 1325 W. 11th Ave., Denver
Acreage: 15
Amenities: Recreation center, playground, amphitheater, outdoor pool, basketball court, picnic shelter, picnic tables, benches, football field, tennis court, baseball/softball field, picnic area, fitness zone, skate park

GETTING THERE

BY CAR Take I-25 to Colfax Ave. Take a right on Osage St. to the park. **BY TRANSIT** Light rail lines C, D, F, and H stop nearby. **BY BIKE** Take Cherry Creek Trail to W. 11th Ave. Go west to the park.

Lincoln Park (Denver's fourth park) and the attached La Alma Recreation Center are the heartbeat of a vibrant neighborhood with a long history of advocacy from the Chicano movement. Starting in 1885, the neighborhood grew out of the rise of the railroad yards just to its west where immigrants found jobs. Soon, single immigrants grew into loving families who populated the communities along the railroad, where Lincoln and Auraria to the north shared common visions and neighborliness.

When the 1965 flood took out most of Lincoln and Auraria (see Confluence Park), and Denver's leaders decided to build the Auraria Higher Education Campus, residents were forced to find new places to live. Many of the Aurariarans moved to the Lincoln Park neighborhood. Fearing that the neighborhood could get redeveloped again without resident input, the locals organized to protect and save their community.

Led by the Benavidez family, and with the help of César Chávez, the Chicano movement fought against porn shops along Broadway, rallied to keep the Byers library open, and preserved many of the neighborhood's historic structures. Fighting the outside threats that would harm it, the community grew strong. At this time, with the influx of many Hispanics moving from Auraria to Lincoln Park, the neighborhood began being called La Alma, or "The Soul."

In the 1980s, Denver park maps started to show the park as La Alma/Lincoln Park, and the city council officially changed the name in 2013.

The park itself is an active area that thrives with community interaction. On summer days, neighborhood kids float in the pool and use the diving board and waterslide. Any day of the year, the vibrant artwork, reflecting the community's heritage, invites all viewers to reflect and enjoy. In the evening, picnic tables swarm with families who often share with anyone who stops by, and the open space always attracts informal soccer games and drills. The playground, decorated

The soul of the community, La Alma/Lincoln Park is popular with families year round.

with butterflies, or *mariposas*, sprawls across the park with climbing nets, rubber hills, and swings. The fitness center is within the playground, providing an all-family good-time atmosphere. Surrounding the playground are fun cement blocks painted in rainbow colors.

EXTEND YOUR VISIT

Stop in the **Buckhorn Exchange** just south of the park on Osage. It's a local hangout, notable for obtaining Colorado's first liquor license. The plethora of taxidermy hanging on the walls, which gets decorated for the holidays, is a must-see.

50   GOVERNORS PARK

A diminutive park with a starter-slide for little ones and some intriguing artwork for adults to contemplate

Location: 701 N. Pennsylvania St., Denver
Acreage: 1.9
Amenities: Benches, drinking fountain, picnic tables, playground, public art, bike/pedestrian path

TOUR SOME SEATS OF POWER

The Grant-Humphreys Mansion, named after the two families who lived there, was built in 1902 in a neoclassical style. Grant made his money in the smelting industry and his wife established a home for destitute children. Humphreys was a wildcatter who discovered oil in Oklahoma, Texas, and Wyoming. He and his wife raised two boys, who started Denver's first airfield in Park Hill and became influential in the aviation industry. The mansion is owned and rented out by History Colorado.

Built in 1908 to house two families, the Governor's Residence is also known as the Cheesman-Evans-Boettcher Mansion, named after its previous owners. You can tour it for free. Boettcher made his fortune in sugar, livestock, cement, potash, steel, securities, utilities, and transportation. In 1959 the state accepted the mansion as a gift from the Boettcher Foundation, and it's now used for the governor's residence (if the governor so desires).

The mansions' respective websites note the hours of operation and fees.

The Governor's Residence, located in Governors Park, offers free tours if you plan in advance.

GETTING THERE

BY CAR Take I-25 to E. 6th Ave. Take a left on Pennsylvania St. to the park. **BY TRANSIT** Buses 0, 6, and 52 stop nearby. **BY BIKE** Take the Cherry Creek Trail to Pennsylvania St. Go north to the park.

Sitting in the shadow of mansions, this intimate terraced park has just enough shade, play space, and artwork to keep most folks interested.

At the south end of the park, you'll see a piece of artwork, *Valedictorian*, by Abe Vigil. *Valedictorian*, also known as *Redwood*, is an abstract tree constructed of wood and metal. Next to the art is a small wooden playground. It's big enough for the little ones to try out their first slide. In the center of the park, you can find the names of all of the Colorado state governors stamped in concrete.

EXTEND YOUR VISIT

Be sure to visit the mansions next to the park. The **Grant-Humphreys Mansion** to the east or the **Boettcher Mansion** to the north, where Colorado's governor lives, will start your imagination firing.

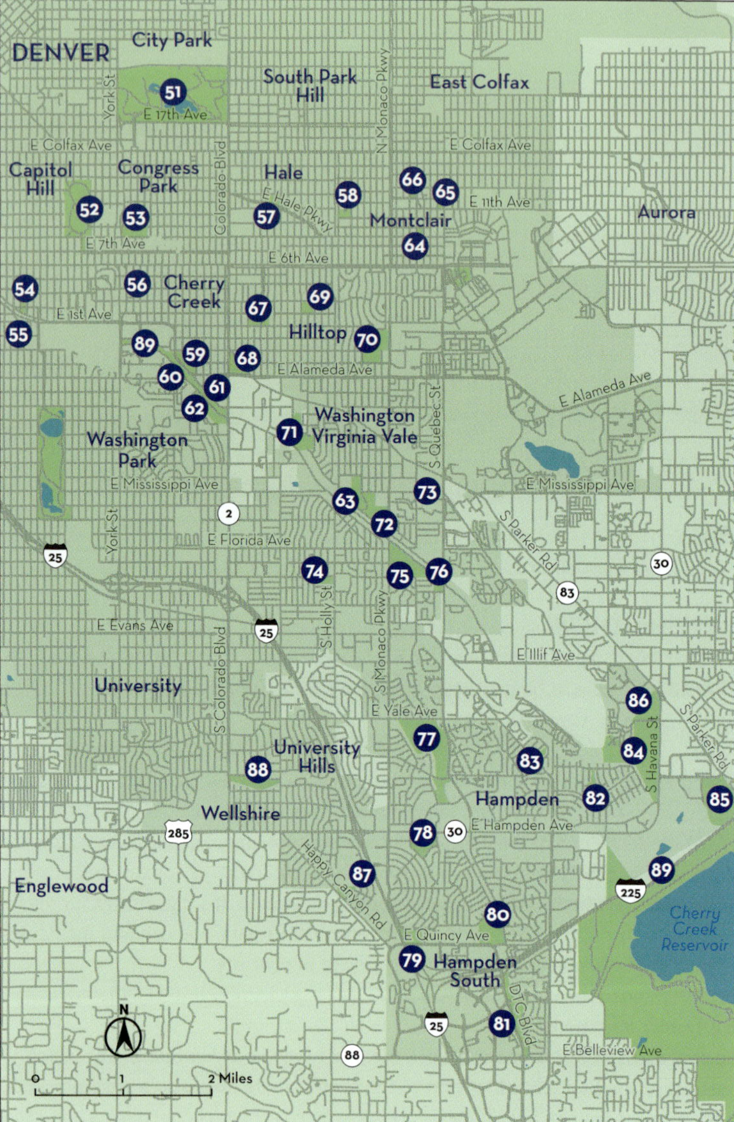

DENVER
City Park
South Park Hill
East Colfax
Capitol Hill
Congress Park
Hale
Montclair
Aurora
Cherry Creek
Hilltop
Washington Virginia Vale
Washington Park
University
University Hills
Wellshire
Englewood
Hampden
Hampden South
Cherry Creek Reservoir
York St
E 17th Ave
E Colfax Ave
E 7th Ave
E 1st Ave
E Hale Pkwy
E 6th Ave
E 11th Ave
E Colfax Ave
Colorado Blvd
N Monaco Pkwy
E Alameda Ave
E Alameda Ave
E Mississippi Ave
E Mississippi Ave
S Quebec St
S Parker Rd
S Parker Rd
E Florida Ave
E Evans Ave
E Illif Ave
S Colorado Blvd
S Holly St
S Monaco Pkwy
E Yale Ave
E Hampden Ave
Happy Canyon Rd
E Quincy Ave
E Belleview Ave
S Havana St
DTC Blvd
York St
N
0 1 2 Miles

EAST PARKS

The city's biggest park

Location: 1700 N. York St., Denver
Acreage: 314
Amenities: Benches, drinking fountain, picnic tables, playground, flower beds, walking/jogging path, interactive fountain, lake, baseball/softball field, handball court, soccer field, football field, tennis court, horseshoe pits, museum, zoo, picnic area

GETTING THERE

BY CAR Take Colorado Blvd. to the park's east entrance through the Joshua Monti Gate at the Museum of Nature and Science. **BY TRANSIT** Buses 20 and 32 stop nearby. **BY BIKE** Take E. 17th Ave. to the park's south entrance up through the City Park Esplanade and through the Richard E. Sopris Gateway.

City Park started as a crazy idea fueled by Mayor Richard Sopris, the grandfather of City Park, who envisioned a grand parkway (Colfax Avenue) that would connect the newly acquired Sloan's Lake Park to City Park. See "A Vision Starts with Water" sidebar for the fascinating history of how this crown jewel of Denver parks came to be and then make plans to experience the park's inexhaustible charms yourself. Its monuments, playgrounds, water features, and trails are only touched on here.

City Park Golf Course
E 23rd Ave
E 23rd Ave
Mile High Loop Trail
ball field
mixed-use fields
Denver Zoo
museum parking garage
N Colorado Blvd
Museum of Nature and Science
Joshua Monti Gateway
McLellan Gateway Entrance
tennis courts
horseshoe pit
Duck Lake
H2Odyssey
City Park
Dustin Redd Playground
Robert Burns Memorial
Prismatic Fountain
Ferril Lake
City Park Gardens
Grizzly's Last Stand
N York St
Martin Luther King Jr Memorial
City Park Pavillion
bandshell
boathouse
mixed-use fields
Children's Fountain
mixed-use fields
mixed-use fields
Joseph Addison Thatcher Memorial Fountain
Mile High Loop Trail
E 17th Ave
Richard E. Sopris Gateway Entrance
Lily Pond
E 17th Ave
City Park Esplanade
N
0   500   1,000 Feet

Gateways

Four gateways serve as entrances into the park. The first, William W. McLellan Gateway, was erected in 1904. McLellan, a member of the city council, advocated for the state to purchase the land for City Park. This gate sat at the East 18th Avenue entrance and was later moved to East 21st Avenue at York. McLellan donated half of his savings to erect the gateway. He considered that it was a civic duty for all citizens to give back in their own way.

The second gate, Richard E. Sopris Gateway, designed by F. E. Edbrooke, was erected in 1912 at the 17th Avenue entrance. It is made of pink sandstone and was engraved to honor the spirit of Sopris as a "pioneer, miner, legislator, explorer, soldier, sheriff, mayor, and park commissioner."

The third gate, on Colorado Boulevard, the Joshua Monti Gateway, was erected in 1916. Joshua Monti was a Denver pioneer, miner, and land owner. It is constructed of Platte Canyon granite and invites visitors to visit the Museum of Nature and Science.

The fourth gate, now known as the City Park Esplanade, was erected in 1917 on ground the state donated to the city. The gate was originally named the Dennis Sullivan Gateway, after a Denver pioneer banker. It was built to honor agriculture and mining. Leo Lentelli sculpted two pylons out of terra cotta brick, one of a miner and his burro, and the other of two women gathering wheat.

Prismatic Fountain

During Mayor Robert Speer's reign, electricity became the norm. To dazzle and wow the electorate, he installed the large lake's Prismatic Fountain, which was inspired by a fountain he had seen in Mexico City. Designed by Fred Darlington, it illuminated at night with dark and light reds, blues, oranges, yellows, and lavenders. People still enjoy the renovated fountain lights today.

Joseph Addison Thatcher Memorial Fountain

At the north end of City Park Esplanade, you'll find a bronze female figure. She represents Colorado and holds the state's shield and sword. She honors loyalty, learning, and love. Lorado Taft sculpted this piece; it was presented by Joseph Thatcher, a Denver banker.

Martin Luther King Jr. Memorial

In 1976, Ed Rose took up the challenge of sculpting the Martin Luther King Jr. Memorial. Many felt that the squat figure of King with Emmett Till, the young man from Chicago who was lynched while visiting relatives in Mississippi which

City Park, the jewel of the City Beautiful movement, has surprises in every corner; you'll want to take a day or more to explore it.

prompted King into the civil rights movement, should have been more lifelike and not so representative. The Martin Luther King Jr. Memorial Foundation had commissioned the statue and felt the head was too large for the body and refused to pay until it was fixed. Although Rose was finally paid, the statue was moved to the Denver Art Museum's basement in 1976. In 2002 it was moved to the Martin Luther King Jr. Museum and Cultural Center in Pueblo, Colorado.

A second statue, fashioned by Ed Dwight, replaced the original in 2002. This is the Martin Luther King Jr. Memorial that now stands in City Park. It includes King, who figuratively stands on the shoulders of Mohandas Gandhi, Rosa Parks, Sojourner Truth, and Frederick Douglass. Surrounding the monument on the plaza, you'll find panels depicting relevant moments in civil rights history and a re-creation of how slaves laid in ballast in the bottom of ships as they were transported to slave auctions.

Robert Burns Memorial
Near Duck Lake, you'll find the Robert Burns Memorial sculpture of the Scotsman poet and lyricist, Robert Burns. The Scots Caledonian Club of Colorado donated the sculpture in 1904.

Grizzly's Last Stand
Southwest of the east museum entrance, you'll find *Grizzly's Last Stand*. Donated by J. A. McGuire, editor of *Outdoor Life* magazine, this mascot of the museum was sculpted by Louis Paul Jonas in 1930.

City Park Gardens

Throughout the park, you'll find formal gardens. They started with a donation of French hybrid lilacs from Milton Keegan, with an additional donation of forty-seven varietals of crabapple trees from S. R. DeBoer. Over the years, the gardens' many plantings have been donated by groups such as the Denver Rose Society, the American Iris Society, the Men's Garden Clubs of Colorado, and other citizens.

H2Odyssey

Kids can squeal and parents can chase them through the water fountain between the rose gardens and the museum. *Grizzly's Last Stand* overlooks the melee as spurts of water randomly dash up from the ground, offering wet surprises to anyone who dares challenge them.

Dustin Redd Playground

On the other end of the park from H2Odyssey is the city's largest playground and certainly a fan favorite. You'll find a giant 25,000 square foot treasure trove built on a kid scale. Within the wood beam–rope park, you'll find three-story towers, six slides, three sets of swings, and enough space for kids to run and use outdoor voices to their heart's content. Once slated to be upgraded to a park like the new one in Sanchez (see Paco Sanchez Park), the playground was saved by citizens who rallied at public meetings with Denver Parks and Recreation. The playground, built by over three hundred volunteers and funded by donations from the Broncos and Phil Long car dealerships, is named after Dustin Redd, a five-year-old who drowned in Ferril Lake in 1996.

Trails

A walk around Ferril Lake will clock you about one mile. Within the park, you'll also see the Mile High Loop, a meandering 5K paved path at 5280 feet in elevation. In each corner of the park, you can continue to make larger and larger loops on both paved and unpaved trails, weaving among spruce, cottonwood, elm, and hawthorn trees.

Boathouse

At the boathouse, you can rent paddleboats, stand-up paddleboards, canoes, kayaks, and water bikes. Or you can bring your own. In the winter, if the ice is thick enough, you can skate and play ice hockey.

EXTEND YOUR VISIT

After enjoying the park, visit the **Museum of Nature and Science** or the **Denver Zoo**. Both are in the park. Check out their websites for information about attractions, visiting hours, and entrance fees.

A VISION STARTS WITH WATER

At the turn of the twentieth century, saloons were the gathering places for the public; the idea of community parks was just forming. While he was the city's mayor, and then the city's first park commissioner, Mayor Richard Sopris came to realize that in order for his idea for City Park to flourish, it would need water. After some wrangling, the city council purchased what became City Ditch. Meandering from the South Platte River through Washington Park (see Washington Park) and then going underground at City Park, it filled Ferril Lake, Duck Lake, and ultimately the pond at the zoo.

With a good water source now in place, Sopris hired Henry F. Meryweather to design the park. Meryweather, heavily influenced by Frederick Law Olmsted Jr., who had just developed New York's Central Park, created ambling carriageways for horses and carriages, water features, formal gardens, statues, and fountains. Development of the park was slow—the city had to manage all of the squatters along York Street, and the park budget was minimal.

Sopris raised $500 from adjacent landowners to plant the first row of cottonwoods, and he motivated youngsters to come to the park on Arbor Day to plant trees. By 1890 over 13,000 trees were planted in what was once sage prairie.

Despite the 1893 silver crash that depressed Denver, the city continued to fund City Park and make it a priority. Soon the large lake, which would later be named after Thomas Ferril, Colorado's first poet laureate, was dug. John J. Humphreys and William E. Fisher designed and built the pavilion, which included a jail cell in the basement for the unruly. Also during this time, Mayor Thomas McMurray donated his bear cub, Billy Bryan (named after famed orator and politician William Jennings Bryan), and the zoo began. Continuing the fun at the turn of the century, the city built a horse track, which doubled as a speedway. World records for horse and car speed were established there (the track was closed in 1950).

When cable cars reached the park as the twentieth century dawned, demand for its beauty skyrocketed. Sopris's last great act in the park was to fund and build a floating bandstand. In order to encourage tram usage to get to the park, the cable car companies sponsored the bands that played nightly concerts on the floating bandstand. People flocked to City Park.

Although the floating bandstand no longer exists, the tradition of free-to-the-public concerts lives on.

City Park continued to grow and become the centerpiece for outdoor excitement in Denver. In 1904, Denver elected Robert Speer as mayor, and the national movement called City Beautiful came to Denver. Promoted at the Chicago World's Fair, urban parks became the centerpiece of many mayors' visions throughout the United States. Inspired by what he saw in Chicago and Europe, Speer he was determined to create the prettiest city in the West on his return to Denver.

He marched forward to pave roads, light parks, flower fields, and beautify any area he could. Speer hired the best architects and planners available, including Charles Robinson, who submitted the plan for Civic Center Park; George Kessler, who envisioned the boulevard system; and S. R. DeBoer, a landscape architect. Together, they drafted and executed Speer's big ideas, many of them within City Park. When Mayor Speer visited Düsseldorf, he couldn't get over its beauty. While there, he came across a fountain called *Six Legs* and sought permission to duplicate it. This recreation, by Max Blondet, is called *Children's Fountain* and is on the west side of the park. It's the bronze sculpture of children reading as frogs squirt water up to them.

52 CHEESMAN PARK

A lovely park to walk, but with a ghostly past

Location: 1599 E. 8th Ave., Denver
Acreage: 80.7
Amenities: Benches, drinking fountain, pavilion, picnic tables, playground, flower beds, fountain, walking/jogging path, bike/pedestrian path, shelter, scenic views, picnic area

GETTING THERE

BY CAR Take I-25 to E. 6th Ave. to Josephine St. Turn north to the park. Park in the garage. **BY TRANSIT** Buses 6 and 24 stop nearby. **BY BIKE** Take the Cherry Creek Trail. Turn left toward Gilpin St. Slight right onto Gilpin St. Turn right onto E. 4th Ave. Turn left onto Williams St. Turn right onto E. 7th Ave./E. 7th Ave. Pkwy. Turn left onto Josephine St. Bike racks are on York.

This is one of Denver's larger parks and it has a jaw-dropping history. Cheesman Park is named after Walter Cheesman, a forefather and major political influencer in Denver's history. The park features miles of paved and unpaved trails, a gorgeous

The park may have a reputation for ghostly and ghastly happenings, but the Cheesman Park Pavilion has hosted presidents and weddings.

forest of pines, firs, oaks, and elms, and its wide open, grassy fields have beckoned Denverites for over a century. But the story of this park starts before Cheesman. William Larimer Jr., who founded Denver (see Confluence Park), soon realized that the city needed a cemetery, and in 1858 he declared this area, which was an old Arapahoe Indian burial ground, to be Mt. Prospect Cemetery, or Prospect Hill.

In the rough and tumble world of the western frontier, the first person to be buried in the new cemetery was Jack O'Neill, a victim of a barroom brawl and gun fight. His murderer, John Stoefel, soon followed. Despite Larimer's vision of the wealthy and famous being buried here, the area soon fell into disrepair, and State Senator Henry Teller requested that the United States Congress allow Denver to turn the area into a park. Congress agreed and Denver in turn designated the area Congress Park.

What followed was the gruesome work of relocating the bodies. Denver notified its citizens to come within ninety days and claim the dead to reinter them elsewhere. Most of the bodies eventually ended up in either Riverside Cemetery or Fairmount Cemetery. But since many of the buried were homeless and scoundrels, they weren't claimed.

At the time, Mt. Prospect Cemetery was subdivided into sections, including Odd Fellows, Society of Masons, Roman Catholics, Jewish, the Grand Army of the

Republic—there was even a segregated section at the south end for the Chinese. Because the Roman Catholic section was so large, Mayor Joseph E. Bates sold that 40 acres, which is now the Denver Botanic Gardens (see their website for more information about the fabulous gardens), to the archdiocese and named it Mount Calvary. Eventually the Catholics reinterred most of the bodies at Mt. Olivet Catholic Cemetery in Wheat Ridge. The Chinese bodies were sent to China.

Once a majority of the bodies were moved, the city hired undertaker E. P. McGovern to dig up and relocate the remaining five thousand or so bodies to Riverside Cemetery for $1.90 each. After digging and working for a while, McGovern couldn't locate enough adult-sized coffins and ended up breaking up skeletons and putting different parts in different child-size caskets just to get the job done. Soon, he was exposed for his behavior. Said the *Denver Republic* in 1893: "The line of desecrated graves at the southern boundary of the cemetery sickened and horrified everybody by the appearance they presented. Around their edges were piled broken coffins, rent and tattered shrouds and fragments of clothing that had been torn from the dead bodies. . . . All were trampled into the ground by the footsteps of the gravediggers like rejected junk."

The city stopped the work and began the process of creating the new park. Under the vision of Mayor Robert Speer and his City Beautiful movement, Reinhard Schuetze was hired to design the park. Trees, gardens, and pavilions appeared in the design, but it wasn't until Walter Cheesman's family donated $100,000 to build the pavilion that the park finally framed up as a landmark for the Mayor's park vision. At that time, renowned city and landscape architect George Kessler designed the Temple in the Sun of white Colorado marble, and Mayor Speer had the park's name changed from Congress to Cheesman. Thus, Congress Park to the east of Cheesman Park keeps its original name (and never had any bodies buried in it), the Botanic Gardens stands alone, and Cheesman Park became the park as it is today.

Nowadays, after a sprucing up of the pavilion and the park in the 1970s by The Park People in a partnership with Denver Parks and Recreation, the park beckons citizens to enjoy its grassy fields, urban forests, manicured gardens, and at least 3 miles of walking paths. While visiting the park, be sure to go into the Cheesman Memorial and view the bronze plaque showing the outline of the Front Range and names of all its peaks, gifted to the city by the Colorado Mountain Club. While looking west into the park, also notice the dips in the grass. These dips could be indicators of the dug-up graves or locators for the over four thousand bodies still assumed to be buried here in Cheesman Park. Many folks come to the park during Halloween to find ghosts!

EXTEND YOUR VISIT

If you didn't get enough fresh air and ghoulish enjoyment at Cheesman Park, be sure to extend your visit to the **Denver Botanic Gardens**.

53   CONGRESS PARK

Come fly a kite—or maybe get into a pick-up pickleball game

Location: 850 N. Josephine St., Denver
Acreage: 19
Amenities: Benches, drinking fountain, picnic shelter, picnic tables, playground, outdoor pool, restroom, basketball court, football field, baseball/softball field, soccer field, tennis court, pickleball court, parking lot, picnic area

GETTING THERE

BY CAR Take I-25 to E. 6th Ave. to Josephine St. Turn north to the park. **BY TRANSIT** Buses 6 and 24 stop nearby. **BY BIKE** Take the Cherry Creek Trail. Turn left toward Gilpin St. Slight right onto Gilpin St. Turn right onto E. 4th Ave. Turn left onto Williams St. Turn right onto E. 7th Ave./E. 7th Ave. Pkwy. Turn left onto Josephine St.

This park, and the area where Cheesman Park and the Denver Botanic Gardens were eventually created, started as Prospect Hill, otherwise known as Denver's cemetery. A place where the rich buried their family members, it soon became an eyesore on a windswept hill with little access to water. State Senator Henry Teller, seeing the development opportunities of the area, thought it might be good to turn a neglected cemetery into a glorious park and appealed to Congress. Congress agreed, demanding that the bodies get reinterred elsewhere and that the city pay $1.25 an acre for the land. In return, the city named the park after Congress, thus, Congress Park. Eventually, the area to the west of the park would become Cheesman Park and the Denver Botanic Gardens. No bodies were buried in what became Congress Park; all the bodies were buried in what became Cheesman or the Botanic Gardens. (See Cheesman Park.) In the 1940s, Victory Gardens were planted by the public as part of the war effort.

The north end of the park holds the 911 dispatch tower, thus the park is also sometimes called Signal Hill. Down the hill, you'll find the park's pool, opened seasonally, a playground with a tunnel slide, swings, and a bridge. Covering the grassy areas are many types of fields for outdoor activities, including soccer, tennis, pickleball, basketball, and football. This park with its active open space draws kite flyers, too.

EXTEND YOUR VISIT

Head to the **Denver Botanic Gardens** for manicured gardens. Don't miss the sensory garden on the right after you enter the gates. See their website for more information.

54 ALAMO PLACITA PARK

These days you make your own amusement at Alamo Placita Park

Location: 300 N Emerson St., Denver
Acreage: 4.6
Amenities: Benches, drinking fountain, picnic tables, playground, basketball court, flower beds, picnic area

GETTING THERE

BY CAR Take I-25 to Speer Blvd. Go south to N. Clarkson St. Take a left. Turn right on E. 3rd Ave. to the park. **BY TRANSIT** Buses 6, 12, and 83 D/L stop nearby. **BY BIKE** Take the Cherry Creek Trail to N. Emerson St. to the park.

With a fun past and formal gardens Alamo Placita Park is worth a visit.

This gorgeous little park and garden has a long and fun history. It started as Chutes Park in the 1880s, when it was an amusement park where Denverites could watch circus shows featuring a herd of elk diving off a platform into a pool below. After watching the elk, they might see a female bicyclist from Paris braving the dive, and then gawk at Henri Maurice Canon, a 617-pound performer, making a giant splash. Next they could marvel at the Last Days of Pompeii, a show that reenacted the famed volcanic disaster, complete with a "real" ten-foot-high simulated volcano. Sadly, Chutes Park burned to the ground and went bankrupt more than a century ago.

The area was renamed Arlington Park. Mayor Richard Speer, who owned land in and around the area at the time, decided the park was "overgrown with mammoth cottonwoods," cleared it, and divided it into lots that were subsequently sold for development. But right before he left office in 1911, the city repurchased portions of the land and declared it a public park for the citizens of Denver. Cherry Creek, which Mayor Speer had channeled and walled around the same time, ran through this contested area. The north side became known as Alamo Placita Park, which means "little tree park," and the south side is now Hungarian Freedom Park. (See Hungarian Freedom Park.) You can access either from the Cherry Creek Trail.

While in the park, be sure to enjoy the formal gardens, which bloom nicely in the spring and summer. A small playground, which is popular with late morning caregivers and preschoolers, sits beneath cottonwood shade. Picnic tables host impromptu meals.

EXTEND YOUR VISIT

Head south across Speer Boulevard to enjoy **Hungarian Freedom Park**, the other half of the original Arlington Park.

55 HUNGARIAN FREEDOM PARK

Revolt!

Location: 901 E. 1st Ave., Denver
Acreage: 1.7
Amenities: Picnic tables, benches, fountain

GETTING THERE

BY CAR Take I-25 to Speer Blvd. south to the park. **BY TRANSIT** Buses 1, 12, and 83L stop nearby. **BY BIKE** Take Cherry Creek Trail to the park.

Stately lions on the fountain and a significant memorial are two reasons to visit Hungarian Freedom Park.

Like its sister park, Alamo Placita Park, which is just across Speer Boulevard and Cherry Creek, this park has a long history. It started as a dump, became Arlington Park under the vision of S. R. DeBoer, and was split in two. Ultimately the southern portion was renamed to commemorate the 1956 revolt of Hungarians against Soviet oppression.

DeBoer originally designed this side of the park to offer a forested respite for the local neighborhoods. You can still see the pine, spruce, fir, honey locust, and hawthorn at its southeast end. In 1963 the Hungarian Club of Colorado, led by Janos Benko, petitioned the city to create a memorial to honor the people killed in the Hungarian-Soviet conflict. The city agreed. The club hired sculptor Zoltán Popovits to design the Hungarian memorial, the first of its kind in North America. You'll find this solemn memorial of concrete and bronze at the southeast end of the park.

In 1976 a Baroque two-tiered fountain with lion heads, copying the one in Benedict Fountain Park, in northwest Denver, and designed by Maurice Bardin, moved in. Children used to dip their toes in the fountain while chatting with the lions until the public health department ended the conversation. In 1986 the Hungarian Freedom Park was listed in the National Register of Historic Places as a contributing feature of the Denver Park and Parkway System.

EXTEND YOUR VISIT

Be sure to read the engravings and poems at the monument, then head over to **Alamo Placita Park** across Speer Boulevard to see the other half of the original Arlington Park.

56 JAMES N. MANLEY PARK

A treasured neighborhood park that commemorates a school principal

Location: 400 N. Josephine St., Denver
Acreage: 1.43
Amenities: Benches, drinking fountain, picnic tables, playground, bike/pedestrian path

GETTING THERE

BY CAR Take I-25 to Speer Blvd., which turns into E. 1st Ave. Take a left on Josephine St. to the park. **BY TRANSIT** Buses 6 and 83L stop nearby. **BY BIKE** Take Cherry Creek Trail. Turn north on S. University Blvd. Jig over to N. Josephine St. to the park.

This pocket park is named after principal James N. Manley, who led nearby Bromwell Elementary School from 1973 to 1984. He revived the school and helped it transition after two fires threatened to close it permanently. In 1996, the neighbors petitioned to have the park just north of the school named after Manley. Now the park is the go-to for local children for a mid-morning romp or an after-school recess. Although it's not a big park, the neighborhood loves it and keeps its eye on its local treasure.

EXTEND YOUR VISIT

Head over to **Cherry Creek Mall** for some shopping or lunch.

57 HENRY S. LINDSLEY PARK

Awaiting your return

Location: 4601 E. Hale Pkwy., Denver
Acreage: 7
Amenities: Benches, picnic shelter, drinking fountain, picnic tables, playground, basketball court, bike/pedestrian path, horseshoe pits, baseball/softball field, tennis court, picnic area

GETTING THERE

BY CAR Take I-25 to E. 6th Ave Pkwy. Go east to Eudora St. Take a left on E. Hale Pkwy. to the park. **BY TRANSIT** Bus 15 stops nearby. **BY BIKE** Take the Cherry Creek Trail to E. 12th Ave. through Cheesman Park. Turn right on Colorado Blvd. and left on E. Hale Pkwy. to the park.

In 1954, Judge Henry S. Lindsley was the youngest person ever elected to the District Bench. He subsequently went on to become a Colorado Supreme Court Justice. His most famous rulings included allowing the San Luis Valley to pump water from an underwater reservoir, which established the agricultural economy in San Luis Valley. Additionally, he authored the decision to uphold the rights soldiers have to return to their jobs after deployment.

A gorilla greets you at Lindsley Park; be sure to scratch its nose for good luck.

This cute little Mayfair neighborhood park, named in honor of the judge, has a camel and gorilla for the littles to tackle. A large sandpit, decorated with the neighborhood's shovels and pails, awaits the curious digger. Informal games of baseball or softball occur on the field, and a tennis court welcomes those who want to try their hand at love.

EXTEND YOUR VISIT

Across the street is the **Rose Medical Center**. Head over that way to explore the campus and enjoy the many pieces of public art on display.

58 MAYFAIR PARK

Play with the ponies!

Location: 1000 N. Ivy St., Denver
Acreage: 4.8
Amenities: Benches, picnic tables, playground, basketball court, bike/pedestrian path, flower beds, natural areas

GETTING THERE

BY CAR Take I-25 to Colfax Ave. Go east to Ivy St. Take a right to the park. **BY TRANSIT** Buses 6 and 40 stop nearby. **BY BIKE** Take Cherry Creek Trail to turn to E. Bayaud Ave. Turn left onto S. Steele St. Turn right onto E. 1st Ave. Turn left onto Ivanhoe St. to the park.

This well-loved neighborhood park welcomes aspiring thoroughbred race jockeys. You'll find Mayfair, the statue pony, politely kneeling, waiting for her next rider. Next to her is a rich array of playground equipment, organized for bigs and littles. And, as with most neighborhood parks, you can also enjoy running freely in the grassy open fields or along the trails that loop the park.

EXTEND YOUR VISIT

Head over to Montclair's famous **Richthofen Castle**, built by the Baron Walter von Richthofen, uncle of the famous Red Baron. It is located at 7020 E. 12th Avenue.

59   PULASKI PARK

A facility that serves up plenty of love

Location: 3300 E. Bayaud Ave., Denver
Acreage: 13 combined
Amenities: Drinking fountain, picnic tables, playground, restroom, tennis court, Gates Tennis Center, picnic area

GETTING THERE

BY CAR Take Colorado Blvd. to E. Bayaud Ave and turn west. **BY TRANSIT** Buses 3, 40, and 83D stop nearby. **BY BIKE** Take the Cherry Creek Trail to E. Bayaud Ave.

Pulaski Park and Gates Tennis Center join together to provide plenty of fun for everyone. The park, named after Casimir Pulaski, a Polish military commander and American Revolutionary War hero, features wide-open fields with grassy areas for kite flying and picnicking. An action-packed playground with two sets of equipment allows kids of all ages to go wild while their caretakers relax in the sun.

Next door at the Gates Tennis Center, grab your racquet, reserve a court, and play tennis to your heart's content. The facility was gifted to the people of Denver by the late Charles C. Gates of the Gates Corporation. The center, awarded the USTA Outstanding Large Public Facility of the year in 2008, allows you to pay as you play; there are no residency requirements. With twenty unlit courts, the facility offers year-round lessons, camps, and tournaments for adults and kids. Be sure to check the center's website for hours and reservations.

EXTEND YOUR VISIT

Jump on over to the Cherry Creek Trail and head in either direction to visit several **Denver Sister City parks**.

60   CITY OF KARMIEL PARK

Some Denver Jewish history

Location: 3300 E. Cherry Creek North Dr., Denver
Acreage: 3.3
Amenities: Benches, bike/pedestrian path, Cherry Creek Trail

GETTING THERE

BY CAR Take Colorado Blvd. to Cherry Creek N. Dr. **BY TRANSIT** Buses 40 and 83D stop nearby. **BY BIKE** Take the Cherry Creek Trail to the park.

The fourth of Denver's Sister City parks, and one of three on the Cherry Creek Trail, City of Karmiel Park celebrates the Denver Jewish community. You'll find their stories in the plaques within the park, including one about Prussia-born Fred Sadek Solomon. He owned the first general mercantile store in Denver and also served on the city council and as a territory governor. During this time, a Jewish woman named Francis Wisebart Jacobs arrived and formed the Denver Hebrew Ladies Relief Society which ultimately morphed into the National Jewish Health hospital.

When the city purchased the land to create the park in response to frequent flooding in this area, it decided to name the park after their newly formed relation with the city of Karmiel in Israel. Karmiel has a similar climate and environment to Denver.

Within the park, you'll see the sculpture *Allies in Life* by Michael Clapper, a local Denver artist. The Cherry Creek Trail meanders through this linear park under shady oaks and connects several Sister City parks.

EXTEND YOUR VISIT

Down the Cherry Creek Trail about 0.3 mile, don't miss the children's garden. Also be sure to check out the **City of Brest Park** and the **City of Takayama Park**. Both are Sister City parks, and they are located nearby along the Cherry Creek Trail.

The Allies in Life *sculpture is just one of the attractions in City of Karmiel Park.*

61   CITY OF TAKAYAMA PARK

Finding peace in Denver

Location: 3700 E. Cherry Creek North Dr., Denver
Acreage: 6.6
Amenities: Benches, bike/pedestrian path, Cherry Creek Trail

GETTING THERE

BY CAR Take Colorado Blvd. to Cherry Creek North Dr. **BY TRANSIT** Buses 40 and 83D stop nearby. **BY BIKE** Take the Cherry Creek Trail.

As with the other two Sister City parks along Cherry Creek, Denver purchased this land to help control flooding. But before that, the town of Harman was here. Named after Edmond Preston Harman, a former slaveholder from Georgia who wanted to create a freedman's plantation, the town of Harman never quite took off and got annexed to Denver after the silver crash. Nevertheless, the original Harman Town Hall still stands at the corner of St. Paul Street and East 4th Avenue; it is now a private residence.

During World War II, the US government interned Japanese Americans. Governor Ralph Carr didn't like this idea, and after the war he developed relationships with the Japanese communities that had relocated to Denver from the internment camps in southeastern Colorado. These ties were the start of Denver's Japanese connection. Ultimately this connection helped create Denver's Sister City relationship with Takayama in 1960 to celebrate the one hundred year anniversary of the Harris Treaty between the United States and Japan.

Although posh now, this area once included the city's dump. Temple Buell, who came to Denver for tuberculosis treatment, turned the dump into one of Denver's first malls in 1955. It grew quickly as people fled the shops of downtown in favor of suburban malls. Thanks in part to the restoration of Cherry Creek and the building of the Cherry Creek Reservoir to control flooding, this area has come a long way from Harman and the city dump.

Enjoy the plaques within the park and the small bonsai garden, then amble along the Cherry Creek Trail in search of the next Sister City park.

EXTEND YOUR VISIT

Head up to the corner of E. 4th Avenue and St. Paul Street to admire—from the street—the former **Harman Town Hall**.

62   CITY OF BREST PARK

Voila! Je suis ici!

Location: 3800 Cherry Creek South Dr., Denver
Acreage: 16.3
Amenities: Picnic tables, bike/pedestrian path

GETTING THERE

BY CAR Take S. Colorado Blvd. to Cherry Creek South Dr. **BY TRANSIT** Buses 40 and 83D stop nearby. **BY BIKE** Take the Cherry Creek Trail to the park.

One of three Denver Sister City parks on the Cherry Creek Trail, this park has French influence. The city of Brest, a medieval city in western France, suffered a heavy toll in World War II. Shortly after the war, to help our French friends, local students and their teacher from East High School raised $32,000 in nickels and pennies to help rebuild Brest's hospital. Their charity work caught the eye of Denver's leadership. Soon, the Denver Sister City program was born. The City of Brest Park was the first park in the program. It's fitting that this park honors the French. Many French fur trappers made their way along nearby Cherry Creek.

INTERNATIONAL SISTERHOOD

The Denver Sister City program, part of Sister Cities International, honors Denver's relationships with cities around the world. Often, those cities have something in common with Denver, such as capitol status, similar elevation, or common geography.

The organization bridges four continents, thirteen municipal governments, at least fifteen languages, and nearly twenty million city dwellers. It hosts festivals, student exchanges, and global experiences throughout the year. Its roots are in the People to People program, an idea facilitated by President Eisenhower to enhance international relationships through education, the exchange of culture, and humanitarian activity. The program was created to help bring about a peaceful climate in response to the Cold War.

Denver's version of Ike's idea celebrates thirteen cities. Not all of these Sister Cities have namesake parks in Denver, but you'll find many of the Sister City parks along Denver's creeks and rivers, although several are located in residential neighborhoods. (See parks 28, 38, 60, 61, 62, 63, 76, 101, 119, and 144 for the Sister City parks included in this book.)

Some believe the Platte River was named by these fur trappers. The French word *plat* means "flat," and this river is famously wide and shallow. But before the land became a Sister City park, this parcel and many acres around it would often flood. In response, the Castlewood Dam was built, but it burst in 1933 and the area was flooded once more. The Kentwood Dam replaced the Castlewood Dam in the 1950s.

The park contains a meandering path off the Cherry Creek Trail that's perfect for an afternoon stroll. Historic plaques encourage you along spruce-lined trails, telling the story of French influence in Denver. Offering a break from the noisy hustle and bustle of Cherry Creek, City of Brest Park encourages visitors to find a quiet spot for meditation and contemplation under the trees or within the nooks along the unpaved path.

EXTEND YOUR VISIT

If you want to learn more about Denver history, head south down the Cherry Creek Trail to **Four Mile Historic Park**.

63   CITY OF POTENZA PARK

A place to play bocce ball in the city!

Location: 1101 S. Holly St., Denver
Acreage: 4.5
Amenities: Benches, playground, bike/pedestrian path, bocce ball court

GETTING THERE

BY CAR Take I-25 to E. Evans Ave. Go east to Holly St. Turn left to the park. **BY TRANSIT** Buses 11, 40, and 83D stop nearby. **BY BIKE** Take the Cherry Creek Trail to the park.

It's not surprising that this Denver Sister City park has courts for the Italian sport of bocce. After all, Potenza *is* in Italy! This park recalls the impact that Italian immigrants have had on Denver, including the agricultural products they provided to its citizens at the turn of the century.

In 1977, Sam Martinelli purchased this 4 acres and donated it to the city to honor the Italian history, but the park was not developed until 1987. The nonprofit organization The Park People supplied funds to put in trees, grass, and an irrigation system to beautify the land. Now younger kids enjoy the drawbridges and

Adults can enjoy a game of bocce at City of Potenza Park, while the younger crowd tries out the playground equipment.

swings while bigger kids run through the grass catching Frisbees. You might even catch a game of bocce on the courts.

EXTEND YOUR VISIT

Take a walk north along the Cherry Creek Trail and visit the several other **Sister City parks** between the City of Potenza Park and the Cherry Creek Shopping Center.

64   KITTREDGE PARK

Some ups and downs for kids, and quiet contemplation for adults

Location: 851 N. Olive St., Denver
Acreage: 2.2
Amenities: Benches, picnic tables, playground, softball field, bike/pedestrian path, drinking fountain

GETTING THERE

BY CAR Take Quebec St. to E. 8th Ave. Go west to the park. **BY TRANSIT** Buses 6, 10, and 15 stop nearby. **BY BIKE** Take the Sand Creek Greenwayto E. 6th Ave. Pkwy. Turn left on Olive St. to the park.

Named after the Kittredge family, who built a castle on Oneida Street that was later turned into the Dean Peck School for Girls, this little neighborhood park sits unassumingly in the middle of the Montclair neighborhood. Charles Kittredge, an engineer, built the McMann and Kittredge Bank on the corner of 16th Street and Glenarm, and later founded the town of Kittredge on the banks of Clear Creek. His banking abilities contributed to him becoming superintendent at the Denver Mint.

This neighborhood park has your typical Denver amenities, plus a great standing seesaw that middles will adore. With its quiet nooks under shady trees, it's an inviting park for a lovely break from the day's hustle.

EXTEND YOUR VISIT

Enjoy a walk up and down the 700–900 block of **Oneida Street** to view the large Victorian homes.

65 DENISON PARK

Read in the shade

Location: 1105 N. Quebec St., Denver
Acreage: 2.4
Amenities: Benches, picnic tables, playground, basketball court, horseshoe pits

GETTING THERE

BY CAR Take Quebec St. to E. 11th Ave. to reach the park. **BY TRANSIT** Bus 73 stops nearby. **BY BIKE** Take Quebec St. to the park.

This corner park services the Montclair neighborhood. Kids love the multi-level play structure with four slides and several bridges. The open grassy area is perfect for throwing a Frisbee or for having an evening picnic. But it doesn't have to be all running and playing: bring a book to the park to honor the park's namesake, Ella Strong Denison, who benefited many libraries throughout the United States, including several on the University of Colorado Anschutz Medical Campus.

EXTEND YOUR VISIT

Right around the corner from the park is the **Richthofen Castle**, built by the uncle of the famed Red Baron. Now restored, its best viewing is around Halloween when the current owners get quite spirited. See it at 7020 East 12th Avenue, Denver.

66 MONTCLAIR PARK

The Molkery, once a place for cows, now a scene for festivities

Location: 6820 E. 12th Ave., Denver
Acreage: 2.3
Amenities: Historic site, Montclair Civic Center (The Molkery), benches, picnic tables, playground, horseshoe pits, tennis court, picnic area

GETTING THERE

BY CAR Take Quebec St. to E. 11th Ave. Turn west to the park. **BY TRANSIT** Buses 10, 15, and 15L stop nearby. **BY BIKE** Take Cherry Creek Trail to E. 7th Ave. Pkwy. Take a left on Newport St. to the park.

Although named after its founder's hometown of Montclair, New Jersey, it was Baron von Richthofen who put it on the map. This baron, not the other less famous scoundrel who founded Park Hill, was an uncle of the famed Red Baron. He came into Denver with a giant reputation and sadly died before his vision of Montclair becoming a world-class health spa destination could flourish. Appendicitis got him.

But before he died, he convinced eighty-eight others to build homes—double the size of typical Denver houses at the time—in the Montclair neighborhood. Three-story mansions of brick and stone grace what is now Montclair's historic district, but the Baron's dwelling topped them all. Fifteen-thousand square feet of opulence sit at Montclair's high point. Surviving renovation after renovation, the beautiful architecture of Montclair's famous mansion is especially highlighted when the current owners host Halloween parties.

The Montclair Park Civic Center was once part of the Baron von Richthofen estate.

In the middle of the park sits what is left of the baron's estate. Now the Montclair Civic Center, purchased by the City of Denver in 1908 as its first community center, it can be rented for events. This building, listed on the National Register of Historic Places, has been a dairy barn, restaurant, and sanatorium for tuberculosis patients.

The park features the usual playground and picnic tables, plus horseshoe pits and a tennis court. Enjoy imagining the parties within The Molkery (German for "dairy barn"), which is the nickname of this civic center, as you relax in the park.

EXTEND YOUR VISIT

Walk around the corner to see the rest of the **Richthofen estate**, including the castle at 7020 East 12th Avenue.

67 CRANMER PARK

A view worth visiting, time after time

Location: 4501 E. 1st Ave., Denver
Acreage: 24
Amenities: Benches, drinking fountain, picnic tables, plaza, flower beds, football field, soccer field, baseball/softball field, scenic views, picnic area

GETTING THERE

BY CAR Take I-25 to Alameda Ave. Go east and turn left on Colorado Blvd. Turn right on E. 1st Ave. to the park. **BY TRANSIT** Buses 1, 3, and 40 stop nearby. **BY BIKE** Take the Cherry Creek Trail to E. Bayaud Ave. Turn left on Colorado Blvd. and right on E. 1st Ave. to the park.

Sitting as the centerpiece of Denver's highest neighborhood of Hilltop, the jewel of Cranmer Park is its historic sundial and mountain range diorama. Looking west from the sundial, you can see the mountain range laid out in stone on the edge of the steps, identifying popular peaks and ranges. The remainder of the park is open space and flower beds, with soccer and softball fields available seasonally.

Once called Mountain View Park, and for good reason, it was renamed after George Cranmer, who strongly impacted the beauty of Denver. He had the vision to create Red Rocks Park and the Denver Mountain Parks system, including his personal victory, Winter Park. Under Mayor Benjamin Stapleton, Cranmer's can-do attitude got him appointed as Denver's Manager of Parks and Improvements. In that role, he successfully implemented many of the ideas that had arisen during

Mayor Robert Speer's tenure. He also purchased the land for what became the Stapleton Airport. (See Central Park and Westerly Creek Park.)

Cranmer's father was a Confederate soldier who moved west to get into ranching. The younger Cranmer's love for the outdoors kept him motivated to tackle the ups and downs of the time period, completing projects under budget and with flair. Just take a look at Red Rocks Park!

The sundial itself resulted from Cranmer viewing a six-inch model of it in a Chinese curio shop. Designer Steven Ionides took his notes and designed a 2.5 ton landmark, which was destroyed by vandals in 1965. Milt Erickson sculpted a replacement and the Colorado Mason Contractors installed it. In 2018, the sundial and the accompanying stone panorama of the mountain range were restored once again.

EXTEND YOUR VISIT

The Hilltop neighborhood has several jewels, including the famous mansion **Cableland**. Built by TV mogul Bill Daniels, the home engulfs eight lots. Upon Daniels' passing, the property was donated to the city and county of Denver as the official residence of the mayor. It is also used by nonprofit organizations for fundraising. Since 1986 millions of dollars have been raised on the estate, which includes a multi-level outdoor pool, a heated driveway, and squirrel condominiums. Inside, you'll find a grand room for two hundred people and a closed-circuit television system. The address is 4150 East Shangri La Drive. Check the Cableland website (cableland.org) for times to see inside.

68 DC BURNS PARK

An inspiring open space where you'll find intriguing sculptures to contemplate

Location: 250 S. Colorado Blvd., Denver
Acreage: 12
Amenities: Picnic tables, public art, open space

GETTING THERE

BY CAR Take I-25 to Colorado Blvd. Go north to the park. **BY TRANSIT** Buses 1, 3, 40, and 83L stop nearby. **BY BIKE** Take Cherry Creek Trail to S. Steele St. Continue onto Cherry Creek North Dr. Slight left onto E. Alameda Ave. Turn left onto S. Colorado Blvd. to the park.

Originally just a temporary art exhibit, DC Burns Park has endured for decades.

This park is named after Daniel Cochran Burns, founder of the D. C. Burns Realty & Trust Company. The Burns family paved the way for home ownership throughout Denver by providing low-income housing and creative financing in a time when many people had no access to home ownership. After D. C. died, his nephew Franklin, and Franklin's wife, Joy, took their seat at Denver's business and social tables. Together, they changed how people bought homes and how women invested in banks, and along the way they grew the hotel and tourism industry in Denver. The Colorado Business Hall of Fame honor both of these Denver pillars.

As for the park and its sculpture, the vision began one night in the 1960s when Bev and Bernie Rosen dreamed up a sculpture park with their artist friends, Roger Kotoske and Wilbert Verhelst. They lamented to one another that there was no place for sculpture in Denver, and so they created the one-time-only Denver Sculpture Symposium. Proposed to be a temporary exhibit, sculptors Kotoske and Verhelst, along with Anthony Magar, Dean Fleming, Peter Forakis, Robert Morris, Robert Mangold, Richard Van Buren, and Angelo Di Benedetto, crafted temporary pieces out of marine lumber.

Over time, the sculptures deteriorated or were taken down, ultimately leaving only the works of Verhelst, Kotoske, Magar, Fleming, and Di Benedetto. In the 1990s Di Benedetto's piece was recreated in concrete. Fleming's work was demolished, and Kotoske's was rebuilt. A new sculpture was added—Barbara Baer's

Jazz, which has a different style than the minimalist others. Thus, Magar and the Verhelst are the only originals remaining from the Denver Sculpture Symposium.

Yet, regardless of the history of the sculptures, DC Burns Park is a great open, grassy space for passive enjoyment of the Cherry Creek area. It's a good place to go to get away from the hustle of Colorado Boulevard and Alameda Avenue. Be awed at the giant sculptures as you while the day away.

EXTEND YOUR VISIT

Once you've had your fill of art, head across the street to any of the many great places to eat in Cherry Creek and its mall.

69   ROBINSON PARK

Is there anything more fun than a good sledding hill?

Location: 200 N. Fairfax St., Denver
Acreage: 6.7
Amenities: Drinking fountain, benches, picnic tables, playground, restroom, basketball court, football field, baseball/softball field, bleachers, picnic area

GETTING THERE

BY CAR Take I-25 to E. 6th Ave. Turn south on Fairfax St. to the park. **BY TRANSIT** Buses 3 and 6 stop nearby. **BY BIKE** Take the Cherry Creek Trail to E. Bayaud Ave. Take a left on Fairfax St. to the park.

The Robinson family owned the land this park now sits on, but when they moved their Robinson Brick Yard (now owned by General Shale) to another location, they donated the original brickyard property to the city. Thanks to their generosity, Hilltop neighborhood kids and their parents can now enjoy a good snow romp when the flakes fly. With gently sloping hillsides that run into large open space, no one has to worry about a wayward sled heading into a busy street.

A sidenote: after the brickyard left the area, the EPA discovered large amounts of radium at the site. They designated it as a Superfund site, cleaned it up, and now generations of kids have run, skipped, and giggled here.

EXTEND YOUR VISIT

Go southeast to discover **Crestmoor Park** if you want to enjoy activities such as soccer and tennis. Go west to view the historic sundial in **Cranmer Park**.

70   CRESTMOOR PARK

The choicest neighborhood includes this very choice park

Location: 99 S. Monaco Pkwy., Denver
Acreage: 37
Amenities: Benches, drinking fountain, picnic tables, playground, restroom, bike/pedestrian path, soccer field, baseball/softball field, tennis court, picnic area

GETTING THERE

BY CAR Take I-25 to Speer Blvd., which turns into 1st Ave. Turn right on Steele St. onto Cherry Creek North Dr. Take a left on E. Alameda Ave. Take a left on S. Kearney St. Take a right on E. Cedar Ave. Take a left on S. Locust St. to the park on Monaco. **BY TRANSIT** Buses 6, 75, and 83L stop nearby. **BY BIKE** Take the Cherry Creek Trail to Vale Dr. Turn east to S. Flamingo Ct., take a left to E. Exposition Ave., and take a right. Take a left on S. Kearny St. to the park.

Hoping to attract the affluent to a high-end neighborhood, the Crestmoor Realty Company advertised this area as being "the choicest." A protected, residential park featured in their promotion in 1936. Since then, beautiful custom homes have been built here. And the neighborhood certainly enjoys its namesake park.

The park itself, at over 37 acres, has many nooks and crannies to explore. More than 3 miles of paved and unpaved trail within invite you to tour around the playground, forest, and open spaces. Along the way you'll find a well-appointed set of tennis courts, nice views, and active people. On weekend mornings, the park buzzes with kids' soccer games where parents coach from the sidelines. During the evening, many dog walkers and joggers use the trails to relax.

EXTEND YOUR VISIT

Head west to **Cranmer Park** and check out the historic sundial.

71   FOUR MILE HISTORIC PARK

Experience the pioneering life at this remarkable hands-on historical park

Location: 715 S. Forest St., Denver
Acreage: 10.8
Amenities: Historic site, museum, special events, educational activities, paid admission required

GETTING THERE

BY CAR Take I-25 to W. Alameda Ave. Turn east. Turn right on Cherry Creek Dr. S. Turn left on S. Cherry St. Turn right on E. Exposition Ave. to the park. **BY TRANSIT** Buses 1, 40, and 83L stop nearby. **BY BIKE** Take the Cherry Creek Trail to the park.

This stage coach stop couldn't compete when the trains came, but Four Mile Historic Park still captures the pioneer spirit.

Samuel and Jonas Bratner built a homestead on this property in 1859 after failing at gold panning. They turned to farming and eventually sold the homestead to Mary Cawker. She saw an opportunity. The house was 4 miles from downtown Denver and the last stagecoach stop along the Smoky Hill Trail where folks could freshen up before arriving in Denver. She transformed the farmhouse into a bar downstairs and a tavern upstairs. Dances were held on the second floor. Eventually, the wagon and horse traffic gave way to the railroad traffic, and the building lost its significance as a last stop on the trail.

The Cherry Creek flood of 1864 convinced Mary to move to higher ground, and she sold the farm. Over time, various families owned the piece of land, adding buildings and improving the lot. In the 1960s, when development threatened the farm and Glendale's encroachment tried to eat up this beautiful piece of property, fans of history and preservationists rallied to protect the parcel with landmark status. The City of Denver ultimately purchased the farm-turned-landmark. Generations of Denver children have since learned about the pioneering life through hands-on interactions and enactments at this park.

Oh, the things to do here! You can explore Cherry Creek to view wildlife, take a horse-drawn wagon ride, go on a blindfolded listening walk, learn Native American sign language, cook over an open campfire, live the prairie life, inspect old barns, chase butterflies, and mingle with farm animals, among other things. Admission to the park is minimal and there are often free days. For details, check the park's website (fourmilepark.org). Regardless of age, everyone will enjoy their time here. From bee history to gardens, horse-drawn carriages to goats, the kid inside of you will jump for joy at this fabulous historic park.

EXTEND YOUR VISIT

Catch the Cherry Creek Trail up to **Cherry Creek Shopping Center** to grab a frozen yogurt and other modern treats. After your visit back in time, the wonders of electricity and refrigeration may just amaze you.

72   DAVID T. GARLAND PARK

For birders and ballplayers alike

Location: 6300 E. Mississippi Ave., Denver
Acreage: 50
Amenities: Lake, benches, flower beds, drinking fountain, picnic tables, playground, restroom, baseball/softball field, basketball court, bike/pedestrian path, football field, sand volleyball court, tennis court, picnic area

GETTING THERE

BY CAR Take I-25 to E. Evans Ave. Go east to S. Monaco Pkwy. Turn left to E. Mississippi to the park. **BY TRANSIT** Buses 11 and 65 stop nearby. **BY BIKE** Take the Cherry Creek Trail to the park.

Dave Garland has been called "the saint of Denver sports." Due to its namesake, many people might think of this park as a sports park—and they wouldn't be wrong. Garland befriended all baseball and basketball kids, advocated for their well-being, and made friends with everyone he met. The Colorado Sports Hall of Fame inducted him, the University of Denver awarded him, and the community embraced him. Many a kid went to sleep in Denver with a baseball mitt wish fulfilled by Garland. Denverites attribute the city's success in baseball to Garland. His namesake park's large baseball fields with bleachers attract the members of the community both on-and-off season.

But this park also has a lollipop-shaped trail around Lollipop Lake, which is a haven for pelicans, herons, red-winged blackbirds, swallows, gulls, geese, and ducks. Bats flutter through the nearby canopy. In the water, you can fish for largemouth bass, orangespotted sunfish, sucker, yellow perch, bluegill, bullhead, channel catfish, crappie, and green sunfish.

Just to make it that much more perfect, this park also has a small playground for the kids.

EXTEND YOUR VISIT

Cross the Cherry Creek Trail and check out one of Denver's Sister City parks, the **City of Potenza Park**. It's located just across the creek.

73 FRANCES WEISBART JACOBS PARK

Everyone deserves hope

Location: 1101 S. Quebec St., Denver
Acreage: 12
Amenities: Benches, drinking fountain, picnic tables, bike/pedestrian path, multi-purpose field (lacrosse, rugby, soccer)

GETTING THERE

BY CAR Take I-25 to E. Evans Ave. Go east to Quebec St. Head north to the park. **BY TRANSIT** Buses 11, 65, and 83L stop nearby. **BY BIKE** Take the Cherry Creek Trail to S. Kearney St. Turn right on E. Mississippi Ave. The park is on the left before reaching Quebec St.

When Frances Weisbart Jacobs arrived in Denver in 1872, she couldn't get over how the citizens of Denver ignored the destitute tuberculosis patients who were coughing and hacking their way from street to tent to soup kitchen. She began bringing them coal, food, and medicines, nursing them back to health and advocating on their behalf. While her husband worked in the OK Clothing Store he owned, she

Sunny pathways are appropriate in Jacobs Park, named for the woman who established the first hospital for tuberculosis sufferers in Denver.

made her benevolent way through Denver, ultimately starting what has become the National Jewish Health hospital. Jacobs was highly honored by many organizations, and was inducted into the National Women's Hall of Fame. You can also find a stained glass window of Jacobs in the Colorado state capitol rotunda. This sunny park, which her patients would have enjoyed, is named in her honor.

When you visit the park, you may want to bring your lacrosse gear to play a match, or maybe leave the gear at home and just lie in the grass and watch clouds drift overhead. Or stretch your legs along the few paved trails that offer short 0.5-mile loops through the park for strollers, skaters, and runners, taking a break on one of the benches that dot the trailside. You could make a day of it and pack along a blanket and a picnic basket to spend hours gratefully basking in the sunshine. When you're searching for bright bluebird-blue skies in the depths of winter, this is a good place to hunt.

EXTEND YOUR VISIT

Head over to National Jewish Health at the corner of Colorado and Colfax to see a bronze statue of Jacobs in the lobby of **National Jewish Medical and Research Center**. Also along Colorado Boulevard, just south of the medical center, you can admire a large urban garden and chicken coop maintained by Denver Urban Gardens.

74   ASH GROVE PARK

Excuse me, I've got to make a call

Location: 1701 S. Holly St., Denver
Acreage: 7.3
Amenities: Benches, picnic tables, playground, basketball court, soccer field, bike/pedestrian path

GETTING THERE

BY CAR Take I-25 to E. Evans Ave. Go east to S. Holly St. Turn left to the park. **BY TRANSIT** Bus 65 stops nearby. **BY BIKE** Take the Cherry Creek Trail to Holly. Go south to the park.

This darling park sits where carnations, horseradish, and grain first grew in the Sullivan area of unincorporated Arapahoe County. Down the street, Mrs. Henderson once managed the Sullivan telephone exchange from her home, connecting calls to Denver for a long-distance toll. When your kids play with the voice stations at the park, be sure that they call Mrs. Henderson!

The playground's fun tree house overlooks the tot-oriented bike track, a small concrete route for the littles to practice their striding and balancing on two wheels. Dr. Seuss–style megaphones invite outdoor voices to echo. In addition to passing time in the playground, plan to fly a kite in the open space or just lie in the grass and whistle. There are also several good geocaches in this park.

EXTEND YOUR VISIT

Walk over to **Mrs. Henderson's old place** at 1640 South Holly Street, which still stands. Although the original phone equipment has been removed, you can imagine the days of long-distance phone rates and per-minute charges.

The "kids only" tree house is only one of the Ash Grove Park's attractions for little ones.

75 JUDGE JOSEPH E. COOK PARK

For the kids

Location: 7100 E. Cherry Creek South Dr., Denver
Acreage: 37
Amenities: Recreation center, outdoor pool, benches, picnic shelter, picnic tables, playground, restroom, drinking fountain, basketball court, bike/pedestrian path, soccer field, baseball/softball field, natural areas, picnic area

GETTING THERE

BY CAR Take I-25 to E. Evans Ave. Go east to S. Monaco Pkwy. and go left to Cherry Creek South Dr. to the park. **BY TRANSIT** Buses 21, 65, and 73 stop nearby. **BY BIKE** Take the Cherry Creek Trail to the park.

With a recreation center, plenty of outdoor space, a quirky playground, and nice walking paths that combine for about 2 miles of trail, this park has plenty for children

Who doesn't love a small bridge over a quiet creek? C'mon down to Cook Park!

and adults alike to love. That's fitting, as it's named after one of Denver's biggest advocates for kids, Judge Joseph E. Cook. Judge Cook, originally from Uxbridge, Massachusetts, started his life in Denver as a reporter for the *Rocky Mountain News*. He then did a stint in the US Army, becoming a lieutenant. He went on to attend Westminster Law School, which ultimately became the Sturm College of Law at the University of Denver. His soft spot for the welfare of kids informed his work with the Boy Scouts, Big Brothers, Big Sisters, the YMCA, and the PTA. He advocated for kids throughout the judicial system, so be sure to give him a virtual thanks as your kids enjoy this park with its great open spaces and outdoor pool.

The grounds include beautiful, meandering trails and a pedestrian bridge that spans a quiet creek. Next to the picturesque creek is a large playground with a teeter-totter, towers, tunnels, and bridges that littles, middles, and bigs will enjoy.

EXTEND YOUR VISIT

Situated along the Cherry Creek Trail, **Judge Joseph E. Cook Park** lies in the shadows of several other parks along the trail, including a number of **Sister City parks** just to the northwest.

76   CITY OF CHENNAI PARK

Once the home to prairie dogs, now a delightful spot for gregarious neighbors

Location: 1600 S. Quebec St., Denver
Acreage: 7.7
Amenities: Benches, bike/pedestrian path, natural areas

GETTING THERE

BY CAR Take I-25 to E. Evans Ave. Turn east to S. Quebec St. Go north to the park.
BY TRANSIT Buses 21, 73, and 83D stop nearby. **BY BIKE** Take the Cherry Creek Trail to Quebec St. Go north to the park.

Although they no longer live here, many black-tailed prairie dogs once roamed this stretch of land along the old Cherokee Trail, now the Cherry Creek Trail. The park is named for Chennai, a city on the Bay of Bengal in India that is a magnet for Indian actors; many films for the entertainment industry are produced there. The locals call it Kollywood. The City of Chennai is the seventh in the Denver Sister City program.

This park is really good for just passing time, gathering with neighbors, and getting some fresh air. A walking path in the park connects with the nearby Indian Creek neighborhood.

EXTEND YOUR VISIT

Just across Quebec Street is the large and engaging **Judge Joseph E. Cook Park**.

SOPHISTICATED, BUT DON'T GET TOO CLOSE

Black-tailed prairie dogs live in colonies underground and can burrow up to 12 feet in any direction. The dogs bark in a series of complicated calls, including warning and all-clear, to the members of their community while they harvest nearby grasses for food. Their language is sophisticated enough such that they differentiate between an individual and a group. At one time, prairie dogs were collected from their burrows and sold as pets, a practice that was discontinued when it was discovered they could carry bubonic plague. Local rangers and game wardens now manage the wild populations for plague, often encircling the burrows with pesticide to kill the fleas that carry the disease. Be aware that these critters can still cause occasional public land closures.

77 JAMES A. BIBLE PARK

Boredom doesn't have a prayer at this park!

Location: 6802 E. Yale Ave., Denver
Acreage: 66
Amenities: Benches, drinking fountain, picnic tables, playground, restroom, baseball/softball field complex, basketball court, tennis court, bike/pedestrian path, High Line Canal Trail, fitness zone, football field, natural areas, picnic area

GETTING THERE

BY CAR Take I-25 to E. Yale Ave. Go east to the park. **BY TRANSIT** Bus 27 stops nearby. **BY BIKE** Take the High Line Canal Trail to the park.

Life's rewards can often come late, but when it comes, the recognition can be wonderful. That's the case for James A. Bible. A hard worker for Denver Parks and Recreation, he toiled in the parks for almost fifty years, starting in the field and working his way up to supervisor. At his retirement, the City of Denver honored him and named this park after him. Welcome to James A. Bible Park, where the closest thing to a pulpit might be a mile marker on the High Line Canal Trail, which travels the park's perimeter.

In the middle of the park, you'll find fine baseball fields with stadium seating and dugouts next to restrooms and concessions. Tennis courts beckon in the

Giant Bible Park offers quiet walks by the water, as well as baseball fields and more.

distance, while an outside gym begs you to sit up and push up. The opposite end of the park, to the northeast, invites children to swing and slide. If you're lucky, you might spot owl nests and coyote tracks along the High Line Canal. Goldsmith Gulch wanders through the park for about a mile, offering bridges to cross and reeds to shelter wildlife.

When a good snow has fallen, this park is heaven for cross-country skiing. You can ski along its perimeter on the High Line Canal Trail or get your heartbeat up by snowshoeing along the undulating hills. The open fields entice the ambitious to build a family of snow people. Don't forget the snow dog!

James A. Bible Park is both a destination and a pass-through while hiking along the Goldsmith Gulch Trail or the 71-mile High Line Canal Trail. Either trail adventures through the park and provides great connectors to the regional trail system.

EXTEND YOUR VISIT

Stay in the park and catch a softball game, then stroll the nice 3-mile loop hike on the **High Line Canal Trail**.

DON'T DITCH THE TRAIL

The High Line Canal is a 71-mile ditch that runs from Waterton Canyon to Green Valley Ranch. Built in 1880 as an economic development tool to bring water to dry areas, the ditch never fulfilled its vision to bring water all the way to Green Valley. Drought and improper engineering measurements defeated the canal's far northern end. After the need for water at the Rocky Mountain Arsenal dried up, Denver Water committed to moving water only as far north as Fairmount Cemetery. If conditions are right and it's wet along the South Platte River (the canal's water source), Denver Water moves water in the canal, but not more than twice a year.

The trail that runs along the canal has always been the maintenance road for Denver Water and its ditch riders. In 1985 the trail opened up for recreational users, and for more than thirty years Denverites have loved this urban treasure. Now under the vision of the High Line Canal Conservancy, the trail is approaching its next generation of use. The conservancy plans to unite many ideas and visions from the eleven jurisdictions the trail travels through to produce a high quality, omnipresent trail for everyone to access and love.

78 SOUTHMOOR PARK

Sledding abounds!

Location: 3551 S. Poplar St., Denver
Acreage: 17
Amenities: Benches, drinking fountain, picnic shelter, picnic tables, playground, basketball court, bike/pedestrian path, soccer field, baseball/softball field

GETTING THERE

BY CAR Take I-25 to E. Hampden Ave. Go east to Poplar. Take a right to the park. **BY TRANSIT** Buses 65 and 105, and light rail E and H stop nearby. **BY BIKE** Take Goldsmith Gulch Trail. Turn right onto E. Eastman Ave. Continue onto E. Girard Ave. Turn left onto S. Oleander Ct. Turn left onto E. Hampden Ave. to the park.

With a sledding hill that all ages will like, this two-story park features big open spaces for sledding, running, or rolling downhill. On the top level you'll find a good playground that should appeal to most kids, and on the bottom level, you'll find plenty of courts and fields. The trail that circles the perimeter of the park for about three-quarters of a mile is great for both walking and bicycling.

EXTEND YOUR VISIT

If you're looking for more outdoor activities, especially those geared toward adults, head north up to **James A. Bible Park**. There you'll find tennis courts, an outdoor gym, and softball/baseball fields.

Great for sledding, sure, but Southmoor Park also offers some glorious fall color.

79 EASTMOOR PARK

A "just right" park with neighborhood appeal

Location: 6900 E. Princeton Ave., Denver
Acreage: 12
Amenities: Benches, drinking fountain, picnic tables, picnic shelter, playground, basketball court, bike/pedestrian path, soccer field, natural areas, picnic area

GETTING THERE

BY CAR Take I-25 to E. Hampden Ave. Turn east to S. Monaco Pkwy. and then south to E. Princeton Ave. **BY TRANSIT** Buses 65, 105, and light rail H stop nearby. **BY BIKE** Take Cherry Creek Trail to S. Oneida St. Turn right onto E. Iliff Ave. Slight left to stay on Goldsmith Gulch Trail. Turn right onto E. Eastman Ave. Continue onto E. Girard Ave. Turn left onto E. Hamilton Pl. Continue onto S. Poplar St. Continue onto S. Oneida St. Turn right onto E. Princeton Ave.

In 1974 the neighbors of Hampden South organized to improve their parks and trails. At the time, Eastmoor Park had few facilities and little development, but the group drafted out what they wanted in the park. Now, Eastmoor Park provides a nice buffer to the noisy I-25 on its western boundary. With ball fields and a playground that includes toy chipmunks just waiting to be ridden, this neat park offers a quick getaway to South Hampden neighbors and their friends.

EXTEND YOUR VISIT

If you want a bigger park with a giant lake and a world of activities, head on over to **Cherry Creek State Park** or the close-by **Rosamond Park**.

80 ROSAMOND PARK

A great park for team sports or individual exploration

Location: 8051 E. Quincy Ave., Denver
Acreage: 35
Amenities: Benches, drinking fountain, playground, basketball court, bike/pedestrian path, football field, soccer field, tennis court, flower beds, picnic tables, picnic shelter, parking lot, picnic area

GETTING THERE

BY CAR Take I-225 to Tamarac/DTC Blvd. Go north. Turn left on E. Quincy Ave. to the park. **BY TRANSIT** Bus 105 and light rail H stop nearby. **BY BIKE** Take the Cherry Creek Trail. Turn right to stay on Village Greens N. Trail. Turn left onto S. Boston St. Turn right onto E. Nassau Ave. Turn left onto S. Yosemite St. Take the Tamarac St. exit toward I-225 S/DTC Blvd. Turn left onto Quincy Ave.

Lighted tennis courts, lacrosse, soccer and football fields: what else could you want in a regional park? How about a few walking paths for a combined 2 miles with the Goldsmith Gulch running alongside? This sweet community park invites all comers, and it's a great park in which to push a stroller, thanks to the concrete paths undulating throughout the shady paths. You'll often find kids sinking their bare feet into the Goldsmith Gulch, which runs north–south through the park, while they look for aquatic adventures. In the winter, a good snowball fight can be had here.

EXTEND YOUR VISIT

Head along Goldsmith Gulch Trail to the north where you can connect with the High Line Canal Trail, then make your way to Waterton Canyon. Alternatively, you can go south on the trail to **George M. Wallace Park**—or, for bigger fun, jump over to **Cherry Creek State Park**.

81   GEORGE M. WALLACE PARK

Nature and tech thrive side by side

Location: 4700 SDTC Blvd., Denver
Acreage: 24
Amenities: Benches, picnic tables, playground, flower beds, bike/pedestrian path, Goldsmith Gulch Trail

GETTING THERE

BY CAR Take I-225 to Yosemite St. Go south to DTC Blvd. Take a left to the park. **BY TRANSIT** Buses 64 and 73 stop nearby. **BY BIKE** Take the High Line Canal Trail to the Cherry Creek Trail. Turn left on Dayton St. Right on E. Union Ave. Continue on Temple Dr. Left on DTC Blvd. to the park.

Smack in the middle of technology, thinkers, and futurists lies the park named after George MacKenzie Wallace, the founder and visionary of the Denver Technological

Technology and nature blend together at Wallace Park near Denver Tech Center.

Center. Wallace believed that nature and technology could be in harmony together, and in 1971 he envisioned a campus of both. At the north end of the park, near the fitness equipment, you can see engraved stones erected in his honor and memory that tell this harmonic story.

On the south end of the park, woven between the lush stands of trees and green grassy open spaces, you'll find an amphitheater that hosts lunchtime concerts and summertime events. Connecting both ends is a system of trails, one that passes by a rich outdoor fitness center for adults.

While ambling the 1- to 2-mile trail, enjoy the seasonal flower beds. During lunch, DTC workers use the park for brown bagging and cloud gazing. Locals enjoy concerts at lunchtime and in the evening. In the winter, grab your cross-country skis for a couple laps around the park or don your snowshoes for some ups and downs.

EXTEND YOUR VISIT

The Goldsmith Gulch Trail runs through the park. You can hop on your bike and take the trail north up to **James A. Bible Park** or south almost as far as the **Arapahoe Lake Reservoir**.

82 HAMPDEN HEIGHTS PARK

A hidden gem with many a twinkling facet

Location: 3301 S. Clinton St., Denver
Acreage: 32
Amenities: Benches, picnic tables, playground, basketball court, bike/pedestrian path, soccer field, baseball/softball field, drinking fountain, picnic area

GETTING THERE

BY CAR Take I-25 to E. Hampden Ave. Go east to S. Yosemite St. Take a left to E. Cornell Ave. Turn right on S. Boston Ct. Take a left on S. Clinton St. to the park. **BY TRANSIT** Buses 21, 83D, and 105 stop nearby. **BY BIKE** Take High Line Canal Trail. Turn left on the Cherry Creek Trail. Turn right on Hampden Heights Trail. Turn right onto E. Cornell Ave. Turn right on S. Boston Ct. Take a left on S. Clinton St. to the park.

A hidden gem in the shadow of the Cherry Creek and High Line Canal confluence area, Hampden Heights Park offers a nicely wooded open space popular with little and big soccer players alike. The newly remodeled playground has rope structures for climbing. Local neighborhood trails lead from the park toward the Cherry Creek Trail and the High Line Canal Trail. On any given Saturday, you'll find the park loaded with families cheering for their brothers and sisters on the soccer fields. If your kids aren't soccer fans, the giant rope climbing structure that reaches to the sky might motivate them to try their balance skills, Spider-Man style. The playground for the smaller kids has a moonscaped boulder waiting for landings. In the winter, wide open fields beg for snow angels and snow forts.

EXTEND YOUR VISIT

Head north out of the park to pick up the Cherry Creek Trail or the High Line Canal Trail. Venture along the Cherry Creek Trail into **Paul A. Hentzell Park** or up to **Babi Yar Park**.

83 GOLDEN KEY PARK

Sometimes all you need to unlock a treasure is a tiny golden key

Location: 2900 S. Syracuse Way, Denver
Acreage: 2.8
Amenities: Picnic tables, playground, basketball court, bike/pedestrian path, benches

It may be small, but Golden Key Park is big enough to offer respite to at-home workers or passers by.

GETTING THERE

BY CAR Take I-25 to E. Yale Ave. Turn east to Syracuse Way. Turn right to the park. **BY TRANSIT** Bus 73 stops nearby. **BY BIKE** Take Cherry Creek Trail to S. Wabash St. Take a right to E. Yale Ave. Turn left on Syracuse Way to the park.

Built roughly in the shape of a key, this quaint neighborhood park has just about everything you need for a quick recess in a tiny space. There's a one-hoop basketball court, a small playground for your littles, a swing set with four swings, a small open space, and a 0.5-mile path to walk around. After you get your play on, you can relax at the picnic tables in the shade of pine and oak trees.

EXTEND YOUR VISIT

The High Line Canal Trail is located nearby. Hop on the trail and travel in either direction to reach larger parks such as **Paul A. Hentzell Park** or **Hampden Heights Park**.

84   PAUL A. HENTZELL PARK

Is it a park or open space?

Location: 10300 E. Yale Ave., Denver
Acreage: 59
Amenities: Bike/pedestrian path, Cherry Creek Trail, open space, natural areas

A burbling brook runs through Hentzell Park, the site of a contentious battle that redefined how the city of Denver manages its parks.

GETTING THERE

BY CAR Take I-25 to E. Evans Ave., which becomes E. Iliff Ave. Turn right on S. Parker Rd. Turn right on S. Havana St. Turn right onto E. Yale Ave. to the park. **BY TRANSIT** Buses 21, 35, 83L, and 105 stop nearby. **BY BIKE** Take the Cherry Creek Trail to the park.

Welcome to the land of park controversy! In 2013 the city wanted to swap a portion of this park with Denver Public Schools. The plan was to build a school and a center for domestic violence recovery and information in this location. This prompted the Friends of Denver Parks to sue the city. The Friends believed that the city had no right to give away a public park without a vote of its citizens. The city argued that this area never was designated a park; nevermind the NORTH HAMPDEN HEIGHTS PARK sign and DENVER PARKS AND RECREATION sign with a list of park rules. Ignore also the concrete bike paths through the park that the city had installed.

After research and testimony, the judge ruled in favor of the city, going back to a 1955 law about park designations, and so the Friends lost and the swap happened. As a result of the lawsuit, the city inventoried its lands and went through formal reviews to designate parks as either parks or open space so that misunderstandings could be eliminated in the future. Now, depending on how a park is categorized, Denver Parks and Recreation creates management plans relevant to those categories.

The now-diminished park is named after Paul A. Hentzell, Denver City Council member for twenty-eight years. A friend of historic preservation, Hentzell successfully lobbied for the historic designation of the Daniels & Fisher clock tower in downtown Denver and the creation of several parks throughout Denver.

Even though the park is a bit smaller than it used to be, it still features 59 acres of open space with Cherry Creek running through it. You'll find coyotes, foxes, deer, beaver, birds of prey, and a fairly intact ecosystem that connects the many open spaces and trails in the Cherry Creek area. Explore the territory on more than 5 miles of trails that feature bridges, and enjoy ambling in cottonwood groves and rabbit bush thickets.

EXTEND YOUR VISIT

Head up the hill north to **Babi Yar Park** for a quiet, reflective time in honor of the Ukrainian Jews killed during the Holocaust.

WHAT IS THIS CHERRY CREEK TRAIL THAT LEADS EVERYWHERE?

Cherry Creek Trail, part of the Denver Regional Trail System, runs about 40 miles. The southern point is Cherry Creek Reservoir, and the northern point is the creek's confluence with the South Platte River. This picturesque trail connects Denver to the municipalities of Parker, Centennial, and Franktown. Usually 8 feet wide, the concrete trail provides a speedy and direct way for cyclists to commute to downtown Denver. It also provides a good platform for athletes to train for long-distance hikes and rides. Although the trail is designated as multimodal, walkers and runners alike might feel more comfortable on the dirt goat trail that parallels the concrete.

85 KENNEDY BALLFIELDS COMPLEX

Play some serious ball

Location: 3398 S. Kenton St., Denver
Acreage: 94
Amenities: Baseball/softball field complex, press box, restroom, drinking fountain, parking lot, shade structure, natural areas, dog park, soccer field complex

If you're looking for high-quality softball and base-ball fields, Kennedy Ballfields is your go-to place.

GETTING THERE

BY CAR Take I-225 to N. Parker Rd. Head north to E. Dartmouth Ave. and take a left. Turn left on S. Kenton St. to the park. Note that there are several access points into the park that differ greatly from the official street address. **BY TRANSIT** Bus 105 and light rail H stop nearby. **BY BIKE** Take the Cherry Creek Trail to the park.

After John F. Kennedy visited Denver, the city got JFK fever. This giant outdoor ballpark, named after him, is the biggest and nicest baseball/softball field complex in Denver. It features eight fields, and if you're planning to watch a game, or play in one, you'll probably need a map just to find the right field (you can download a map from denvergov.org). Huge fences and backstops keep the games contained on their own fields, and each field comes complete with stands for fans and dugouts for players. Turfed fields, snack bars, and lots of parking attract tournaments throughout the season.

The Kennedy Golf Course is located on the northwestern side of this giant park complex. At the golf course, you can play twenty-seven holes of regulation golf, nine holes of par 3 golf, a round of foot golf, some putt-putt golf, or just hit a bucket of balls on a driving range that is open until ten o'clock at night in the summer. Farther west in the park, and maybe not as lush as the baseball fields, are four soccer fields that invite tournaments and leagues.

Your dog will love the dog park, located just to the west of the soccer fields. It can fantasize about chasing all the soccer balls out on the field.

EXTEND YOUR VISIT

Jump on the Cherry Creek Trail and make your way south to **Cherry Creek State Park** to splash in the lake on a hot day.

86   BABI YAR PARK

Holocaust remembrance

Location: 10451 E. Yale Ave., Denver
Acreage: 25.2
Amenities: Benches, fountain, memorial/monument, natural areas, bike/pedestrian path, parking lot

GETTING THERE

BY CAR Take I-25 to E. Hampden Ave. Go east to E. Yale Ave. Go left to the park. **BY TRANSIT** Buses 83D and 83L stop nearby. **BY BIKE** Take Cherry Creek Trail to S. Elmira St. Turn right on E. Yale Ave. to the park.

Visiting this park, completed in 1982, requires a meditative mind and a calm heart. Babi Yar's designers, Lawrence Halprin and Satoru Nishita, wanted to commemorate the Ukrainian Jews and others from Kiev who were murdered by the Nazis between 1941 and 1943. These massacres were carried out in Kiev, Ukraine, at a site known as Babi Yar.

Dirt from the original Babi Yar Ravine is buried beneath People's Place in Babi Yar Park.

Enter the park on a path that passes between two large pieces of dark, inscribed granite monoliths that set the tone for your thoughts within the park. Following a descent through cottonwoods and willows, take a moment in the bowl-shaped amphitheater known as People's Place. From there, choose any of the pathways. The paths are configured as a Star of David and walking them allows you to contemplate the one hundred lindens planted throughout the park, which represent the over two hundred thousand people killed at Babi Yar in Kiev.

On your way to the rear of the park, be sure to pause and view the water that flows across a black granite disk. Then cross a ravine that is reminiscent of where the dead were buried in Kiev. The narrow bridge features high, black walls that are meant to evoke the trains used by Nazis to transport these citizens to their deaths.

Although the park is quite solemn, the setting is peaceful. It is a place for contemplation and reflection. Kids can certainly experience the importance of the place through the earnest, yet solemn placement of stones, trees, and shapes.

EXTEND YOUR VISIT

Paul A. Hentzell Park, located to the south, offers a nice walk along Cherry Creek.

87 JEFFERSON SQUARE PARK

Experience a park that feels bigger than it is

Location: 5773 E. Happy Canyon Rd., Denver
Acreage: 4.55
Amenities: Benches, picnic tables, playground, multi-purpose field (lacrosse, rugby, soccer), baseball/softball field

GETTING THERE

BY CAR Take I-25 to Hampden Ave. Turn left on Happy Canyon Rd. to the park. **BY TRANSIT** Buses 40 and 65/105 stop nearby. **BY BIKE** From the Cherry Creek Trail, turn right onto Hampden Heights Trail. Slight left at S. Yosemite St. Turn left onto E. Eastman Ave. Continue onto E. Girard Ave. Turn left onto E. Hamilton Pl. Continue onto S. Poplar St. Continue onto S. Oneida St. Turn left onto E. Princeton Ave. Turn right toward E. Quincy Ave. Sharp right onto E. Quincy Ave. Slight right onto Happy Canyon Rd.

Sharing lacrosse fields and other facilities with Thomas Jefferson High School, this triangle-shaped park welcomes Southmoor residents and visitors to the neighborhood. Although the actual park is small, with playground equipment for little kids

Playground equipment and sheltering trees make Jefferson Square Park a popular neighborhood attraction.

and a mixed-use field, it appears to be big. You can see the tennis courts and ball fields of the high school next to the park, which adds to the open space feel of this neighborhood gathering spot.

EXTEND YOUR VISIT

Not too far away to the north is **Mamie Doud Eisenhower Park**, which offers a recreation center, more playgrounds, and a larger mixed-use area.

88   MAMIE DOUD EISENHOWER PARK

Ode to Mamie

Location: 4300 E. Dartmouth Ave., Denver
Acreage: 20
Amenities: Recreation center, grills, picnic shelter, picnic tables, playground, outdoor pool, restroom, bike/pedestrian path, football field, soccer field, horseshoe pits, tennis court, baseball/softball field, flower beds, benches, picnic area

Picnic tables just call out for you to make it a full day of fun at Mamie D. Eisenhower Park.

GETTING THERE

BY CAR Take I-25 to Colorado Blvd. Turn south. Turn left on Dartmouth to the park.
BY TRANSIT Bus 40 stops nearby. **BY BIKE** Take the High Line Canal Trail to the park.

As you can see, this park is named after the former first lady Mamie Doud Eisenhower, whose family migrated from Iowa to Denver for the health of Mamie's sister. The sisters grew up in a Denver Square home at 750 Lafayette Street (near Cheesman Park). Mr. Doud made his money in the meatpacking business.

The park sits along the High Line Canal Trail. Take a walk to the south side of the park where the High Line Canal abuts the perimeter. Walk along the trail for about half of the length of the park to the east, away from the recreation center, and you'll stumble upon a single concrete bench dedicated to the High Line Canal. Be sure to read the inscription and notice how it references areas north of the park. Elsewhere in the park, which has some of the greenest grass in the Denver park system, you can settle down with your picnic blanket, kick around a ball, hit a pitch, or count clouds. Just west of the park is a recreation center with pool and facilities.

In the winter, strap on your cross-country skis and enjoy practicing your moves in the open fields, or ski over to the High Line Canal Trail and ski along it for up to 71 miles. Snowshoes can take you in the same direction, or you might choose to just fall backward into the drifts and leave your snow angel print. Swish those limbs!

EXTEND YOUR VISIT

Across Colorado Boulevard, you can golf on one of the City of Denver's finer public golf courses, **Wellshire**. Featuring eighteen holes and putting and chipping greens, it's the only golf course west of the Mississippi designed by pro golf course designer Donald Ross. Its clubhouse was built in 1926 and is a popular landmark for weddings and events.

89   CHERRY CREEK STATE PARK

A fully-stocked oasis next to Denver

Location: 4201 S. Parker Rd., Aurora
Acreage: 4,200
Amenities: Boating, camping, fishing, hiking, swimming, sailing, remote control field, gun range, biking, open space, dog park, picnicking, horseback riding

GETTING THERE

BY CAR Take I-225 to S. Parker Rd. Drive south. Turn right on E. Leigh Ave. to enter the park. **BY TRANSIT** Bus 83L and light rails H and R stop nearby. **BY BIKE** Take Cherry Creek Trail to the park.

Throughout the City of Denver, you can see evidence of how the flooding of Cherry Creek affected the city's ability to grow and flourish. In the early 1900s, Denver mayor Robert Speer recognized that the waterway could wreak havoc on the city. He had the banks of the creek cemented along Speer Boulevard (see Alamo Placita Park). In 1950 the Army Corps of Engineers formally addressed the problem of Denver's flooding and built the Cherry Creek Reservoir. Since then, most of Denver's flooding has been controlled, and those who live down river are finally able to heed the flooding warnings that the Native Americans gave many years ago. The main purpose of the Cherry Creek Reservoir is to control the creek's flow, but it also does double duty as Denver's watery oasis.

Within the park are 133 campsites for overnight camping; trout, walleye, bass, and wipers to catch on your line; sailboats to maneuver and jet skis to speed;

Right outside of Denver's city limits, Cherry Creek State Park features a giant reservoir and plenty of land-based activities too.

880 acres of lake and many miles of shoreline to discover; a small airfield to fly remote craft; horses to gallop; targets to shoot; and over 25 miles of hiking trails to discover. Phew! Even your dog will be thrilled: one of the area's best off-leash dog parks is here. It features more than 100 acres of open space, including a creek for your pup to get muddy in.

The best way to enjoy the park is to take your time. Start in the northwest corner of the park at the marina and grab the water vehicle of your choice: you may even want to stand up on a paddleboard! Or launch your own boat; sail away in lessons; rent a pontoon, speed boat, and even jet skis; paddle your kayak; or trawl away while fishing to your heart's content. Whatever your craft, you'll have a lot of cool, flat water to float upon.

Next, grill along the sandy beach, then head out to the wetlands preserve in the south for just under a mile and a quarter hike around the Wetland Loop Trail. If you're a shooter, go west to the gun range for some target practice; you can either bring your own guns or rent one there. If you'd rather fly than shoot, bring a remote control airplane for great flying conditions nearby.

Although there's no hunting in the park, you can "hunt" with your binoculars all along the western and southern edges of the park for eastern cottontail rabbit, coyote, beaver, muskrat, raccoon, weasel, ground squirrel, mule deer, white-tailed deer, and scampering black-tailed prairie dogs. You can also just sit in the sun in the summer, or do a little ice fishing in the winter. This park is a year-round playground.

Finally, consider renting or bringing your own horses for a ride in the park. Designated trails are available for trail rides, wagon pulls, hay rides, and horse lessons. Be sure to check the park's website for hours, restrictions, and fees (https.//cpw.state.co.us).

EXTEND YOUR VISIT

The **Cherry Creek Trail** runs about 7 miles through the park. It then continues south for another 20 miles to the Franktown community, and it goes north for about 12 miles into Denver. The trail is perfect for a full day's walk or a good cycle between downtown Denver and Franktown, and the park is a good midway point for taking a break.

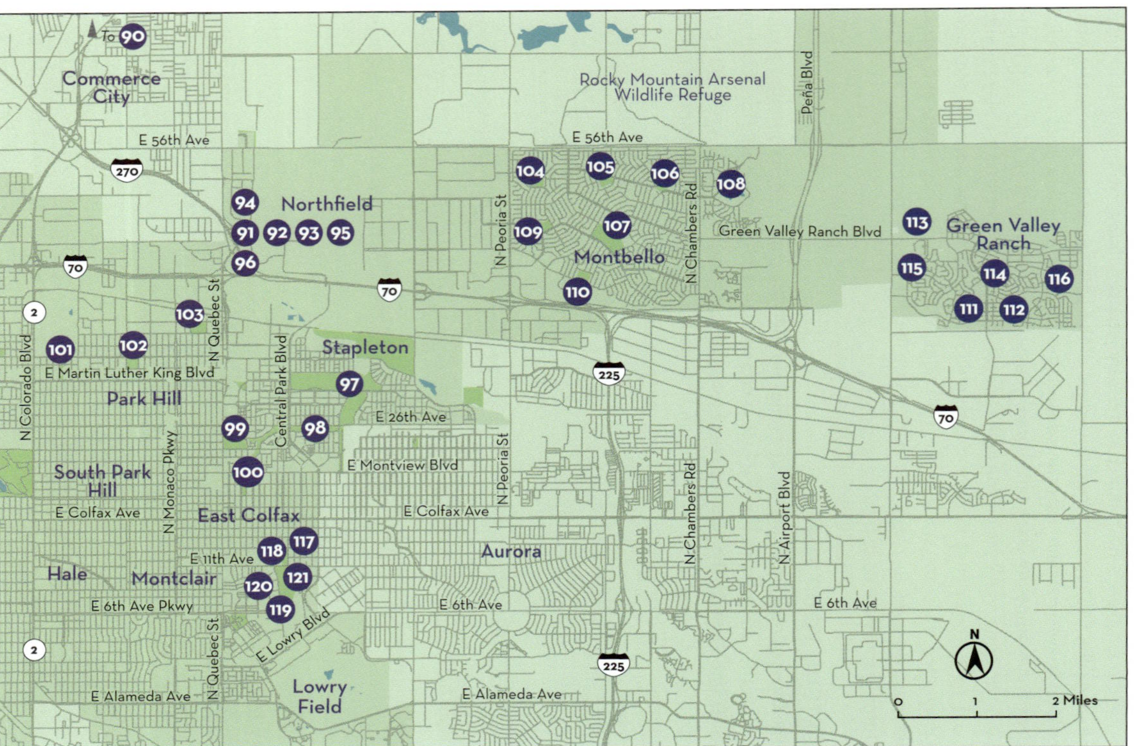

To 90
Commerce City
Rocky Mountain Arsenal Wildlife Refuge
Peña Blvd
E 56th Ave
270
E 56th Ave
104
105
106
108
94
Northfield
91
92
93
95
96
N Peoria St
109
107
Montbello
N Chambers Rd
Green Valley Ranch Blvd
113
Green Valley Ranch
115
114
116
70
110
111
112
70
2
103
N Quebec St
Central Park Blvd
Stapleton
225
101
102
E Martin Luther King Blvd
N Colorado Blvd
Park Hill
N Monaco Pkwy
97
E 26th Ave
99
98
E Montview Blvd
70
South Park Hill
100
N Peoria St
E Colfax Ave
E Colfax Ave
East Colfax
Aurora
N Chambers Rd
N Airport Blvd
118
117
E 11th Ave
Hale
Montclair
120
121
E 6th Ave Pkwy
119
E 6th Ave
E 6th Ave
2
E Lowry Blvd
225
E Alameda Ave
Lowry Field
E Alameda Ave
N
0   1   2 Miles

NORTHEAST PARKS

90   BARR LAKE STATE PARK

An outdoorsy paradise just north of Denver

Location: 13401 Picadilly Rd., Brighton
Acreage: 2,715
Amenities: Fishing, hunting, hiking, biking, canoeing, kayaking, picnic tables, hunting, archery, duck blinds, nature center, boat ramps, trails, cross-country skiing, limited dog access, horseback riding, ice fishing, sailboarding, snowshoeing. No camping.

GETTING THERE

BY CAR Take I-76 to exit 22. Go east to Picadilly Rd., take a left to the park. **BY TRANSIT** No available transit. **BY BIKE** Take South Platte River Trail to Front Range Trail. Turn right on E. 120th Ave. Turn left on Tower Rd. Turn right on E. 128th Ave. Turn left on Piccadilly to the park.

Offering something for everyone, this park, once a bison wallow, became a wonderland for the outdoor enthusiast once Burlington Canal was dug in the late 1800s. The canal moved water from the South Platte River to the wallow, which created a lake. Nearby Denverites could then hop onto a train for a day of relaxation at what was called Oasis Reservoir. At the turn of the century, after some

Barr Lake State Park, just north of Denver's city limits, offers great fishing, hiking, shooting, and birdwatching.

legal maneuvering with water rights and land ownership, the Farmers Reservoir and Irrigation Company joined the lake with the existing and smaller Burlington Reservoir to increase its size. The result was Barr Lake, which was named after one of the civil engineers at Burlington Northern Railroad.

Over time, Denver's filth and garbage floated downriver to Barr Lake. The historic 1965 Denver flood, and various pieces of legislation, cleaned it up. Barr Lake soon became the jewel of Brighton, just north of Denver.

Now Barr Lake is an outdoor enthusiast's paradise. Whether you want to do an 8.8-mile hike, horseback ride, bike ride around the lake, practice your archery, or do a bit of canoeing, Barr Lake will accommodate you. Be sure to bring your own gear and horse. The trail near the dam (Dam Crest Trail) is open to hikers and bicyclists except on Wednesdays and Saturdays from October through February when it is closed due to hunting.

If you want to hunt, grab your license and try your luck bagging waterfowl, doves, and geese. You can sign up for time at a duck blind, or if you'd rather try your hand at arrows and not bullets, practice your aim in the many archery lanes open to the public. Prefer to fish? Cast your line into the ice during the winter or from your boat in the summer. Only sailboats, hand-propelled craft, and boats with electric trolling motors or gasoline motors of 10 horsepower or less are permitted on Barr Lake. Stocked channel catfish, smallmouth and largemouth bass, rainbow trout, walleye, bluegill, wiper, and tiger muskie await your luck. Keep in mind that the southern portion is a wildlife refuge and is off-limits to boating, hunting, fishing, and dogs.

Around the park's nature center you'll find shorter trails and boardwalks through the marsh and along the perimeter of the lake. Stop in the center for history, education, and helpful naturalists. Because Barr Lake is part of the Colorado state park system, expect to pay entry fees. (See cpw.state.co.us for the latest fees and hours.)

EXTEND YOUR VISIT

Although you could easily devote an entire weekend to the lake, you might also enjoy some of the wonderful trails and parks managed by Brighton's Parks and Open Space department. These open spaces are located just west of **Barr Lake State Park**.

91 SANDHILLS PRAIRIE PARK

A park with a spectacular view— and a fun playground too

Location: 5400 Prairie Meadow Dr., Denver
Acreage: 14.6
Amenities: Trails, open space, nature play, vista point, public art

GETTING THERE

BY CAR Take I-70 to Northfield Blvd. Turn north. Take Verbena to the left to the park. **BY TRANSIT** Bus 88 stops nearby. **BY BIKE** Take Sand Creek Greenway to Quebec St. Go north on Northfield Blvd. Veer left under Northfield to Trenton St. Follow the trail through Prairie Basin Park to the park.

Some say that Sandhills Prairie Park is the crowning glory of the Stapleton Northfield parks. Perhaps it's because this park has the best views in Stapleton. Climb 0.25 mile to the high point along concrete and soft surface trails for a 360-degree view. From the top you'll see the entire Stapleton Northfield park system, homes in Northfield, the Rockies to the far west, and a glorious view of downtown Denver to the southwest.

At the base of the high point is a fun nature play area where kids can scramble on the tree trunks and boulders. To the east, the trail goes under Central Park Boulevard on its way to Northfield High School and then to the Rocky Mountain Arsenal Wildlife Refuge. If you walk through the tunnel, pause to enjoy the art installation,

Get views of the Stapleton neighborhood, downtown Denver, and the Front Range in Sandhills Prairie Park.

FROM BOMB FACTORY TO WILDLIFE REFUGE

The Rocky Mountain Arsenal Wildlife Refuge, just north of Stapleton, is the US Fish and Wildlife Service's most urban refuge. Packed with bison, coyotes, prairie dogs, ferrets, and birds of prey, the refuge started as an armory for the war effort of World War II. The arsenal manufactured petroleum bombs and sarin and mustard gas, followed by high-octane fuel for the Space Race during the Cold War. Representative Pat Schroeder led the charge to declare it a Superfund site in the 1980s. After $2 billion was spent to clean up the nasty chemicals, the former arsenal opened in 2013 as a 2,800-acre refuge to preserve bald eagle habitat. Auto trails and hiking trails throughout the park take you on a journey to see American bison.

Drift Inversion, by David Franklin, which echoes the original sand dunes in this area. This is a great tunnel to experience during sunset due to its play of light against the backdrop of the Rockies in the distance.

EXTEND YOUR VISIT

From here, head about a quarter-mile to 56th Avenue and go east a few miles to Peña Boulevard. On the northwest corner of Peña and 56th, you'll find a fabulous trailhead to the **First Creek** at DEN Open Space Trail. It's a must for an easy 4- to 8-mile round-trip amble with kids along First Creek.

92 PRAIRIE MEADOWS PARK

Go up on the ropes or down on the slide—or both!

Location: 5100 Uinta St., Denver
Acreage: 15
Amenities: Slide, bridges, creek, parking, restrooms, rope structures

GETTING THERE

BY CAR Take I-70 to Northfield Blvd. Turn north. Take Uinta St. to the left to the park. **BY TRANSIT** Bus 88 stops nearby. **BY BIKE** Take Sand Creek Greenway to Quebec St. Go north on Northfield Blvd. Veer left under Northfield to Trenton St. Follow the trail through Prairie Basin Park to the park.

Sandwiched between two other Stapleton Northfield parks, this park is really geared to the adventurer. Older kids will enjoy the 25-foot tall rope structure on the western edge of the park, while the younger ones will get a kick out of the giant, curvy red slide that connects the high point of the park to its lower basin.

Flowing through the park is Runway Creek, which has fantastic rock paths to giggle across. You'll find traditional playgrounds and more nature play areas in the parks to the east and north. (See Sandhills Prairie and Cottonwood Gallery Parks.)

EXTEND YOUR VISIT

For lunch options, head south on Uinta Street to **Northfield Boulevard**. You'll find shops on the north side of Northfield Boulevard, or you can cross the boulevard to enjoy the outdoor mall on the south side of the street.

93   COTTONWOOD GALLERY PARK

Experience this varied park in its infancy

Location: 5100 Verbena St., Denver
Acreage: 16
Amenities: Playgrounds, open space, native grasses, creek, benches, bathrooms, trails

GETTING THERE

BY CAR Take I-70 to Northfield Blvd. Turn north. Take Verbena St. to the left to the park. **BY TRANSIT** Bus 88 stops nearby. **BY BIKE** Take Sand Creek Greenway to Quebec St. Go north on Northfield Blvd. Veer left under Northfield to Trenton St. Follow the trail through Prairie Basin Park to the park.

Part of the Stapleton Northfield collection of parks that connect to Prairie Meadows Park and Sandhills Prairie Park, this large open space features smaller areas within that invite different types of adventurers. Near the center of the park on the north side, you'll find two playgrounds, one for littles, one for bigs, with a set of swings connecting the two. Farther on is a native flower prairie that is anchored by a set of picnic tables and a meditative forest of tall junipers. Although this park is new, and the vegetation is still in its infancy, don't let the newness keep you from going on a wonderful 2-mile walk or bike ride through it, connecting to the other parks to the south and west. (See Prairie Meadows, Prairie Basin, and Sandhills Prairie Parks.)

EXTEND YOUR VISIT

The **Rocky Mountain Arsenal Wildlife Refuge** can be

Two playgrounds for kids sit in a prairie and wildflower setting in Cottonwood Gallery Park.

reached by foot or by bike from this park. Head north through **Sandhills Prairie Park**, go under Central Park Boulevard, and continue along the connector trail to the refuge.

94 WILLOW BARK PARK

You've got to love a park with a punny name!

Location: 5300 Spruce St., Denver
Acreage: 3
Amenities: High-energy and low-energy sections, shade structure, water, open spaces, off-leash dog areas

GETTING THERE

BY CAR Take I-70 to Northfield Blvd. Turn north. Take a left on Prairie Meadow Dr. to the park. **BY TRANSIT** Bus 88 stops nearby. **BY BIKE** Take Sand Creek Greenway to Quebec St. Go north on Northfield Blvd. Veer left under Northfield to Trenton St. Follow the trail through Prairie Basin Park to the park.

This isn't Stapleton's largest dog park—that'd be Greenway Park—but it is newer than the one on the south side of the Stapleton neighborhood. And like the southern park, this one has two areas: one for low-energy dogs, the other for high-energy dogs. A nice shade structure protects dog parents from the elements while their pups play. A baggie station helps keep the area clean, and a water fountain for you and your pup is on during season. Locals have left a broom for sweeping up wayward gravel. Be sure to do your part by brushing up the concrete as your dogs romp.

EXTEND YOUR VISIT

Put the dog's leash back on and enjoy longer walks through any of the **Stapleton Northfield parks** that connect to Willow Bark Park.

95 UPLANDS PARK

Ping-pong your way from one end to the other of this narrow park

Location: 5000 Uinta St., Denver
Acreage: 9
Amenities: Benches, open space, ping-pong tables, picnic tables, concrete paths, running paths, public art, volleyball courts, basketball courts, playgrounds

GETTING THERE

BY CAR Take I-70 to Northfield Blvd. Turn north. Take Uinta St. to the left to the park. **BY TRANSIT** Bus 88 stops nearby. **BY BIKE** Take Sand Creek Greenway to Quebec St. Go north on Northfield Blvd. Veer left under Northfield to Trenton St. Follow the trail through Prairie Basin Park to the park.

A nice linear park made for strolling and striding, this park connects the west and east sides of the Stapleton Northfield neighborhood. While enjoying the park, you can catch a game of ping-pong or eat at the large concrete picnic tables designed for a neighborhood feast. Throughout the walk, keep an eye out for native plants. You might even see some edible fruits and berries. The park also features the sculpture *Woven Light* by Catherine Widgery. This open, airy structure simulates an outdoor room where light shines through the slats and colored dichroic glass. If you continue your walk through the park toward Northfield Boulevard, you'll find an active area of volleyball courts, a playground, an open space, more ping-pong tables, and a basketball court.

EXTEND YOUR VISIT

Just around the corner and west from the volleyball courts is an outdoor shopping center, the **Shops at Northfield Stapleton**. This mall is full of great places to eat, a movie theater, and shopping.

96   PRAIRIE BASIN PARK

With a view of the mountains plus plenty of closer-up stuff to view

Location: 5099 Uinta St., Denver
Acreage: 33
Amenities: Open space, creek, public art, benches, concrete path, jogging path

GETTING THERE

BY CAR Take I-70 to Northfield Blvd. Turn north. Take Uinta St. to the left to the park. **BY TRANSIT** Bus 88 stops nearby. **BY BIKE** Take Sand Creek Greenway to Quebec St. Go north on Northfield Blvd. Veer left under Northfield to Trenton St. Follow the trail to the park.

Interesting artwork sits in the overlook above Runway Creek at Prairie Basin Park.

Built as a flood control park for the Stapleton Northfield neighborhoods, this park teems with wildlife and artwork. A concrete path, which extends from the Sand Creek Greenway Extension along the west side of the park, can be taken all the way to the Rocky Mountain Arsenal Wildlife Refuge. Within the park, you'll find Runway Creek making its way south to Sand Creek.

On the west side of the park is a new art installation, *Phantom Pavilion*, by Volkan Alkanoglu. Its undulating arcs and playful blue tones capture the spirit of the mountains against the excitement of downtown Denver. From the promontory, you can see the Rockies to the far west and north, downtown Denver to the southwest, and the regional post office directly west.

An 8-foot-wide multimodal trail circles the park for about a mile. A soft surface jogging path complements the east side of the park for about half a mile. Watch for skaters, striders, and runners as they circle the park and its small pond.

EXTEND YOUR VISIT

If you've got your pup with you, head north on the concrete path to **Willow Park Bark** or south under Northfield Boulevard to **Northfield Pond Park**.

97 CENTRAL PARK, PRAIRIE UPLANDS PARK, WESTERLY CREEK PARK

Spirits soar on the grounds of the old Stapleton Airport

Location: 8801 E. Martin Luther King Blvd., Denver

Acreage: 76 (Central Park), 44 (Prairie Uplands Park), 64 (Westerly Creek Park)

Amenities: Lake, benches, picnic shelter, restroom, drinking fountain, playground, soccer field, bike/pedestrian path, natural areas, interactive fountain, picnic area, bocce ball court, climbing rocks, sledding hill

GETTING THERE

BY CAR Take I-70 to Central Park Blvd. Turn left on Martin Luther King Blvd. to the park. **BY TRANSIT** Many bus lines and the A train stop at Central Park station. **BY BIKE** Take Sand Creek Greenway to Westerly Creek Trail to the park.

The crown jewel of the Stapleton neighborhood parks, Central Park links together all the southern Stapleton parks (see Greenway Park). This giant park started as Rattlesnake Holler, the place everyone thought that Mayor Benjamin Stapleton was crazy to put an airport. It was 1929, aviation was just starting to take off, and the mayor saw an opportunity. He lobbied for funding, fought with folks over where the new airport should be, and ultimately got his way.

The day after Stapleton Airport opened, the stock market crashed—proving to his naysayers that an airport "in these times" was a crazy idea. Despite the financial crises of the time, the airport survived. Lindbergh, Earhart, and other noteworthy aviators graced the location, and soon Stapleton Airport was on the map as a wonderful facility for the future of flight.

Over time, the airport expanded to the north. With larger runways came larger and louder planes. The nearby Park Hill neighborhood sued, the FAA put height restrictions on downtown development, and the growth of Stapleton Airport was threatened in the 1980s. The city planners knew it was time to find a new location for the airport and eventually agreed to move it north to its current location.

Developers clamored to turn the abandoned airfield into Denver's next big thing: a sustainable, urban neighborhood that would be walkable, accessible, and close to downtown. Forest City, a development company, earned the rights to turn the ribbons of concrete and asphalt into the Stapleton neighborhood. Part

E Smith Rd
Old Stapleton Runway
Sand Creek Greenway
Sand Creek
Sand Creek Trail
E Smith Rd
Prairie Uplands Park
Paul's Point
E 35th Ave
Central Park Blvd
N Xenia St
E 33rd Ave
overlook bridge
sledding hill
interactive fountain
rock climbing wall
Central Park
recreation center
bocce ball court
soccer & mixed-use fields
main entrance
Alzheimer's Remembrance Garden
E Martin Luther King Blvd
N Xenia St
E 29th Ave
N Beeler St
Westerly Creek Park
N Dayton St
E 26th Ave
E 26th Ave
Greenway Park
N Xanthia St
Central Park Blvd
Akron Ct
N Beeler St
Westerly Creek
E Montview Blvd
N
0
1,000
2,000 Feet

Find Stapleton's old flight tower on the edge of Central Park as the walkway links to the bridge to nowhere, pointing to the new flight tower at Denver International Airport.

of the plan, happily, was to create green spaces including Central Park, Sand Creek Greenway, and Westerly Creek Park (as well as others).

In Central Park, you'll find over 10 miles of wide multimodal trails for bikes, skates, walks, dogs, and strides. On the southwest side of the park, the trails connect you to the Alzheimer's Remembrance Garden, soccer fields, a water park (in season), a Dr. Seuss–inspired oasis for bouldering, climbing, and swinging, and a lake for floating toy boats. You'll also find Stapleton's best sledding hill.

Located in the middle of the park you'll encounter a bridge that looks like it goes nowhere. This unique overview points conceptually from Stapleton's flight tower (to the west) to the new flight tower out at Denver International Airport to the north.

On Central Park's northeast side, you can walk westerly 0.5 mile along the Sand Creek Greenway to find what's left of where the planes once crossed the creek and to take off to the north. Look for the concrete walls along the banks of Sand Creek. These were the tunnel walls of the taxiway.

Remarkably, this section almost never happened. After the northeast side of the park sat dormant as a weedy field for a dozen years, Paul Frohardt organized his Eastbridge neighbors to remind the city, the county, Stapleton's developer, Forest City, and Denver Parks and Recreation that Central Park wasn't quite finished.

This area, known as Prairie Uplands Park, was still just weeds until its renovation, including trails and groomed areas, was completed in 2017. The high point on this northeast side of the park is a ring of sandstone boulders known as Paul's Point. It's a fabulous place to watch the sunset.

Attached to the southeast corner of Central Park is Westerly Creek Park. Westerly Creek, which ran underground during the airport's time here, became daylighted. The park now invites kids to play in the creek water or ride the more than 3 miles of trail beside it. Along the west side of Westerly Creek, you'll find large, adobe-colored pots on their sides. These beauties, which were cast from tree root balls and sculpted by Thomas Sayre, are called *Chorus*.

Together, Central Park and Westerly Creek Park create a giant open space with trails and creeks running through them. There's never a day that hikers, walkers, dogs, kids, bikes, rollers, skaters, or skippers aren't enjoying what used to be an old airport tarmac.

EXTEND YOUR VISIT

To the west of Central Park is a restaurant complex called **Punch Bowl Social Stapleton**. It occupies the location of Stapleton's flight tower. The tower, unfortunately, is currently closed to the public. Even if you can't get up the flight tower, there are some fun aviation artifacts in the restaurant (which is open to all) to enjoy.

98   GREENWAY PARK

From tennis to fun for dogs to rock climbing

Location: 8180 E. 26th Ave., Denver
Acreage: 40.5
Amenities: Dog park, picnic tables, restroom, drinking fountain, playground, skate park, tennis court, bike/pedestrian path, Stapleton Greenway Trail, picnic shelter, community garden, natural areas, picnic area

GETTING THERE

BY CAR Take I-70 to Central Park Blvd. Go south to the park. **BY TRANSIT** Bus 88 stops nearby. **BY BIKE** Take Sand Creek Greenway to Westerly Creek Trail. Go south to the park.

Part of the system of parks in the Stapleton neighborhood (and the original Stapleton Park), Greenway Park connects Fred Thomas Park on its west, Westerly Creek

Linking several parks, Greenway Park also contains secret playgrounds and climbing walls along the way.

Park on its east, and Central Park to the north. Running through the middle of this linear park, you'll find a 3-mile-long, wide, multimodal concrete path. Starting on the west end, the path ribbons its way past four tennis courts, a dog park, a community garden, a skate park, and two playgrounds including a rope climbing structure, finally reaching a rock wall and observation deck on its eastern end. The path in Greenway Park provides a pleasant strolling experience, transit for kids on bikes going to school, and a jogging escape. It's a great place to try out your new rollerblades. Located at the west end of the park, the giant dog park is separated into two sections, one for active and another for not-so-active pups.

EXTEND YOUR VISIT

Continue northeast to **Westerly Creek Park** to hunt for tadpoles in the creek.

99   FRED N. THOMAS PARK

Never underestimate how a small group can change the world

Location: 2400 N. Quebec St., Denver
Acreage: 29
Amenities: Pavilion, benches, picnic tables, picnic shelter, playground, restroom, drinking fountain, basketball court, football field, soccer field, baseball/softball field, tennis court, sand volleyball court, bike/pedestrian path, picnic area

GETTING THERE

BY CAR Take I-70 to Quebec St. Go south to the park. **BY TRANSIT** Buses 20, 28, and 43 stop nearby. **BY BIKE** Take E. 26th Ave. bikeway to the park.

This park, which sits on the border between the Park Hill and Stapleton neighborhoods, is a fitting place to honor its namesake. Fred N. Thomas was a giant in the local and then national stage in the fight to integrate schools. A Park Hill icon, he saw how segregation was impacting the education of his kids and other kids around the neighborhood, both white and African-American. Highly educated himself, he became a thinker and advocate for civil rights and school integration. He

SEPARATE ISN'T EQUAL

Although Fred Thomas made great strides in racial equality for our society, within his own federal jobs he was often denied opportunity. Prior to moving to Denver and attending University of Denver and the University of Colorado, he worked as an administrative assistant in Washington, D.C. Because he was African-American, he was not allowed to work with the all-white clerical staff and was categorized as a custodian. He often ate his lunch alone because he was banned from the all-white cafeteria. Later, when the Supreme Court decided the *Keyes* case, he was invited to sit in the court to listen, which he took great satisfaction in doing. In 1979 he received the third annual Martin Luther King Award from the Denver Martin Luther King Foundation and Black Educators United.

With a giant play structure and plenty of open space for ball playing, Thomas Park is a great place for an afternoon outdoors.

attended trainings, organized forward thinkers, and helped fund the civil actions that culminated in *Keyes v. School District No. 1*, the local court case that ended up in the Supreme Court and decided mandatory busing.

Bring your ball of choice. The many types of fields in Thomas Park give you lots of options for which sport to play. You can always find a pick-up game to play or watch. Trails snake through the park, offering visitors many paths to watch the games or to continue on to the network of Stapleton parks. A playground on the south side is large enough for your bigs while still offering smaller tunnels and spring-loaded totters for your littles.

EXTEND YOUR VISIT

This park connects with the Stapleton park system. Head east out the park to **Greenway Park** and beyond to enjoy miles and miles of trails and outdoor spaces.

100 WILLIAM H. MCNICHOLS PARK

Find a gorilla park

Location: 1700 N. Rosemary St., Denver
Acreage: 3.2
Amenities: Picnic tables, playground, football field, baseball/softball field, benches, bike/pedestrian path, picnic area

GETTING THERE

BY CAR Take Colorado Blvd. to E. 17th Ave. Pkwy. Take a left on Rosemary St. to the park. **BY TRANSIT** Buses 15L and 20 stop nearby. **BY BIKE** Take E. 17th Ave. Pkwy. to Rosemary St. Go north to the park.

With a fun gorilla perched on lookout keeping an eye on this neighborhood park, this is a great park for little kids. Open fields also invite visitors to an evening game of soccer and benches welcome an afternoon of book reading.

The park is named after Denver's former three-time mayor, William McNichols, who was a visionary leader. His credits include the 16th Street Mall, the Denver Center for the Performing Arts, the McNichols Sports Arena (demolished in 2000), the Auraria Higher Education Campus, the North Building addition at the Denver Art Museum, the expansion of Mile High Stadium, and twenty new pools and recreation centers. The old Carnegie Library at Civic Center Park now bears his name as well.

EXTEND YOUR VISIT

If you want a good cup of coffee, be sure to stop in at **Quince Coffee House**. It's a few blocks southwest of the park, just off Colfax Avenue on Quince Street.

101 CITY OF AXUM PARK

Also known as Obelisk Park

Location: 3200 N. Birch St., Denver
Acreage: 5
Amenities: Drinking fountain, picnic tables, picnic shelter, playground, restroom, basketball court, benches, walking/jogging path, picnic area

GETTING THERE

BY CAR Take I-70 to Colorado Blvd. Go south to Bruce Randolph Ave. Take a left, then right on Birch St. **BY TRANSIT** Buses 33 and 43 stop nearby. **BY BIKE** Take the Sand Creek Greenway to 48th Ave. Go west to Holly St. Turn south to Bruce Randolph Ave. to the park.

Another park in the Denver Sister City program, this park honors many parts of Denver's history. Its beginning is rooted in the history of the Prussian barons von Winckler and von Richthofen, who platted this area. Then James Cooke developed the area, bringing in the tramway to connect what was once called "the North Division of Capitol Hill." Cooke was friendly with George Clayton, a Denver

You'll have fun pretending to be a caterpillar crawling through the play structure at City of Axum Park.

philanthropist and kind heart to orphanages, who left his fortune to help the cause of early childhood development. Clayton Early Learning on the corner of Colorado and Martin Luther King Boulevard continues this philanthropic mission that started in the early 1900s.

In 1995, Mayor Wellington Webb cemented Denver's Sister City relationship with the city of Axum in Ethiopia. The name of this park changed accordingly. Axum is believed to be the home of the Queen of Sheba and Ethiopia is where famed paleontologist Richard Leakey discovered the remains of Lucy. In addition, in the city of Axum there are ancient obelisks believed to be among the oldest man-made structures in the world. To honor Denver's Sister City relationship, the city of Axum named one of the streets leading up to the famous obelisks as "Denver Street."

Within the park itself, you'll find a modern play structure where middles can crawl and climb. A long slide leads to a fun landing. A smaller play structure welcomes little kids to climb on a small make-believe rock cropping. Be sure to look for the obelisk in the center of the park next to the fun mural depicting Denver Street.

EXTEND YOUR VISIT

Commonwealth Coffee Roasters, northeast of the park on E. 38th Street and Forest Street, is a great place to relax after enjoying the Ethiopian flavor of the park.

102 SKYLAND PARK

The park near Holly Square offers fun for all ages

Location: 3334 N. Holly St., Denver
Acreage: 8
Amenities: Recreation center, benches, playground, basketball court, football field, baseball/softball field, tennis court, pickleball court, bike/pedestrian path

GETTING THERE

BY CAR Take I-70 to the Holly St. exit. Go south. The park is at the corner of 35th Ave., on the left. **BY TRANSIT** Buses 34, 43, and 65 stop nearby. **BY BIKE** Take the Sand Creek Greenway to 48th Ave. Go west to Holly St.

Not to be confused with the Skyland neighborhood to the west, Skyland Park is tucked behind the Hiawatha Davis Jr. Recreation Center. Its fun spiderweb-shaped climbing apparatus inspires kids to pretend they're superheroes as they climb through the playground. There's a nicely paved 0.5-mile walking path around the park that gives you a 360-degree view of the park. Adults can enjoy a walk while the kids play.

Inside at the recreation center is a pool for laps and exercise, a fitness center, and a place to check out gear for a game of pickleball. The center is named after city councilman Hiawatha Jones, who advocated for feeding senior citizens, playgrounds for children, and fairness in small-business economics.

EXTEND YOUR VISIT

On Holly Street, you'll find a variety of community facilities, including a **Boys & Girls Club** and the **Pauline Robinson Branch Library**.

103 MARTIN LUTHER KING JR. PARK

So all can play

Location: 3880 N. Newport St, Denver
Acreage: 11.3
Amenities: Recreation center, playground, basketball court, bike/pedestrian path, football field, soccer field, baseball/softball field, ping-pong, tennis court, pickleball court, picnic tables, benches, picnic area

GETTING THERE

BY CAR Take I-70 to Monaco Pkwy. Head south. Turn left on Smith Rd. Turn right on Newport. **BY TRANSIT** Buses 34 and 88 stop nearby. **BY BIKE** Take Sand Creek Greenway to E. 48th Ave. Turn south on Holly St. Turn left on Smith. Right on Newport.

A large park with a large grassy field marked for soccer, this park welcomes tennis, pickleball, and ping-pong players. It also invites imagination on the playground, which features a dinosaur fashioned in an abstract way and swinging bridges. In addition, there's a more traditional playground of tunnels and swings. Next to the park is the Martin Luther King Jr. Recreation Center.

Martin Luther King Jr. visited the Park Hill neighborhood in 1964, making visits and speeches at Macedonia Baptist Church. He then spoke at Montview Boulevard Presbyterian Church. Crowds overflowed the churches, spilling into the streets of Park Hill. King chose Park Hill because of the community's vision to integrate peacefully and its history in the fight for integrated schools.

Throughout Park Hill you can find historically relevant areas that figured in the civil rights movement, including the first school to integrate in Denver. From

Park Hill came the case that rose to the US Supreme Court that settled the issue of mandatory busing and desegregation. (See Fred N. Thomas Park and City Park.)

EXTEND YOUR VISIT

Stop at the two churches mentioned in this entry to pay tribute to Dr. King's visit to Denver. Also, look for the busts of King embedded in the median flowerpots along Martin Luther King Blvd. If you have time, visit the **Martin Luther King Jr. Memorial** in **City Park**. (See City Park.)

104 ELMENDORF PARK

Pretend to fly across the United States or just spin in circles at this park inspired by a high-flying pilot

Location: 12701 E. Elmendorf Pl., Denver
Acreage: 5.7
Amenities: Benches, picnic tables, playground, basketball court, baseball/softball field, soccer field

GETTING THERE

BY CAR From I-70, take Peoria north. Take a right on E. 51st Ave. then a left on Scranton St. **BY TRANSIT** Buses 42 and 121 stop nearby. **BY BIKE** Take the Sand Creek Greenway to the Dahlia St. trailhead. Head north to 56th Ave. Turn east to Peoria. Go south to E. 54th Avenue Dr. Take a left on E. Elmendorf Pl.

Named after Captain Hugh M. Elmendorf, a World War II high-altitude, record-breaking flyer in the Air Force, Elmendorf Park shares its site with John H. Amesse Elementary, abutting its playground. Although parts of the playground are fenced off

Shared with an elementary school, Elmendorf Park includes a map of the United States for kids to skip across.

for the younger kids, the playgrounds of both the school and Elmendorf Park are currently available all day. Kids have fun on the giant painted map of the United States. They also enjoy circling the sphere in the middle of the park or playing on several different sets of playground equipment. Most are geared toward younger, elementary-sized kids. In the corner of the park are two softball fields. In 2017, Denver Public Schools voted to restart this school. Expect changes to the playground.

EXTEND YOUR VISIT

The **High Line Canal Trail**, located south of the playground, meanders through Green Valley Ranch for 5 miles. Travel east, and you can discover three additional parks along the way that are just off the trail.

105 FALCON PARK

Small but packs a punch!

Location: 13650 E. Maxwell Pl., Denver
Acreage: 9.6
Amenities: Benches, picnic tables, playground, basketball court, football field, baseball/softball field, bike/pedestrian path

GETTING THERE

BY CAR Take I-70 to Peoria St. Turn right onto E. 46th Ave. Turn right onto Albrook Dr. Turn left onto Crown Blvd. Turn left onto 51st Ave. Turn right onto Xanadu St. Turn right onto Maxwell Pl. **BY TRANSIT** Bus 121 stops nearby. **BY BIKE** Take the Sand Creek Trail. Turn right onto Peoria St. Turn right onto E. 46th Ave. Turn right onto Albrook Dr. Turn left onto Crown Blvd. Turn left onto 51st Ave. Turn right onto Xanadu St. Turn right onto Maxwell Pl.

Falcon Park is a small neighborhood spot with a high-energy playground of many elevations. Kids love to climb the tower of power, zip down the slide, then run through the simulated creek to the bridge. And even though this park is pretty basic, the playground encourages kids to run from apparatus to apparatus.

EXTEND YOUR VISIT

Nearby, on the corner of Albrook Drive and 46th Avenue, is the brand-new **Montbello Open Space Park**. It's loaded with outdoor play items like a stump field, boulder nature play, and rope climbing course. It also has a giant climbing wall.

106 BARNEY L. FORD PARK

You never know where you'll end up

Location: 14480 E. Maxwell Pl., Denver
Acreage: 4.3
Amenities: Benches, picnic tables, soccer field

GETTING THERE

BY CAR Take I-70 to Peoria St. Turn right onto E. 46th Ave. Turn right onto Albrook Dr. Turn left onto Crown Blvd. Turn left onto 51st Ave. Turn right onto Xanadu St. Turn right onto Maxwell Pl. Pass Falcon Park to arrive at Ford Park. **BY TRANSIT** Bus 121 stops nearby. **BY BIKE** Take the Sand Creek Trail. Turn right onto Peoria St. Turn right onto E. 46th Ave. Turn right onto Albrook Dr. Turn left onto Crown Blvd. Turn left onto 51st Ave. Turn right onto Xanadu St. Turn right onto Maxwell Pl. Pass Falcon Park to arrive at Ford Park.

The park is a bit pedestrian, offering just a few soccer fields and a couple of benches, but its namesake sure is interesting! The park is named after Barney, a fugitive slave who escaped off a riverboat in Mississippi, entered the Underground

There's room to run in Ford Park.

Railroad, and eventually landed himself in Chicago where he met his future wife, Julia Lyoni. She encouraged him to create a middle and last name, and when he saw a locomotive named Lancelot Ford, he claimed the name.

From Chicago he headed out to discover gold by way of a ship voyage around Cape Horn. On his way he decided to open a hotel and restaurant in Nicaragua. It was hugely successful. Still with the idea for gold ruminating in his head, he headed to California to strike it rich, only to end up in Denver instead. When he got to Colorado, he found out that African-Americans could not stake claims, so instead he opened several very successful businesses: a barbershop, a restaurant, and several hotels, including the Inter-Ocean Hotels in Denver and Cheyenne, Wyoming.

The building that housed his People's Restaurant stands in downtown Denver, and is now called the Barney L. Ford Building. Ford was the first African-American to be nominated to the Colorado Territorial Legislature, and he played a giant role in ensuring that Colorado entered the Union as a free state. Before Ford passed away, he was generating the fourteenth highest income in Colorado.

Within the park, kick or throw around your favorite ball, spread a blanket out to enjoy a picnic, or maybe plant the park's first geocache. You might even find a few birds' nests in the pine trees.

EXTEND YOUR VISIT

Although not close by, the **Barney L. Ford Building** at 1514 Blake Street in downtown Denver is of interest. It is currently occupied by Hapa Sushi.

107 MONTBELLO CENTRAL PARK

Beautiful mountain views and terrific playground equipment

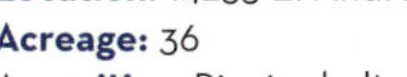

Location: 14255 E. Andrews Dr., Denver
Acreage: 36
Amenities: Picnic shelter, playground, baseball/softball field complex, press box, soccer field, tennis court, restroom, drinking fountain, picnic tables, benches, bike/pedestrian path, parking lot

GETTING THERE

BY CAR Take I-70 to Peoria St. Go north to Andrews Dr. Take a right to the park. **BY TRANSIT** Buses 42 and 45 stop nearby. **BY BIKE** Take Sand Creek Greenway to Central Park Blvd. Go north to E. 47th Ave., which turns into Albrook Dr. Take a left on Crown Blvd. to the park.

Sitting in the middle of a planned subdivision called Montbello, this large park invites the neighborhood to come out and play. Kids can remain occupied for hours on the brand-new play structure that shoots at least 20 feet into the air, complete with giant rope bridges to cross. Around the corner from the playground, you'll almost always see a game of pick-up football underway or locals shooting hoops. In the spring, Montbello Central Park offers a beautiful display of bulb flowers, and in the summer the park offers much-needed shade from which to admire the fantastic views of the amazing Rockies to the west. In the winter, kids wrestle in the snow and play hide-and-seek behind snow bunkers. Montbello's name comes from *mont* for mountain and *bello* for beautiful. The name succinctly conveys what you'll see in this neighborhood park.

EXTEND YOUR VISIT

Not far from **Montbello Central Park** is the **Rocky Mountain Arsenal Wildlife Refuge**. Go there to find some bison and enjoy a great hike.

108 PARKFIELD LAKE PARK

There's so much to choose from here; make a day of it!

Location: 15555 E. 53rd Ave., Denver
Acreage: 88
Amenities: Recreation center, natural areas, picnic shelter, benches, picnic tables, restroom, playground, skate park, tennis court, basketball court, baseball/softball field, football field, soccer field, interactive fountain, lake, picnic area, dog park

GETTING THERE

BY CAR From I-70, exit 283, north on Chambers Rd. to the park. **BY TRANSIT** Buses 45 and 121 stop nearby. **BY BIKE** Take the Sand Creek Trail. Turn onto Chambers Rd. Go north to the park.

A large regional park in the Montbello neighborhood, this donut-shaped funland circles the Montbello Recreation Center. You could easily spend the entire day here, first starting with a few ups and downs in the skate park! Next, watch or play some football on the field covered in turf, run through the interactive fountain, climb the octagon, and let your dog chase balls in the dog park. After you've gotten your aerobic activity in, head to the wetlands where you can identify several species of dragonflies while hunting for toads and frogs. Or maybe you'll just sit back and enjoy the waving bulrushes.

This park is always busy, and many tournaments and events happen on the ball fields, so be sure to take tournament schedules into account when planning your day. Although there is ample parking, you may want to approach the park by foot or bike. In addition, several moms are trying to start walking groups in the park; check in at the recreation center for more info.

Within the park, you can meander along the trails around the lake, through the ball fields, and by the dog park. You could easily walk 2 to 3 miles on the trails within the park. As the sun sets, see if you can catch one of the concerts or performances at the stage just south of the recreation center and overlooking the lake. On the east side of the park is the Derby Lateral Trail, which parallels the High Line Canal that once delivered water to the Rocky Mountain Arsenal. There are plans to connect the Derby Lateral Trail to the Rocky Mountain Arsenal Wildlife Refuge. Derby used to be the name for Commerce Town, née Commerce City!

EXTEND YOUR VISIT

Since you're so close, head up to the **Rocky Mountain Arsenal Wildlife Refuge**.

109 MELVIN F. SILVERMAN PARK

Vibrant and energetic spaces offer a workout and family time

Location: 12875 E. Andrews Dr., Denver
Acreage: 9
Amenities: Benches, picnic shelter, picnic tables, playground, restroom, drinking fountain, basketball court, football field, bike/pedestrian path, picnic area, fitness zone

GETTING THERE

BY CAR Take I-70 to Peoria St. Go north to Andrews Drive. Take a right to the park. **BY TRANSIT** Buses 42 and 45 stop nearby. **BY BIKE** Take Sand Creek Greenway to Central Park Blvd. Go north to E. 47th Ave. which turns into Albrook. Take a right on Andrews Dr. to the park.

Named after Melvin Silverman, a famous Denver artist who died young, this park's bright playground and outdoor fitness center have an air of vibrancy and energy. Silverman was an outstanding baseball pitcher at North High School, and he was

Get a workout in and enjoy some family time at energetic Silverman Park.

offered a contract from a minor league team with the Yankees organization. But art was his first love, and he passed on a baseball career in order to attend the Art Institute of Chicago. He married, moved to New York City, and traveled extensively. From many types of media, he produced collages, oils, wood sculptures, metal sculptures, charcoals, pencil drawings, cartoons, and book illustrations. Sadly, Silverman died in 1996 from cancer.

In the park, all ages can enjoy the fitness zone, playground, and basketball courts. Families play and picnic together in the evening. The fitness zone offers several sets of outdoor equipment for you to tone your arms, legs, and full body. Try balancing as you step along the multilevel posts. It's a great place to get fit while watching the kids effortlessly zip down the orange and purple slides or practice their dunking on the basketball court. The small kids will love the brightly colored teeter-totters.

EXTEND YOUR VISIT

Head east over to the large **Montbello Central Park** and climb on the new playground equipment that reaches to the moon.

110   VILLAGE PLACE PARK

Senior stepping, plus a zip line for the kids!

Location: 14029 E. Albrook Dr., Denver
Acreage: 9.7
Amenities: Benches, drinking fountain, picnic shelter, flower beds, picnic tables, playground, basketball court, soccer field, baseball/softball field, bike/pedestrian path, picnic area

GETTING THERE

BY CAR Take I-70 to Peoria St. Go north to Albrook Dr. Take a right to the park. **BY TRANSIT** Bus 42 stops nearby. **BY BIKE** Take Sand Creek Greenway to Central Park Blvd. Go north to E. 47th Ave., which turns into Albrook, to the park.

Near several senior centers, this park is hopping with seniors who go out for a half-mile lap around the park. A nice shady pavilion with good barbeque grills is a very popular attraction for groups and families. In addition, there's an added surprise for the kids—a zip line!

EXTEND YOUR VISIT

If you want some more space or would like to see some nice flower beds, head north about a mile to **Montbello Central Park**, where you'll also get some great views of the Rockies to the west.

111   41ST & ENSENADA PARK

Mile 64 on the High Line Canal

Location: 4100 N. Ensenada St., Denver
Acreage: 5
Amenities: Benches, picnic tables, playground, picnic shelter, bike/pedestrian path

GETTING THERE

BY CAR Take I-70 east to Tower Rd. Drive north. Turn right on E. 38th Ave. Turn left to Ensenada St. to the park. **BY TRANSIT** Bus 42 stops nearby. **BY BIKE** Take the High Line Canal Trail to Green Valley Ranch. Exit at mile marker 64.

This roadside park may be nondescript, but it is significant, especially for hikers doing the High Line Canal Trail. After making their way northward on the High Line Canal along Tower Road, hikers jig along 38th Avenue to rejoin the High Line Canal Trail here at the park before continuing north. It's a great place to stop and enjoy the picnic tables under the spruce and cottonwoods. For those who are checking off all 71 miles of the High Line Canal Trail, look for mile marker 64 at the south edge of the park. On the west side of the park, you can pick up the Derby Lateral Trail that will, eventually, make its way to Derby Lake in the Rocky Mountain Arsenal Wildlife Refuge.

EXTEND YOUR VISIT

Walk along the High Line Canal Trail north out of the park. Go through the neighborhoods for a bit more than 5 miles to enjoy **Green Valley Ranch**. The terminus of the High Line Canal is at 64th Avenue.

112   42ND & LISBON PARK

Green Valley's community park has everything—except a proper name

Location: 4000 N. Kirk St., Denver
Acreage: 18
Amenities: Benches, picnic tables, picnic shelter, playground, restroom, drinking fountain, basketball court, tennis court, bike/pedestrian path, baseball/softball field, disc golf course, picnic area, parking lot

GETTING THERE

BY CAR Take I-70 to Tower Rd. Go north. Turn right on 38th Ave. Turn left on Himalaya Rd. Take a right on E. 42nd Ave. to the park. **BY TRANSIT** Bus 42 stops nearby. **BY BIKE** Take the Sand Creek Trail. Turn right onto Chambers Rd. Turn right onto E. 32nd Ave. Turn left onto N. Airport Blvd. Take the exit. Turn left. Slight right. Turn right onto E. 40th Ave. Continue onto E. 38th Ave. Turn left on Himalaya Rd. Turn right onto E. 42nd Ave.

This large yet compact park has every activity you might imagine, and you could easily spend an entire day here. As they enter the park, kids run to the art installation, *Global Rhythms*, by Bill and Mary Buchen. This multipart installation of a steel echo chamber, steel drums, and steel noisemakers encourages visitors to use their loudest outdoor voices and musical talents. A disc golf course invites you to play a

A sound garden at the unnamed park at 42nd and Lisbon invites kids to shout and scream in their outdoor voices.

round through large grassy fields and natural areas. Climb the hills to launch a kite, walk the 3 miles of concrete paths, watch butterflies in the natural area, encourage your kids to play tag and chase, or let them loose on the two different playgrounds. One playground attracts your climbers while the other calls out to your wobblers. If you want to be chill, find a shady spot under the oaks or sit for a spell near the picnic shelter eyeing the mountains or looking for satellites at dark. It's surprising that such a well-appointed park doesn't have an official name. What would you name it?

EXTEND YOUR VISIT

If you haven't tried disc golf yet, this is a great park to give it a try. Although you can buy specific discs for the sport at outdoor stores, why not grab the old Frisbee you have in the garage and try it out?

113   TOWN CENTER PARK

A community gathering place where pelicans, gulls, and people mingle

Location: 5050 N. Argonne St., Denver
Acreage: 25
Amenities: Recreation center, lake, restroom, drinking fountain, playground, benches, picnic shelter, baseball/softball field, basketball court, skate park, bike/pedestrian path

In the middle of Green Valley Ranch, Town Center Park provides a venue for concerts, farmers markets, and beer gardens.

GETTING THERE

BY CAR Take I-70 to Peña Blvd. Turn right on Green Valley Ranch Rd. Turn left on Tower Rd. Turn right on E. 50th Ave. to the park. **BY TRANSIT** Buses 45 and 169L stop nearby. **BY BIKE** Take the Sand Creek Trail. Turn right onto Chambers Rd. Turn right onto E. 32nd Ave. Turn left onto N. Airport Blvd. Take the exit. Turn right on E. 40th Ave. Turn left on Tower Rd. Turn right on E. 50th St. to the park.

Right in the middle of Town Center, but still on the west side of the Green Valley Ranch neighborhood, sits this park. It is mixed in with a governmental complex and commercial district. The lake draws pelicans and seagulls, while its northern shore hosts a different type of visitor—softball and baseball players! In the summertime, there is a concert series and a farmers market where locals share community stories about what's happening in Green Valley Ranch. Schools and their playgrounds back up to the park. The Green Valley Ranch Recreation Center is on the park's southeastern edge; it offers more playground facilities.

Take a walk around the lake for about half a mile, grab some fruit from the farmers market, then socialize with friends at the beer garden located just west of the park.

EXTEND YOUR VISIT

On the edge of the park, on the west side, is a fabulous beer garden. It's a nice place to relax after a game of baseball.

114   GREEN VALLEY RANCH EAST PARK

Pass, set, spike!

Location: 4455 N. Jebel St., Denver
Acreage: 13.4
Amenities: Dog park, benches, drinking fountain, picnic shelter, picnic tables, playground, football field, baseball/softball field, tennis court, basketball court, outdoor pool, sand volleyball court, parking lot, picnic area

GETTING THERE

BY CAR Take I-70 to Peña Blvd. Turn right on Green Valley Ranch Road. Turn right on Jebel to the park. **BY TRANSIT** Buses 42 and 45 stop nearby. **BY BIKE** Take the Sand Creek Trail. Turn right onto Chambers Rd. Turn right onto E. 32nd Ave. Turn left onto N. Airport Blvd. Take the exit. Turn left. Slight right. Turn right onto E. 40th Ave. Continue onto E. 38th Ave. Turn left onto Ensenada St. Turn right onto High Line Canal Trail. Turn left onto Lisbon St. Turn left onto E. 45th Ave. Turn left onto Jebel St.

This community park is situated compactly on the eastern side of the Green Valley Ranch neighborhood. You, your dog, and your family could spend lots of time here. This park has one of the few sand volleyball courts in the city, so be sure to bring your outdoor volleyballs. You'll also find good tennis courts to get in some serious play or to just volley.

The dog park, like most in Denver, has two areas. One allows active dogs to run and the other is for slower dogs to chill. To the southern side of the park sits playground equipment, which abuts the High Line Canal and its trail. In the fall, local football teams practice in this park, while the cheerleaders jump and yell.

Green Valley Ranch used to be just that! Back in the mid-1800s, the Ebert family cobbled together acre after acre of farmland to ultimately create a 1,400-acre farm. Through its middle ran the Colorado Eastern Railroad, a narrow-gauge line that moved coal from the Scranton coal mine to the Grant smelter in Denver. Time passed, the High Line Canal dried up, and the farmers barely scraped out a living. Denver annexed the land in 1973, and developers began constructing what would become Denver's largest neighborhood. In the 1980s developers bartered with the school board to market the neighborhood to accommodate mandated desegregation.

EXTEND YOUR VISIT

Walk the last segment of the **High Line Canal Trail** north to 64th Avenue. Most people stop at mile marker 66 (just east of this park), not realizing the trail continues for another 5 miles to mile marker 71. Until the final segment of the High Line Canal Trail receives its official mile markers, you'll need to travel north through the neighborhoods to get to the end of the High Line Canal.

115   GREEN VALLEY RANCH WEST PARK

Digging for treasure

Location: 4500 N. Argonne St., Denver
Acreage: 3.5
Amenities: Picnic tables, grills, playground, basketball court, football field, baseball/softball field, picnic area

GETTING THERE

BY CAR Take I-70 to Peña Blvd. Turn right on Green Valley Ranch Rd. Turn right on Tower Rd, left on E. 45th Ave., and left on Argonne St. to the park. **BY TRANSIT** Bus 42 stops nearby. **BY BIKE** Take the Sand Creek Trail. Turn right onto Chambers

Not as big as its sister park to the east, Green Valley Ranch West Park still competes with a fun playground, barbeques, and even a place to dig!

Rd. Turn right onto E. 32nd Ave. Turn left onto N. Airport Blvd. Take the exit. Turn right on E. 40th Ave. Turn left on Tower Rd. Turn right on E. 45th Ave. Turn left on Argonne St. to the park.

Smaller than Green Valley Ranch East Park, this neighborhood park is a good one for little kids. The ample playground equipment geared to littles includes a fun simulated front-end loader that kids can use to dig big buckets of sand. Perhaps they'll build their sand castle in the sky or find buried treasure! Additionally, a nicely situated grill with picnic tables welcomes a summer barbeque under shady trees.

The neighborhood around this park, the Green Valley Ranch subdivision, used to be the Green Valley Ranch. To convince the last remaining farmer to sell, the developer built a home for him and his family, allowing the old farmhouse to be demolished. Now, with about 10,000 homes, Green Valley Ranch is only 30 percent built out. Many new subdivisions are planned in the city of Aurora to abut Denver's Green Valley and to squeeze in around the Gaylord Rockies Resort and Convention Center. This tiny park could get crowded!

EXTEND YOUR VISIT

For a larger park with a different focus, head to the **Town Center Park** just a mile or so away to enjoy a walk around the lake or the outdoor farmers market.

116 FIRST CREEK PARK

A small, linear park offers a chance for a short nature walk

Location: 4055 N. Picadilly Rd., Denver
Acreage: 37
Amenities: Bike/pedestrian path, First Creek Trail, open space, natural areas

GETTING THERE

BY CAR Take I-70 to Tower Rd. Head north. Take a right on Elmendorf Rd. Park is on the left. **BY TRANSIT** Bus 45 stops nearby. **BY BIKE** Take Sand Creek Trail. Turn left onto Airport Blvd. Turn right on Green Valley Ranch Blvd. Turn left on Tower Rd. Turn right on Elmendorf Rd. to reach park.

The City of Denver redesigned the old Clear Point Park and reopened it in 2019 as First Creek Park. With three fun natural play areas for smalls, middles, bigs, and

Great natural play areas await you at First Creek Park.

parents alike, the park offers plenty of entertainment for all ages. Work up a sweat swinging, climbing, and tunneling through, then relax at the wooden picnic tables beneath cottonwoods for a spell. After your rest break maybe you'd like to take a stroll on the two miles of gravel paths that meander over First Creek. Be sure to pause to pick raspberries (in season) on your way to the concrete path that takes you to the First Creek Open Space at DEN.

EXTEND YOUR VISIT

Head up the path a few more miles to visit the American bison at the **Rocky Mountain Arsenal Wildlife Refuge**.

117   NEW FREEDOM PARK

A place for gardens and community

Location: 8800 E. 13th Ave., Denver
Acreage: 2.13
Amenities: Picnic tables, synthetic field, playground, community garden, bike/pedestrian path, Westerly Creek Trail

GETTING THERE

BY CAR Take Colfax Ave. to Yosemite. Go south. Turn right on E. 13th Ave. to the park.
BY TRANSIT Buses 15, 15L, and 105 stop nearby. **BY BIKE** Take E. 13th Ave. to the park.

In 2012 the immigrant and refugee community around this park organized and turned a vacant lot into a neighborhood gathering place. Although not a glamorous

Westerly Creek runs through New Freedom Park.

park, the locals love it—and why not? Filled with urban gardens that overflow with crops and flowers from around the world, this newer park invites neighbors to congregate.

A small play area on concrete and a few play structures keep kids entertained as their parents tend the gardens. Westerly Creek, which runs through the middle of the park, is great for exploring. The park received a Frontier Parks Award from the City Parks Alliance for its community work and outreach.

EXTEND YOUR VISIT

If you're hungry, head a couple of blocks north on **Colfax**: you'll find a variety of ethnic-influenced restaurants from Ethiopian to Mexican.

118   VERBENA PARK

Play in a tree then grill up some dinner

Location: 1151 N. Verbena St., Denver
Acreage: 7.1
Amenities: Picnic shelter, picnic tables, benches, playground, basketball court, baseball/softball field, soccer field, bike/pedestrian path

A canopy of trees and shade await you for good climbing and resting at Verbena Park.

GETTING THERE

BY CAR Take Colfax Ave. to Verbena St. Go south to the park. **BY TRANSIT** Buses 10 and 15L stop nearby. **BY BIKE** Take 12th Ave. to Verbena St.

Although you may find a few species of verbena in the park, what this park is great for is climbing trees. With large and inviting specimens of spruce, elm, oak, and ash, you're sure to find a branch to climb or just some welcome shade. This is an active park in the evening when everyone comes out to play ball and grill.

EXTEND YOUR VISIT

Just to the south of the park is the **Kelly Road Dam**. At sunset, you can climb to the top of the dam for great views across the open spaces of the Lowry neighborhood while catching magnificent views of the Rockies.

119 CITY OF ULAANBAATAR PARK

Also known as Red Hero Park

Location: 500 N. Roslyn St., Denver
Acreage: 5.1
Amenities: Benches, playground, natural areas, drinking fountain, bike/pedestrian path, shade structure

GETTING THERE

BY CAR Take Quebec St. to E. 6th Ave. Pkwy. Turn right on Rosalyn St. to the park. **BY TRANSIT** Buses 65 and 73 stop nearby. **BY BIKE** Take Quebec St. to E. 6th Ave. Pkwy. Turn right on Rosalyn St. to the park.

The name of this park recognizes the tenth Sister City in the Denver Sister City program. In turn, Ulaanbaatar, Mongolia, recognizes that Denver has one of the largest Mongolian populations outside of Mongolia. Ulaanbaatar, located on the Trans-Siberian Railway, is the capital of the area. The name, pronounced "u-la-an-Ba-a-tur," literally translates to "red hero" in honor of military leader Damdin Sükh-baatar, whose warriors liberated Mongolia from Chinese occupation in 1921. The cities of Denver and Ulaanbaatar exchange students each year.

From the park's high point, you can catch views into the downtown of the Lowry neighborhood. Enjoy the arched sculpture that towers over the park,

The artwork at City of Ulaanbaantar Park reflects on how the hearth is the center of the home.

or grab your sled for a good downhill thrill in winter. The tower, or *Tulga*, an impressive stainless steel sculpture, was created by artist Tsogtsaikhan Mijid in 2009. It represents the most important area of the home, the fireplace, where families and communities gather to eat, share, and commune. The three rings of the sculpture represent the sun, moon, and stars while the four legs point to the cardinal directions. Altogether, the sculpture relays a feeling of warmth and comfort.

EXTEND YOUR VISIT

The Lowry neighborhood is loaded with great parks and a fabulous museum, **Wings Over the Rockies**, which is just down the hill in downtown Lowry. Be sure to visit.

120 CRESCENT PARK

Walk a half-moon around the park

Location: 782 N. Roslyn St., Denver
Acreage: 7
Amenities: Benches, drinking fountain, picnic tables, picnic shelter, playground, natural areas, bike/pedestrian path, picnic area

GETTING THERE

BY CAR Take Colorado Blvd. and turn east on 8th Ave. to the park. **BY TRANSIT** Buses 6, 10 15, and 73 stop nearby. **BY BIKE** Take Colorado Blvd. and turn east on 8th Ave. to the park.

A nice neighborhood park with a large grassy field, Crescent Park appeals to Lowry neighborhood kids who like to play here. Caretakers often gather in the late mornings with their younger kids to enjoy the playgrounds, while the older kids play tag on the grass. Shaped like a half-moon, the park sits at the juncture of many private schools in Lowry. Kids enjoy the park after school, as well. There is also a mini-auditorium where locals can act out school plays or practice their quartet ensemble.

EXTEND YOUR VISIT

Head over to the **Wings Over the Rockies** museum in the downtown area of Lowry.

121   GREAT LAWN PARK (PLUS!)

Great it is!

Location: 101 N. Yosemite St., Denver
Acreage: 228 (all lands combined)
Amenities: Benches, picnic tables, picnic shelter, restroom, drinking fountain, playground, lake, bike/pedestrian path, overlook plaza, natural areas, picnic area, natural areas, wetlands, pedestrian path, soccer field complex, tennis court, drinking fountain, restroom, benches, basketball court, synthetic field, baseball/softball field complex, press box, pavilion, dog park

GETTING THERE

BY CAR Take Colorado Blvd. to E. 6th Ave. Pkwy. to the park. **BY TRANSIT** Buses 6 and 10 stop nearby. **BY BIKE** Take Colorado Blvd. to E. 6th Ave. Pkwy. to the park.

Great Lawn Park and the surrounding fields, open spaces, and the neighborhood now known as Lowry once made up the Lowry Air Force Base, a military compound for soldiers being taught the technical skills they needed to sustain operations during World War II, the Korean War, the Cold War, and the Vietnam War. Charles Lindbergh landed at Lowry Field as a publicity stunt to promote aviation, and Dwight D. Eisenhower attended church on the base when he was in Denver vacationing with his wife (see Mamie Doud Eisenhower Park). The Base closed in 1994 to be replaced by a thriving mixed-use neighborhood and some splendid public lands.

It's a large area with lots of features. First off, there's Great Lawn Park itself where you'll find sweeping open spaces, concerts during the summer, ponds for toy boat floating, enticing paths, and what might be the world's largest sundial. The park sits next to Kelly Road Dam to the north; visit the natural fields in the fall to see amazing autumn colors as the grasses turn, and keep an eye peeled for birds.

It's well worth walking north along the dirt trails from Great Lawn Park toward Kelly Road Dam to reach the giant sundial. Designed by Jesse Clark and fabricated by Mike Mancarella, the aluminum-clad spear climbs to the sky and shadows the time to the ground. A reflection pond captures you and the sundial.

Feeling more sporty than contemplative? Save the sundial for another day and instead head across the street on the south side of Great Lawn Park to the Lowry Sports Complex Park and the Jackie Robinson Fields Park. Grab your ball of choice to play tennis on lighted courts, baseball and softball on lighted fields, or soccer.

With a giant sundial and a meandering creek, Great Lawn Park is the gathering spot in Lowry.

A giant sundial both tells the time and harkens back to Lowry's aviation past.

With a plethora of fields and courts, the Lowry Sports Complex rivals the offerings at Kennedy Ballfields Complex and Veterans Park.

Big as they are, the sports complex and the Jackie Robinson Fields are dwarfed by Lowry's open space to the south. With fields of native grasses and trails galore, you can explore this bird-watching haven, take an urban hike on nice 2-mile loops, or let your dog romp in the generous dog park. The dog park not only has two areas, one for low-energy dogs and one for high-energy dogs, it also has an agility area with hoops and tunnels. There's even a fire hydrant!

In the winter, the area offers an opportunity to strap on your cross-country skis and carve out a nice route.

EXTEND YOUR VISIT

You can find the historic **Eisenhower Chapel** in Lowry at 293 Roslyn Street or visit the **grave of Lt. Francis B. Lowry**, for whom the base was named; he was killed in aerial combat while serving as a photographer in 1918. His grave is located in nearby Fairmount Cemetery.

Stop by and view the home at 7400 East 6th Avenue. Before Lowry Field appeared, this area was home to the **Agnes C. Phipps Memorial Sanatorium**, a 150-bed facility boasting the curative properties of Colorado's climate. Although the Sanatorium's function is gone, the home at 7400 East 6th Avenue is the oldest structure still standing in Lowry; it was built in 1904, and is now a private residence. Looking for still more? Head over to the **Wings Over the Rockies** museum for some indoor fun.

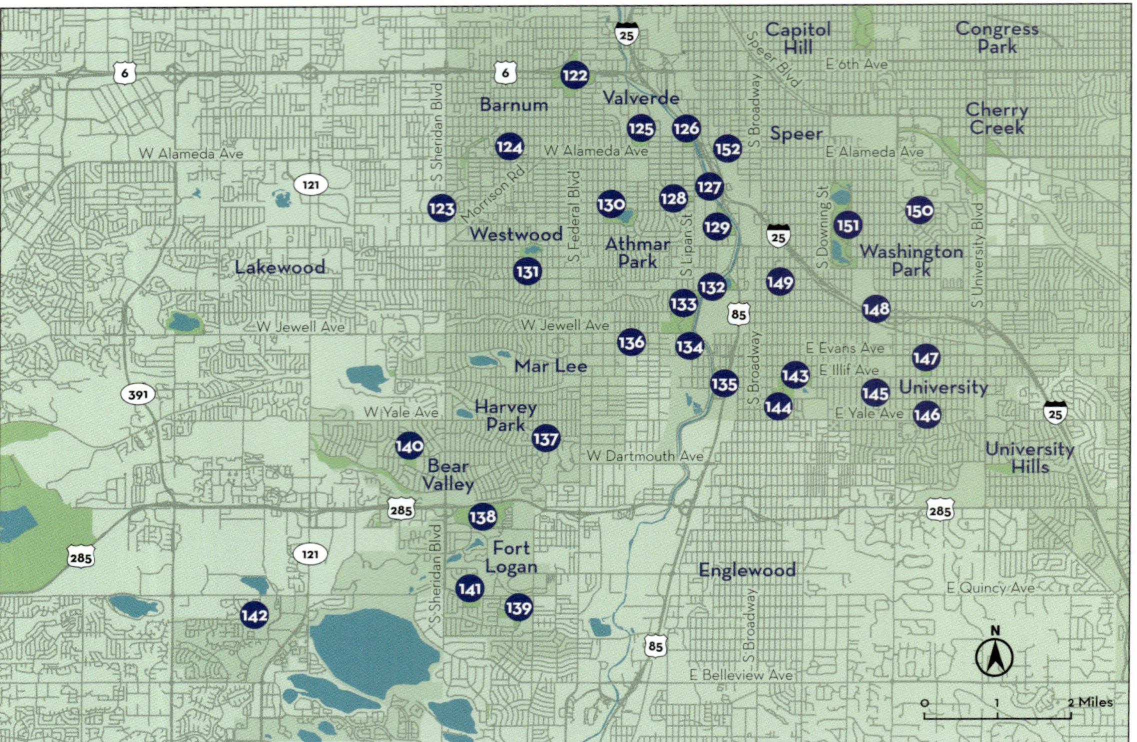

Capitol Hill
Congress Park
Cherry Creek
Barnum
Valverde
Speer
Washington Park
Athmar Park
Westwood
Lakewood
Mar Lee
Harvey Park
Bear Valley
Fort Logan
Englewood
University
University Hills
W Alameda Ave
E 6th Ave
Speer Blvd
E Alameda Ave
S Broadway
S Downing St
S University Blvd
S Sheridan Blvd
Morrison Rd
S Federal Blvd
S Lipan St
W Jewell Ave
W Dartmouth Ave
E Evans Ave
E Illif Ave
E Yale Ave
W Yale Ave
E Belleview Ave
E Quincy Ave
N
0 1 2 Miles

SOUTHWEST PARKS

122   BARNUM PARK

Location: 360 N. Hooker St., Denver
Acreage: 60
Amenities: Soccer field, baseball/softball field complex, natural areas, bleachers, bike skills course, recreation center, outdoor pool, dog park, restroom, playground, basketball court, tennis court, lake, picnic tables, picnic shelter, benches, bike/pedestrian path, picnic area, drinking fountain, restroom

GETTING THERE

BY CAR Take I-25 to exit 209C to the west on 6th Ave. Take a left on N. Knox Ct. to a left on W. 4th Ave. to arrive at the recreation center parking lot. **BY TRANSIT** Buses 9 and 30/31 stop nearby, as does the W line. **BY BIKE** Take the South Platte River Trail to the Lakewood Gulch Trail. Go west. Go south on Grove St. Take a left on 6th Ave./Weir Gulch Trail and enter the park.

This large park spans both sides of 6th Avenue and scoops up several parks into one large area called Barnum, making one large attraction for the whole family. Starting on the north side of 6th Avenue, you'll find a highly maintained and

Although P.T. never lived there, Barnum Park harkens to his folklore and provides several fun places for the whole family including the dog.

competitive softball/baseball field with nicely cared-for infields, bleacher seating, and ample parking for the whole team. The ball field area of the park is known as Sandos Park. It is named after M. L. "Sam" Sandos, a beloved community leader and the first Hispanic to serve on the Denver City Council. Sandos fought for community empowerment issues and healthy development of children.

Just up the hill to the west, you'll discover the Trestle Bike Park. Young kids and more skilled bicycle riders test their skills on the bike skills' dirt tracks. With one track for beginners and one for the more advanced riders, these tracks get riders' adrenaline going as they pump up and down well-maintained, steep hills. Jump on your bike or just watch and enjoy the show. More advanced riders who want a faster course with more turns should try out the dirt track at Ruby Hill. (See Ruby Hill Park.)

A pedestrian bridge spans 6th Avenue, connecting the northern and southern sides of Barnum Park. On the south side is a large dog park. One side of the dog park is for high-energy dogs and the other side is for low-energy pups. This dog park also features great city views, so you can relax on the benches overlooking the city as your dog romps and rolls. Next to the dog park, there are tennis courts for the racquet set and a bank of swings that have plenty of room for kids to try daredevil tricks into a sand pit.

Just down the hill to the south sits the Barnum Recreation Center complete with a fun pool that's open in season. Sitting next to the recreation center are two playgrounds for littles and middles. They'll squeal with delight at seeing the stone gorilla and lion in the playground; they harken to glory days of P. T. Barnum's famed circus. Although he never lived in the neighborhood, his legend does.

Farther down the hill, enjoy a walk of about a half a mile around the lake. Although small, it offers a refreshing walk. Even though you can see 6th Avenue and I-25, they are, luckily, out of earshot. To the east of the lake and across a busy street sits another set of baseball/softball fields in Barnum East Park, which can be accessed from 5th Avenue.

EXTEND YOUR VISIT

After exploring all aspects of this park, be sure to find the **Weir Gulch Trail**. You can take it west for several miles into the Barnum neighborhood and beyond, or you can take it north about half a mile to the **South Platte River Trail**. You can also head west toward the Lakewood Gulch, where you can jump on the **Lakewood Gulch trail** to go 5 miles or more to the west.

If you'd like to explore some offbeat Barnum folklore, you can find what locals call the **Barnum House** on King Street. It's red and yellow and sits across from the landmark Bowman-Savio house. Although P. T. never lived there himself, at one time a jokester who adopted the Barnum name did. He spread the Barnum folklore, and many believe that the home's style, which the jokester fashioned, captures the spirit of those circus stories.

123   WESTWOOD PARK

Enjoy the buzz of pollinator gardens and the fun of making a watery mess

Location: 4951 W. Kentucky Ave., Denver
Acreage: 5
Amenities: Picnic tables, benches, playground, basketball court, baseball/softball field, bike/pedestrian path, picnic area, nature play, walking loop

GETTING THERE

BY CAR Take I-25 to 6th Ave. Take a left on Sheridan Blvd. Take a left on West Kentucky Ave. to the park. **BY TRANSIT** Buses 11 and 50/51 stop nearby. **BY BIKE** Take South Platte River Trail to Lakewood Gulch Trail west. Go south on 6th Ave. to S. Knox Ct. Take a right on Morrison Rd. Take a left on W. Kentucky Ave. to the park.

The heartbeat of play in the middle of the Westwood neighborhood is this newly renovated park. You'll find enough playground structures for your littles, mediums, and bigs, complete with a nature play area that has a fun manual pump for kids to create a watery, muddy, sandy mess. Kids of all sizes can romp around the fallen timber area, crawling under logs and over branches. Don't miss the short loop through the park that passes several pollinator gardens; adults (and kids, too!) can get a workout on the outdoor fitness machines. Seven laps around the loop puts a mile on your step tracker.

At the northern edge of the park, in what used to be a dirt field where drivers did donuts in their trucks, is a grassy open space. Often, there are impromptu

Newly renovated, Westwood Park offers this fallen timber area for playing, as well as a water pump for making mud pies.

volleyball nets set up by the neighborhood athletes looking for some high-energy recreation.

EXTEND YOUR VISIT

Just south of the park, at the corner of Morrison and Sheridan, is the **entry sign into Westwood**. It's worth a visit to see this fun, lively installation. Look for the big red guitar.

124 CUATRO VIENTOS/FOUR WINDS PARK

Where the four winds come together

Location: 3800 W. Alameda Ave., Denver
Acreage: 2
Amenities: Open space, playground, interactive water feature, turf areas for fitness/sport activities, a picnic shelter, basketball court, skate park

GETTING THERE

BY CAR Take I-25 to 6th Ave. Go west. Go south on Perry St. Turn left on W. Alameda Ave. to the park. **BY TRANSIT** Buses 1, 3, and 31 stop nearby. **BY BIKE** Take the South Platte River Trail to the Lakewood Gulch Trail. Follow W. 12th Ave. to 6th Ave. Turn left on Knox Ct .Turn right on W. 1st Ave. Turn right on W. Byers Pl. Turn left on S. Newton St. Turn right on W. Alameda Ave. to the park.

Rising from the ruins of an old trailer park, Cuatro Vientos/Four Winds Park came together thanks to active community involvement. Together with Great Outdoors Colorado (GOCO) and other efforts, the citizens drew up their idea for a good park. They asked for a skate park, basketball court, two levels of fun playgrounds, an open space, and prettier landscaping. They got it.

When asked what they wanted to call the park, the community decided on Cuatro Vientos to reflect the fact that people came from everywhere to get the park designed, funded, and built. The medicine wheel in the playground honors the diversity and rich cultures of this community. Opened in 2014, it was the first park to be built in the Westwood/Barnum area in thirty years.

Although small, it's full of laughter and activity any time of the day. This is a good, compact park to bring the entire family. You can see everyone playing from one vantage point.

EXTEND YOUR VISIT

Make your way into the **Westwood neighborhood** to see how it's transforming into a cultural hub. You'll find great eats, excellent art, and global music.

The turtle at Cuatro Vientos/Four Winds Park spouts water—and bears the world on its back.

125   WEST-BAR-VAL-WOOD PARK

Three communities into one

Location: 2001 W. Cedar Ave., Denver
Acreage: 12
Amenities: Picnic tables, playground, basketball court, football field, baseball/softball field, bleachers, bike/pedestrian path

GETTING THERE

BY CAR Take I-25 to W. Alameda Ave. Head west to S. Tejon St. Take a right on S. Tejon St. Take a left on W. Cedar Ave. to the park. **BY TRANSIT** Buses 3 and 33B stop nearby. **BY BIKE** Take the South Platte River Trail to W. Bayaud Ave. Go west to S. Tejon St. Take a left. Take a right on W. Cedar Ave. to the park.

When a neighborhood gets a park, usually its name comes from a nearby location, a local person, or someone famous. But in this case, back in 1956, the nearby neighborhoods came together and named their local park in a way that reflected everyone in the area, not just one person. Congratulations to the residents of Westwood, Barnum, and Valverde for coming up with this long park name!

Always a community park, West-Bar-Val-Wood Park is thought of as the front yard of the Valverde neighborhood. The community gathers at the two playgrounds on the top of the park or at the softball/baseball fields at the lower part of the park. In the playground for bigger kids is a fun hoop and rope course they can wiggle through as if they were caterpillars! A nice cottonwood grove graces the middle of the park for cool summer shade, and a wonderful spruce forest stands to the west for year-round color.

EXTEND YOUR VISIT

If you like Asian food, you're in luck. You'll find a plethora of Asian restaurants along **Federal Boulevard**, just to the west.

126   VALVERDE PARK

Take me out to the ball game

Location: 150 S. Navajo St., Denver
Acreage: 5.79
Amenities: Baseball/softball field complex, basketball court, football field, bike/pedestrian path, picnic shelter

GETTING THERE

BY CAR Take I-25 to W. Alameda Ave. Head west to S. Navajo St. and turn right to the park. **BY TRANSIT** Buses 3 and 33B stop nearby. **BY BIKE** Take the South Platte River Trail to W. Bayaud Ave. The park is across the street.

Batter up. This park is all about baseball and softball! Four gorgeous fields form a giant square and turf covers both the infields and the outfields. Each diamond owns its own large backstop, and each baseline has its own bleachers. It's a ballplayer's dream come true.

Actually, it's a dream come true that was funded by Denver media and cable mogul, Bill Daniels. He bequeathed the funds to the Denver Police Activities League (PAL) to build and continue to finance the complex. The fields themselves hold the name Donnie Young Fields, in honor of an officer who was shot and killed in the line of duty.

The accompanying basketball court, also funded by Daniels, was named after Nuggets player and Denver PAL alumni, Chauncey Billups. To reserve any of these ball fields, check the Denver Parks and Recreation website.

EXTEND YOUR VISIT

Just to the north of the park, you'll see a large dog sculpture covered in round reflective discs. It denotes the location of the **Denver Animal Shelter**. Go in and scratch a few pups behind the ears or rub a kitty's belly. You might just find a friend for life.

127 JOHNSON-HABITAT PARK

Fun and history on the South Platte River

Location: 610 S. Jason St., Denver
Acreage: 7.6
Amenities: Benches, picnic shelter, South Platte River Trail, natural areas, river access, playground, interpretive overlook, outdoor classroom

GETTING THERE

BY CAR Take I-25 to W. Alameda Ave. Go west. Take a left on S. Platte River Dr. to Jason St. **BY TRANSIT** Buses 3 and 11 stop nearby. **BY BIKE** Take the South Platte River Trail to the park.

To better understand and enjoy this park, you must look at its past. At one time, Denver citizens dumped their waste and junk into the South Platte River and created a wasted river of pollution in the process. This running sewer ran neglected for years. In 1965, a giant storm dumped 14 inches of rain in three hours. The result was a natural disaster. Bridges, homes, printing presses, and neighborhoods were swept away on the rising waters. Denver lay in ruins.

Grab the whole family and balance your way across logs in the giant nature play area and fort at Johnson-Habitat.

Shortly afterward, local visionaries like Mayor William McNichols Jr. and State Senator Joe Shoemaker founded what would become the Greenway Foundation. The hard work began. Plans, visions, and finally funds came together for the revitalization of the South Platte River and its environs. Thanks to these efforts, Denverites today enjoy the South Platte River Trail, a clean river, and the various parks along the way.

With this park, Denver established its first environmental education-focused park. Through the Greenway Foundation's South Platte River Environmental Education (SPREE) program at Johnson-Habitat Park, kids and adults alike get a great outdoor and riverbank experience. The park itself features an elevated fort-style playground of trees and hideaways, an area for bouldering, and nature play. Add in some cultural education, and everyone can enjoy hours of fun here.

At the park you can amble under raised logs, cross wooden bridges, make shelters, and balance on slanted branches. Folks in wheelchairs can safely reach the water's edge, fish, and learn about water quality and bird habitats. Toddlers will enjoy waddling through stumps and trunks. And anglers can relax and try to catch the big one.

Throughout the year, SPREE sponsors events. From summer camps to river cleanups, the nonprofit maintains areas, raises money, and pursues the vision of how to make the South Platte River and its amenities accessible for everyone.

EXTEND YOUR VISIT

Walk north along the South Platte River Trail and stop in at the **Denver Animal Shelter** (see Valverde Park). Or walk south to **Vanderbilt Park** and play some softball!

128 CLIFFORD ASPGREN PARK

Telling the story of the Denver flood through mosaics

Location: 1201 W. Exposition Ave., Denver
Acreage: 3.68
Amenities: Picnic tables, playground, baseball/softball field

GETTING THERE

BY CAR Take I-25 to W. Alameda Ave. Go west to S. Lipan St. Take a left. Turn right on W. Exposition Ave. **BY TRANSIT** Buses 3 and 11 stop nearby. **BY BIKE** Take the South Platte River Trail to West Virginia Ave. Take a left on S. Lipan St. Turn right on W. Exposition Ave.

Although this park, which is named after Clifford Aspgren, a former Colorado state congressman, does not have many amenities, it does play an important role in commemorating the 1965 flood in the Athmar Park neighborhood. The park's three picnic tables feature mosaic tops that tell the story of how the community came together after the flood. Three additional tables can be found in Huston Lake Park just to the west.

The three tables in Clifford Aspgren Park hold special memories. The first commemorates the 1965 flood, the second references love, and the third is a modern design. Be sure to view all three.

EXTEND YOUR VISIT

Walk west to **Huston Lake Park** to see the other three tables or to use additional park facilities.

The picnic tables at Aspgren Park tell a story you won't want to miss.

129 VANDERBILT PARK

Swing, batter, swing!

Location: 855 S. Platte River Dr., Denver
Acreage: 24.5
Amenities: Restroom, bike/pedestrian path, base-ball/softball field, bleachers, lake, natural areas, benches, picnic tables

GETTING THERE

BY CAR Take I-25 to Santa Fe. Turn right on W. Mississippi Ave. Turn right on S. Huron St. to the park. **BY TRANSIT** Buses 0 and 11, and the E train stop nearby. **BY BIKE** Take the South Platte River Trail to the park.

People come here to play ball. Whether softball or baseball, teams and leagues enjoy great evenings and afternoons of batter up. With diamonds that sit opposite each other, a hit ball can go almost as far as the batter desires—unless it's caught, of course. The park sits along the Platte River, so if you tire of ball playing, you can go to spy ospreys dropping in to catch their dinner. A natural area along the southern edge of the park allows the wanderer to enjoy a small urban forest.

EXTEND YOUR VISIT

Take a jaunt up or down the **South Platte River Trail** on the east side of the park.

130 HUSTON LAKE PARK

A mosaic of fun

Location: 850 S. Bryant St., Denver
Acreage: 82
Amenities: Lake, picnic tables, benches, play-ground, football field, horseshoe pits, basketball court, soccer field, baseball/softball field, tennis court, drinking fountain, bike/pedestrian path, flower beds, picnic area, fitness zone

GETTING THERE

BY CAR Take I-25 to Santa Fe Dr. Exit south. Turn right on W. Mississippi Ave. Turn right on S. Bryant St. **BY TRANSIT** Buses 11, 14, and 31 stop nearby. **BY BIKE** Take the South Platte River Trail to West Virginia Ave. Take a left on S. Lipan St. Turn right on W. Exposition Ave. Turn left on S. Vallejo St. to the park.

Offering stunning views of the Rockies across the lake, Huston Lake Park, the jewel of the Athmar Park neighborhood, welcomes you. The park, named after N. K. Huston, an early landowner in the area, was once swampy area. Originally called Frenchie's Lake, it was a a spot for locals to ice skate and swim. Now, the park's amenities attract football, soccer, baseball, softball, and basketball players. Tennis lovers volley in the courts, and walkers and runners travel around the lake for a mile loop. In the summer, plan to toss your horseshoes or bring your camera to photograph the flower beds and bird life. The playgrounds welcome small and big kids, and the fitness area offers equipment for chin-ups and sit-ups.

On the lake, throw your line in, hunt for tadpoles, or sit along the edge and watch the ducks land. While people-watching, you may catch a few who are out geocaching!

The eastern edge of the park features a trio of do-not-miss picnic tables. After the 1965 flood that devastated Athmar, the community rallied together to tell the story of Athmar, its community, and the flood. One group of citizens decided to remember by making mosaics of their community on top of the picnic tables. You'll find three tables here and three additional in Clifford Aspgren Park to the east. (See Clifford Aspgren Park.)

Here at Huston Lake Park, the first table commemorates the ladies from Valverde Presbyterian Church who gathered every Tuesday for over forty years to create quilts for the less fortunate. The second table was made by children from Valverde Elementary School. It shows a flower mosaic. The third table is a mosaic view of the mountains from Huston Lake. It was created by neighborhood residents and designed by the well-known Colorado oil painter and neighborhood resident, Brenda Hendrix. Find the other three tables, and the one about the flood, at Clifford Aspgren Park.

EXTEND YOUR VISIT

Be sure to walk the few blocks to the east to see the additional three mosaic-topped tables in **Clifford Aspgren Park**.

131 GARFIELD LAKE PARK

Bike across a lake!

Location: 3600 W. Mississippi Ave., Denver
Acreage: 29
Amenities: Lake, benches, picnic tables, outdoor pool, bike/pedestrian path, baseball/softball field, basketball court, fitness course, futsal court, football field, restroom, playground, picnic area, bike skills course

A bike path for new riders winds between trees and across water in Garfield Lake Park.

GETTING THERE

BY CAR Take I-25 to 6th Ave. Turn south on Federal Blvd. Turn west on W. Mississippi Ave. to the park. **BY TRANSIT** Buses 11, 31, 30/36L stop nearby. **BY BIKE** Take the South Platte River Trail to the Lakewood Gulch Trail. Follow 8th Ave. to 6th Ave. Turn left on S. Lowell Blvd. Turn left on W. Exposition Ave., then right to return to S. Lowell Blvd. Continue south to the park.

In the past, folks came to Garfield Lake Park, named after President James Garfield, to walk around the lake and get a little exercise in at the fitness center. A chin-up here, a sit-up there. They might even cast a line for black crappie, largemouth bass, bluegill, channel catfish, and common carp.

But then Great Outdoors Colorado (GOCO) took a look at the park and decided it needed some freshening up. They talked with the neighborhood kids, and they all came out to help build a bike skills course. This 0.5-mile track features small bridges (including a floating bridge), ramps, and dirt bumps. Caregivers can watch from the inside of the track or they can jog along with the smaller tots as they march their way around the track. Once the kids are done on their bikes, they can hustle over to the playground and run across the rope bridges.

Take your chance at futsal off to the southeastern edge of the park. This hard court soccer game, a variant of association football, is usually played indoors, but here at Garfield Lake Park it's played outdoors. Many people think of futsal as five-on-a-side football.

During the summer season, the restrooms and outdoor pool are open. Watch for ice cream carts selling treats! Grab an ice cream after playing tennis, baseball/softball, or basketball. By the way, you can still fish in the lake as long as you have the proper license.

EXTEND YOUR VISIT

On Morrison Road, northwest of the park in the Westwood neighborhood, are some great new places to eat and shop. While there you can also visit some interesting parks. (See **Westwood** and **Cuatro Vientos/Four Winds Parks**.)

132 OVERLAND POND PARK

An oasis in the corner

Location: 955 W. Florida Ave., Denver
Acreage: 8.5
Amenities: Lake, benches, picnic tables, bike/pedestrian path, South Platte River Trail, parking lot, natural areas

GETTING THERE

BY CAR Take I-25 to S. Santa Fe Dr. Take a right on S. Platte River Dr. Take a left on W. Florida Ave. **BY TRANSIT** Buses 0, 12, and 14 stop nearby. **BY BIKE** Take the South Platte River Trail to the park.

Hidden on a busy corner, a secret pond provides a quiet respite from the noise nearby. Your route takes you by benches, a dock, and a few environmental education signs, as you enjoy a nice 0.5-mile walk around this small lake. You might instead opt to kick up your feet in the shade of the cottonwoods. Running along the western edge of the park flows the South Platte River and its trail, while on the eastern edge of the park you can barely see Denver's Aqua Golf facilities.

Although it's in a small quiet area, this park has a long history of fun and noise. At one point, it was home to Denver's first golf course. It then became the Denver Country Club, which later moved to its present location beside the Cherry Creek Shopping Center. The city next opened a racetrack on this space. The track was closed when gambling became outlawed. When Buffalo Bill Cody's Wild West Show folded in the early 1900s, its assets were auctioned off here. For a short time in the 1920s, it was a campground. But now it's this delightful slice of nature in the city.

EXTEND YOUR VISIT

Go play a round of golf at the **Overland Golf Course**, located just to the south. Or hit a bucket of balls at **Aqua Golf**, located just to the east. Or jump on your bike to head up or down the river on the South Platte River Trail.

133 RUBY HILL PARK

A park for all your outdoor needs

Location: 1200 W. Florida Ave., Denver
Acreage: 82
Amenities: Picnic shelter, picnic tables, benches, playground, outdoor pool, restroom, baseball/softball field, bike/pedestrian path, natural areas, drinking fountain, flower beds, pavilion, picnic area, bike courses, ski/snowboard courses

GETTING THERE

BY CAR Take I-25 to S. Santa Fe Dr. Go south and take a right on S. Platte River Dr. Turn right on W. Florida Ave. Take a left on S. Lipan St. to enter the park. **BY TRANSIT** Buses 0, 14, and 42 stop nearby. **BY BIKE** Take the South Platte River Trail to the Sanderson Gulch Trail along W. Florida Ave.

A winter playground in the city, Ruby Hill Park is the place to take your snowboard.

Having everything any outdoor enthusiast might desire, Ruby Hill Park sits on a high point just south of downtown Denver. Originally, people flocked to Ruby Hill

Park to find Denver's first red rocks—rubies, which actually ended up being garnets. Ruby Hill Park has attracted adventure ever since.

Now, you can grab your skis or snowboards in the winter and enjoy the Ruby Hill Rail Yard—the nation's first free, urban snowsports terrain park. The Winter Park Resort, a ski area owned and operated by the city and county of Denver, lends its snow machines to the park in January, and more than thirty volunteers use them to build the ramps and rails for folks to practice their tricks and shredding. It's fun to participate or to watch people of all ages get their tricky workouts on this one-acre frozen oasis.

Adjacent to the Rail Yard is the bike park. Featuring over 7 acres of slopestyle courses, you'll find ramps, jumps, pump tracks, and a skills course for bike riders from small children with pedal-less bicycles to seasoned adult riders. Designed to help everyone improve their skills and balance, you'll find a choice of accessible tracks for beginners to advanced riders. Additionally, a 1.7-mile multimodal, soft surface trail circles the park for extra riding options.

Looking for a playground instead? Near the bike track and above the Rail Yard, you'll find two playgrounds. One is a maze with spinners and curiosities for younger children, while a larger playground invites kids to play on swings, ropes, zip lines, and boulders. There's a fierce dragon garden and a cushioned playfield where kids can be human sundials, using the shadows of their bodies to tell time.

At the top of the hill, revel in the 360-degree view. Downtown Denver is to the north and east, the Rockies are to the west, and the Front Range is to the south. See if you can spot the South Platte River at the eastern edge of the park or Pikes Peak all the way down in Colorado Springs. At the middle of the hill is a concession stand and Levitt Pavilion Denver, an outdoor amphitheater. Catch a (usually free) concert in the summer. Just bring your picnic blanket and hang out on the slope. Continue your adventure down the hill and find the baseball fields and enjoy a neighborhood game.

Throughout the park, you'll find quiet places to relax under the spruce trees. You can also fly a kite along the side of the hill or just chill with your dog and enjoy the activities.

EXTEND YOUR VISIT

Ruby Hill Park sits just off the South Platte River and its trail. Jump on your bike and head downriver toward downtown, or upriver you can go toward **Waterton Canyon** for a day of meandering.

134 PASQUINEL'S LANDING

Pretend to be a fur trader

Location: 801 W. Evans Ave., Denver
Acreage: 3.8
Amenities: Bike/pedestrian path, fitness zone, picnic tables, South Platte River Trail, playground (nature play)

GETTING THERE

BY CAR Take I-25 to S. Santa Fe Dr. Take a right on W. Evans Ave. Turn right on Huron St. to the park. **BY TRANSIT** Bus 21 and light rails C and D stop nearby. **BY BIKE** Take the South Platte River Trail to the park.

This newly renovated park, one in a series of three along the South Platte River, including Grant Frontier Park and Johnson-Habitat Park, takes on the concept of nature play while also including wonderful local history. The park's name comes from a character in James A. Michener's novel *Centennial*. Jacques Pasquinel was a fictional fur trader with many loves, and a friend to the Arapahoe.

Pasquinel's Landing, like the other parks, makes you want to put on your fur trading gear and head out. Packed with fallen logs for climbing over, raised timbers for climbing under, and twigs for fort making, all ages will love this compact park.

Pretend to be a fur trader at Pasquinel's Landing along the Platte River.

There's even an oxbow made from the Platte River and a bridge over it for anyone to splash in the river and hunt for invertebrates. Along the edge of the park next to the South Platte River Trail is an adult fitness zone filled with almost a dozen machines to move your body while letting your mind soak in the natural atmosphere. You'll even hear the sounds of the Platte River float by. Squeezed into the corner of the park is a wonderful tot lot with the same theme as the nature play areas, but on a smaller scale. Your little ones can find a knoll to curl up into and await someone to jump out and say boo!

EXTEND YOUR VISIT

In order to get the full nature play experience, be sure to visit the sister parks to this one, **Grant Frontier Park** and **Johnson-Habitat Park**, both nearby on the Platte River.

135 GRANT FRONTIER PARK

Where the original Montana City was founded

Location: 2300 S. Platte River Dr., Denver
Acreage: 8.8
Amenities: Historical site, picnic tables, bike/pedestrian path, South Platte River Trail, natural areas, playground, drinking fountain

GETTING THERE

BY CAR Take I-25 to S. Santa Fe Dr. Turn right on W. Evans Ave. Take a left on S. Platte River Dr. to the park. **BY TRANSIT** Bus 21 and light rails C and D stop nearby. **BY BIKE** Take the South Platte River Trail to the park.

Children and teachers at Grant Middle School came up with this park name while researching this site. They discovered that this location was the first place along the Front Range that miners panned for gold! Gold diggers from Lawrence, Kansas, arrived with big hopes and empty pockets. After hunting for gold and building several rows of cabins here, they abandoned their new Montana City (named after the Spanish word for mountain) digs and headed north to the more successful Auraria settlement.

Here at the park, you'll find several play areas. There's a fun, Conestoga-style wagon to climb on and yell, "Keep 'em moving!" Wander through the re-created foundation of the old Crookman's Cabin (named after science teacher and river lover Carl Crookman), and then venture through one of several play areas. From

A Conestoga-style wagon awaits pioneers at Grant Frontier Park.

treehouses that climb high to the sky to low logs and stumps for crawling and balancing, kids of all sizes have a variety of ups and downs to enjoy. There's a circle maze made of river rock, an outdoor music studio made of chimes and sticks, and a gold panning sluice that's perfect for pretend panning.

From the environmental point of view, the park takes on the South Platte River's seasonal flood levels. Terraces mark the two-year, ten-year, and one hundred-year flood elevations, and describe the ecological zones from aquatic to riparian to upland. An oxbow from the river invites you to wade, skip rocks, and hunt for critters—or the paw prints they've left behind. Raccoons, possums, squirrels, and coyotes leave their marks all over the shoreline. You could spend hours here.

136 LA LOMITA PARK

A neighborly hangout

Location: 2140 W. Asbury Ave., Denver
Acreage: 5.7
Amenities: Benches, picnic tables, natural areas, bike/pedestrian path

GETTING THERE

BY CAR Take I-25 to S. Santa Fe Dr. Exit south. Go right, then first left on S. Platte River Dr. Turn right on W. Jewell Ave. Turn left on S. Tejon St., right on W. Asbury Ave. **BY TRANSIT** Bus 21 stops nearby. **BY BIKE** Take the South Platte River Trail to Sanderson Gulch Trail. Take a right on W. Mexico Ave., left on S. Tejon St., right on W. Asbury Ave.

Here on the old Goat Hill, the Abeyta family raised their children. They arrived from Trinidad (after stopping in New Mexico along the way) in the 1940s and opened a small grocery store named Evans Height Grocery. The grocery closed due to competition from larger stores but reopened eventually as the La Lomita (meaning "Little Hill") Café. It was popular with the community and people waited in long lines for grandma's homemade tortillas and New Mexican–style homemade dishes. In 2019, when the city was seeking a name for this yet-to-be-named park, the Abeyta family shared the story of La Lomita. The park got its name.

La Lomita offers swings and slides for children to play on while parents stroll its perimeter along the concrete sidewalk. A small basketball court invites a few free throws, and a little gulch running through the center of the park asks for exploration. This park is petite, but the community spirit is large.

EXTEND YOUR VISIT

Not far from this park, just a few blocks to the northeast, is **Ruby Hill Park**. This large park features bike skill courses, a human sundial, a pool, and much more. (See Ruby Hill Park.)

137 LORETTO HEIGHTS PARK

A spot to contemplate change

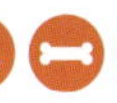

Location: 2800 S. Lowell Blvd., Denver
Acreage: 13.7
Amenities: Picnic shelter, picnic tables, benches, playground, natural areas, bike/pedestrian path, picnic area

GETTING THERE

BY CAR Take I-25 to S. Santa Fe Dr. Turn right on W. Dartmouth Ave. Turn right on S. Federal Blvd. Turn left on W. Amherst Ave. Turn left on S. Lowell Blvd. to the park.
BY TRANSIT Bus 21 stops nearby. **BY BIKE** Take the South Platte River Trail to the Harvard Gulch Trail. Go west. Take a left on S. Zuni St. Take a right on W. Amherst Ave. Take a left on S. Lowell Blvd. to the park.

In 1886 the Sisters of Loretto, a religious organization, felt that Denver needed some saving. Way out in the south of town, away from the hustle and too-much bustle of downtown Denver, they founded the Loretto College Heights Academy for girls. The school grew to become a college for nurses. Men were admitted, additional disciplines were added, and the school set the standard in the south of

From the top of Loretto Park, you can see along the Front Range all the way down to Castle Rock and up to Boulder.

Denver. In 1989 the school was renamed Teikyo Loretto Heights University, and in 2009 it became Colorado Heights University. It closed in 2017. Many of its programs were then transferred to Regis University on the north side of Denver. The future of the campus is uncertain. A development company recently purchased the land, but it has not announced its final plans.

Meanwhile, you can sit and enjoy the fantastic 360-degree views from the top of Loretto Heights Park to look over the campus, its small graveyard, and the western slope of the Rocky Mountains. Contemplate the changes the property has gone through and what it might become.

EXTEND YOUR VISIT

Walk northerly from the park to the fun, throw-back neighborhood of **Harvey Park**, which grew up in the 1950s and really never forgot it. Midcentury homes, influenced by architect Cliff May, beckon you to walk through the neighborhood to go back in time.

138 BEAR CREEK PARK

Also known as Big Hat Park

Location: 3550 S. Raleigh St., Denver
Acreage: 86.4
Amenities: Benches, drinking fountain, picnic shelter, picnic tables, playground, restroom, bike/pedestrian path, Bear Creek Trail, horseshoe pits, soccer field, baseball/softball field, natural areas, picnic area

GETTING THERE

BY CAR Take Hwy. 285 to S. Lowell Blvd. Go north on S. Lowell Blvd./S. Knox Ct. Turn left on W. Girard Ave. Turn right on S. Patton Wy. Turn left on S. Raleigh St. to the park. **BY TRANSIT** Buses 1, 36L, and 50 stop nearby. **BY BIKE** Take the South Platte River Trail to the Bear Creek Trail. Go west on the Bear Creek Trail to reach the park.

Sitting along the Bear Creek Trail, this large park has a sense of humor you'll discover exhibited in the playground, if you can find it. You can approach the park from several directions, and West Kenyon Avenue cuts through the southwest corner of the park, but there is just one access point by car from South Raleigh Street in the northeast corner. It's best to arrive by bike or foot.

Once in the park, whether you're a kid or not, head over to the playground at the west end of the park. You'll be treated to the legend of a giant cowboy, written on the playground walls. Evidence of the giant appears in the playground, where kids and adults alike can slide down the rim of his cowboy hat, barely missing his knees and giant boots. Don't forget to check out the great mural of kids playing on the restroom building near the giant cowboy.

Kids and adults alike will have fun in the cowboy hat at Bear Creek Park.

Once you've had a legendary time, pull up a bench and enjoy the crisp sounds of Bear Creek as it runs through the water feature, or watch the ducks floating near the bridge. There are many geocaches in this park, as well as super places to adventure throughout the natural areas. A soccer or baseball game might pick up on the eastern side of the park.

EXTEND YOUR VISIT

If you have your bike with you, hop on the Bear Creek Trail and head east to the South Platte River. Or go west another 12 miles up the canyon. **Fort Logan National Cemetery** is just south of the park. (See Pinehurst Park.)

139 BOW MAR HEIGHTS PARK

Park with a view

Location: 4000 W. Rutgers Pl., Denver
Acreage: 18
Amenities: Benches, picnic tables, natural areas, bike/pedestrian path

GETTING THERE

BY CAR Take I-25 to S. Santa Fe Dr. Go south to W. Oxford Ave. Take a right. Turn left on S. Irving St. Take a right on W. Quincy Ave. Take a left on S. Quitman St. Turn left on W. Rutgers Place to the park. **BY TRANSIT** Buses 36L and 51 stop nearby. **BY BIKE** Take the South Platte River Trail to the Mary Carter Trail. Go right on W. Oxford Ave. Left on S. Lowell Blvd. Right on W. Quincy Ave. Left on S. Newton St. Right on W. Rutgers Pl. to the park.

Bow Mar Heights Park sits to the north of the tiny town of Bow Mar, overlooking its lakes. The name Bow Mar comes from the two lakes near the area. The smaller is Bowles Lake (named after Joseph Bowles, the Littleton pioneer), and the larger is Marston Lake (named after John Marston, another local pioneer). Offering great views up and down the Front Range, this neighborhood park features a mile or so of concrete and dirt paths that allow you to get up and down the hill. Because the entire park is visible from the hilltop, you can watch your kids on the paths as you take in the views. If you want to get some hills in, this is a good place to do it, either on your bike or your feet. Although there are no playgrounds or other facilities in this park, there are a few benches and tables. In the winter, Bow Mar Heights is a great park to try out your snowshoes.

EXTEND YOUR VISIT

The town of **Bow Mar** is just south of the park. Take a quick spin through this outlier and say hello to the close-knit community. Or, if you're looking for more park time, try out nearby **Bear Creek Park**.

140 BATES & HOBART PARK

You could toss a shoe here

Location: 6000 W. Bates Ave., Denver
Acreage: 6.3
Amenities: Benches, picnic tables, playground, soccer field, bike/pedestrian path, horseshoe pits

GETTING THERE

BY CAR Take I-25 to 6th Ave. Go west to Sheridan Blvd. Go south to W. Bates Ave. Turn right. Go to the park. **BY TRANSIT** Bus 51 stops nearby. **BY BIKE** Take the South Platte River Trail to the Mary Carter Greenway. Then go to the Bear Creek Trail. Go west. Turn right on S. Lamar St. Turn right on W. Bates Ave. to the park.

Sure, it's another neighborhood park with a playground, open space, and benches, but this one also features fun horseshoe pits where you can throw shoes and try your luck. Tucked between a middle school and elementary school, this little gem of a park is a real asset to the neighborhood. The park is named for two of the streets that border it (Bates and Hobart). Perhaps you can come up with a suggestion for a proper name.

EXTEND YOUR VISIT

Jump over to the **Bear Creek Trail** and head west up to the mountains on your bike. Or you can go east to **Bear Creek Park** and discover the legend of the giant cowboy.

141 PINEHURST PARK

In the shadow of Fort Logan

Location: 4600 W. Quincy Ave., Denver
Acreage: 13.7
Amenities: Picnic shelter, picnic tables, benches, playground, basketball court, soccer field, bike/pedestrian path, drinking fountain

GETTING THERE

BY CAR Take I-25 to S. Santa Fe Dr. Go south to W. Oxford Ave. Take a right. Turn left on S. Irving St. Take a right on W. Quincy Ave. to the park. **BY TRANSIT** Buses 36, 36L, and 51 stop nearby. **BY BIKE** Take the South Platte River Trail to the Mary Carter Trail. Go right on W. Oxford Ave. Turn left on S. Lowell Blvd. Turn right on W. Quincy Ave. to the park.

Just south of Bear Creek Park and Fort Logan National Cemetery sits this comfortable neighborhood park. With a playground big enough for most kids, a basketball court, and swings, there's plenty here to attract the whole family. This is a good park to kick around a soccer ball, contemplate a visit to the cemetery, or enjoy a picnic. The paved paths are perfect for a pair of skates or a stroller filled with giggling kids.

EXTEND YOUR VISIT

Head over to the **Fort Logan National Cemetery** and pay respects to our fallen soldiers. The cemetery is just around the corner on W. Kenyon Avenue. Or, take a short drive over to **Bear Creek Park** for a fun play time in a cowboy hat.

142 STANFORD & BALSAM PARK

A linear walk with a view

Location: 8600 W. Stanford Ave., Denver
Acreage: 10
Amenities: Playground, bike/pedestrian path, benches, natural areas

GETTING THERE

BY CAR From I-25, drive south on S. Wadsworth Blvd. (CO-121). Turn left on W. Quincy Ave. Turn left on S. Garrison St. Turn left on W. Stanford Ave. The park entrance is at the end of the street. **BY TRANSIT** Buses 76, 100, and 100L stop nearby. **BY BIKE** Take the South Platte River Trail to the Mary Carter Greenway. Go west on the Bear Creek Trail. Slight left at S. Lamar St. Turn left onto S. Pierce St. Turn right onto W. Quincy Ave. Turn left onto S. Ammons St. Continue onto S. Balsam Way. Turn right onto W. Stanford Ave. (an unmarked concrete path).

Out in southwest Denver, you'll find this yet-to-be officially named park. It's really a flood control area with only a few amenities housed within, yet there is a good trail to walk along the banks of the flood area. It's also a good place to watch the weather come in from the west! A playground on the western side of the park welcomes younger kids, but mostly you'll want to walk the linear trail (good for pushing strollers) through the natural areas.

EXTEND YOUR VISIT

Venture over to **Marston Lake** to see where Denver's drinking water is stored. Or take your littles to the big cowboy hat in the playground at **Bear Creek Park**.

143 HARVARD GULCH PARKS AND ROSEDALE PARK

Rosedale neighborhood's private parks

Location: 550 E. Iliff Ave., Denver
Acreage: Combined 50
Amenities: Recreation center, picnic tables, playground, bike/pedestrian path, outdoor pool, golf course, soccer field, baseball/softball field, basketball court, benches, parking lot, community garden, natural areas, bike/pedestrian path, picnic tables, slack line course

GETTING THERE

BY CAR Take I-25 to Washington St. Turn west on E. Louisiana Ave. Turn left on Logan St. Turn left on E. Iliff Ave. to the park. **BY TRANSIT** Buses 0, 12, and 21 stop nearby. **BY BIKE** Take South Platte River Trail to Cherry Creek Trail east. Turn left on S. Marion Pkwy. Turn left on E. Louisiana Ave. Turn right on S. Franklin St. Turn right on Iliff Ave. to the park.

Three parks merge at Harvard Gulch Park to supply plenty of outdoor and smiles.

It's almost impossible to separate these two parks, as they combine to take up the center of the Rosedale neighborhood. The bigger park is itself actually two parks: Harvard Gulch Park North and Harvard Gulch West Park (separated by East Iliff Avenue). The smaller park is Rosedale Park (separated by South Logan Street). The Harvard Gulch parks that span East Iliff Avenue feature the Harvard Gulch Golf Course (a public, nine-hole, par 3 golf course) and the Harvard Gulch Recreation Center. The Harvard Gulch itself runs along the park's southern edge, which was developed by the US Army Corps of Engineers and the City of Denver. This gulch is part of a plan designed to improve the ecosystem, drainage, and recreational opportunities along the South Platte River, Harvard Gulch, and Weir Gulch.

Harvard Gulch Park offers typical city park attractions: a playground, a basketball court, and soccer fields. In addition, there's a slack line course . . . and a fun golf course! The pro shop building at the golf course is named after Thomas M. Field. Once the city treasurer, Field bought 80 acres between Logan and Downing Streets to use as a farm. He also built a large stone home on the corner of East Iliff Avenue and South Clarkson Street that was sold to Colorado in 1902 to become the State Home for Dependent Children. Over time, the home housed over 16,971 children. The orphanage closed in 1971, and arson destroyed the building in 1987.

On the south side of Harvard Gulch West Park sits the Porter Adventist Hospital. Originally opened as a sanitarium in 1930, the care it offered patients included kindness and tools for healthy living.

Jumping west across South Logan Street is Rosedale Park. The park is named in honor of the roses grown by Amanda Ellis Field, the wife of Thomas M. Field. In Denver's early days, this area was known as the town of South Denver. It was a haven for the straight-laced and moral citizens who fled the boozy and bodacious excesses of Denver proper. When South Denver was annexed to Denver, Rosedale was born. Its park welcomes folks to come, reflect, and enjoy the floral displays. Many short and looping trails run through this park. At the end of the season, you can attend the Rosedale Annual Garlic Fest (tickets required). This event includes a cooking challenge, drinks, and tasting the thirteen different varieties of garlic grown in the vegetable garden.

EXTEND YOUR VISIT

If these three parks, golf course, and recreation center don't entertain you enough, head south across East Harvard Avenue to the **City of Kunming Park** to learn more about Denver's Sister City program.

144 CITY OF KUNMING PARK

From roses to Himalayas

Location: 200 E. Harvard Ave., Denver
Acreage: 3.6
Amenities: Benches, plaza, drinking fountain, flower beds

GETTING THERE

BY CAR Take I-25 to W. Evans Ave. Go west. Turn left on S. Logan St. Turn left on E. Harvard Ave. to the park. **BY TRANSIT** Buses 0 and 12 stop nearby. **BY BIKE** Take the South Platte River Trail. Go east on W. Evans Ave. Turn right on S. Delaware St. Turn left on E. Harvard Ave. to the park.

On this site grew the roses of Amanda Ellis Field, the wife of Thomas M. Field. Field, a city treasurer in the late 1800s, built his career through the development of the railroads. He later ran a series of trading posts along the rails. He once ran for the office of Lieutenant Governor but was defeated.

In the early 1900s, the Field family's home became an orphanage (see Harvard Gulch and Rosedale Park). Eventually, the city took over the family property and divided it into several parks. One section became the City of Kunming Park.

Kunming in China played an important role in the American Pacific Theater of Operations during World War II. The famed Flying Tigers made their flights over the Himalayas to this safe haven. Kunming is, like Denver, a mile-high city sitting in the shadow of a giant mountain range; it maintains an Olympic training center, and is also a capital city. Kunming is the gateway to the Silk Road, much like Denver is the gateway to the Rockies.

From the park, you can enjoy giant views of the valley and the Rockies behind it. At the top of the park are several large sculpted, white pointed rocks. They are meant to symbolize the Himalayas. Kids can play chase around them. Terraced steps lead down to an open, grassy hill that is perfect for tossing down a blanket and counting clouds. In the park, which runs along the Cherry Creek Trail, you'll also find shady areas.

EXTEND YOUR VISIT

Walk across East Harvard Avenue to **Rosedale Park** and enjoy the giant urban garden.

145 S. R. DEBOER PARK

A miniature version of the landscape architect's montane vision

Location: 2505 S. York St., Denver
Acreage: 4.75
Amenities: Drinking fountain, picnic tables, basketball court, playground, bike/pedestrian path, Harvard Gulch Trail

GETTING THERE

BY CAR Take I-25 to University Blvd. Go south. Turn right on E. Harvard Ave. Turn left on S. York St to the park. **BY TRANSIT** Buses 12, 21, and 40 stop nearby. **BY BIKE** Take the High Line Canal Trail to S. Colorado Blvd. Go north. Turn left on E. Yale Ave. Turn right on S. Jackson St. Turn left on the Harvard Gulch Trail. Go west to the park.

What kid wouldn't want to run through the rainbow to get to the heart of DeBoer Park?

Saco Reink DeBoer, born in the Netherlands, began his career in Denver in the 1910s as a landscape architect. He collaborated often with George Kessler and Frederick Law Olmsted Jr., both of whom were hired to beautify Denver during Mayor Robert Speer's time in office. He strongly influenced the Denver aesthetic, and is the design father of several Denver landmarks, including Cheesman Park, Alamo Placita Park, City Park, Speer Boulevard, and the Bonnie Brae subdivision. He strongly lobbied for and helped design the Denver Mountain Parks system and other communities up and down the Front Range.

In his namesake park, you'll see his influence on how the park lays out along the Harvard Gulch Trail, inviting folks for a nice 1-mile walk all the way to Robert H. McWilliams Park. With picturesque little nooks, DeBoer Park has petite views along gentle curves in the Harvard Gulch Trail, pleasant landscaping, and quiet places for people. It feels as if it is a miniature vision of DeBoer's montane ideas.

In the northeast corner of the park, there's a playground that features a fun red sit-and-spin, a rope jungle gym, curvy balancers, and a mini merry-go-round. This equipment makes an active invite for small to middle-sized kids.

EXTEND YOUR VISIT

Meander along the **Harvard Gulch Trail** in either direction for some nice neighborly interactions.

146 ROBERT H. MCWILLIAMS PARK

Find a dinosaur!

Location: 2701 E. Yale Ave., Denver
Acreage: 7.87
Amenities: Drinking fountain, picnic tables, playground, restroom, basketball court, bike/pedestrian path, Harvard Gulch Trail, baseball/softball field, soccer field, picnic area

GETTING THERE

BY CAR Take I-25 to Colorado Blvd. Go south. Take a right on E. Yale Ave. **BY TRANSIT** Bus 27 stops nearby. **BY BIKE** Take the High Line Canal Trail to S. Colorado Blvd. Go north. Turn left on E. Yale Ave. to the park.

Robert H. McWilliams Jr. moved to Denver from Salina, Kansas, in 1927. He attended law school at the University of Denver, and during World War II he worked for the military in some undercover operations. He eventually became a justice on the

Who wouldn't love climbing on top of the giant purple dinosaur at McWilliams Park?

Colorado Supreme Court. In 1970, President Nixon appointed him to the United States Court of Appeals for the Tenth Circuit. A man about town, McWilliams was president of many of Denver's institutions such as the Rotary Club of Denver, the Gyro Club of Denver, and the Colorado Tennis Association. He has the distinction of being the longest sitting judge in the history of Colorado.

The park does not display the seriousness of a judge; it plays to the whimsical. On the western side of the park is a giant purple dinosaur just waiting for its spots to be counted from on top of its back. It watches over his friend, an earless purple camel that welcomes younger kids to tickle its chin. Around behind the slides and swings is a bridge that crosses the Harvard Gulch Trail, which runs through the park. The trail provides a corridor between the dinosaur and the soccer field on the eastern side of the park.

EXTEND YOUR VISIT

Journey along the **Harvard Gulch Trail** in either direction for a nice leisurely stroll.

147 OBSERVATORY PARK

Play by day; observe the heavens by night!

Location: 2100 S. Fillmore St., Denver
Acreage: 10.44
Amenities: Observatory, picnic tables, playground, restroom, drinking fountain, basketball court, multi-purpose field (lacrosse, rugby, soccer), baseball/softball field, tennis court, picnic area

GETTING THERE

BY CAR Take I-25 to S. University Blvd. Head south. Take a left on Buchtel Blvd. S. Turn right on S. Fillmore St. to the park. **BY TRANSIT** Buses 21 and 24 stop nearby. **BY BIKE** Take Cherry Creek Trail to a slight right toward Cherry Creek S. Dr. Continue onto Cherry Creek S. Dr. Turn right onto S. Steele St. Continue onto S. St. Paul St. Turn right onto E. Warren Ave. to the park.

The University of Denver and Denver Parks and Recreation work together to manage the Chamberlin Observatory, named after Humphrey B. Chamberlin, a Denver real estate magnate who pledged $50,000 in 1888 to build and equip the facility. Occupying land on both sides of Warren Street, Observatory Park offers plenty of activities for everyone.

The Chamberlin Observatory and the Denver Astronomical Society host regularly scheduled events for viewing the sky recreationally through its prized 1894 Alvan Clark-Saegmuller 20-inch refracting telescope. Sadly, due to the light pollution from the city, not much research is done here anymore. Yet, with its rusticated red sandstone bricks and Romanesque design, the Chamberlin Observatory still enlightens hearts and minds about space.

The park itself makes room for rugby, volleyball, and lacrosse players in the wide, open fields on both sides of the street. A giant caterpillar of hoops and circles challenges your middle-sized kids to climb and wiggle through it from head to tail. If you want to know what's going on in the nearby community, look at the bulletin board that stands across the street from the observatory near the playground. This active board is always filled with flyers and notes from nearby residents.

To note, when the Colorado Seminary (the University of Denver) donated this land to the city on October 21, 1904, it stipulated that no liquor should ever be sold or manufactured on these lands.

EXTEND YOUR VISIT

Visit the **Denver Astronomical Society**'s website prior to your visit and make plans to attend one of the monthly open houses to see the moon telescopically.

148 VETERANS PARK

A place to remember, give thanks, and play ball

Location: 2100 E. Iowa Ave., Denver
Acreage: 16
Amenities: Drinking fountain, restroom, soccer field, baseball/softball field, bike/pedestrian path

GETTING THERE

BY CAR Take I-25 to S. University Blvd. Go north. Turn left on E. Iowa Ave. to the park. **BY TRANSIT** Light rails E and H stop nearby. **BY BIKE** From Cherry Creek Trail, take S. Marion Pkwy. Turn left on E. Louisiana Ave. Take a right on S. Race St. Continue onto E. Florida Ave. Turn right on S. Vine St. Turn right on E. Iowa Ave.

Sometimes Denver's citizens need to come together to create great parks, as was the case with Veterans Park.

We are indebted to American Legion Post Commander John Perich. It was his idea to create a park honoring our veterans in 1989 and his work of gathering public signatures resulted in Denver Parks and Recreation making it a reality. He envisioned a park that would be a wonderful place to express honor and to hold patriotic events.

In Veterans Park, you'll want to find the thirty-foot flagpole on the east side of the park. Look for the two poems embedded in the rocks around the flagpole. One poem honors the World War I fallen in Belgium and the other pays tribute to all veterans. Perich raised, lowered, and maintained the flag every day for over two decades until he passed away in 2016. Be sure to pass some time at the benches where poppies grow nearby in honor of those American soldiers buried in Belgium and to give thanks to Perich.

The park itself is a haven for ballers. Kickball games take place in the open area and softball is played on the two fields. South High School and a complex of sports fields border the northern edge of the park. On the east side of the park, a 2-mile path runs around the fields in case you want to walk or stroll while your partner plays ball.

EXTEND YOUR VISIT

Washington Park is located just to the north (see Washington Park). For a shortcut, walk north out of the park and past the All-City Stadium. Once past South High School, turn left on East Louisiana Avenue. Washington Park will be across the street.

149 JAMES H. PLATT PARK

A park with a big mansion

Location: 1500 S. Grant St., Denver
Acreage: 3.7
Amenities: Recreation center, library, Fleming Mansion (special use), drinking fountain, benches, picnic tables, playground, basketball court, horseshoe pits

GETTING THERE

BY CAR Take I-25 to S. Santa Fe Dr. Turn left on W. Iowa Ave. Continue east on E. Iowa Ave. Turn left on S. Grant St. to the park. **BY TRANSIT** Buses 11 and 12 stop nearby. **BY BIKE** Take the South Platte River Trail to W. Florida Ave. Turn east. Take a right on S. Santa Fe Dr. Turn left on W. Iowa Ave. Continue east on E. Iowa Ave. Turn left on S. Grant St. to the park.

The Fleming Mansion has anchored Platt Park since its inception.

The Platt Park neighborhood was once home to the town of South Denver's only mayor, James Fleming. His mansion is on the northwest corner of this park. Built in 1882, the grounds of this Denver landmark covered the entire block, where Mayor Fleming had an orchard, known as Fleming's Grove.

Fleming sold the property to the City of South Denver for use as its town hall, jail, and library. Ultimately, South Denver was annexed to Denver. The mansion remained a library until the Decker Branch Library was built on the park's northeast corner in 1913 with Carnegie funds. When the library moved out of the mansion, dances and senior citizen activities moved in, only to move out again in 1974 when the City of Denver built the Platt Park Senior Center between the mansion and the library. Several nonprofits now use the Fleming Mansion as office space.

The park itself has a small playground where the equipment uprights are made of timber rather than plastic, making the playground blend in more with the park. Around the edges of the park are mature trees. In the middle is a mixed-use field where people enjoy time with their dogs. Seniors often throw horseshoes in the nicely appointed pits near the senior center.

EXTEND YOUR VISIT

Be sure to visit the **Decker Branch Library** to marvel at the Carnegie-influenced architecture. The Fleming Mansion is not open to the public but is often open during local home tour events.

150 BONNIE BRAE PARK

Ice cream, mosaics, and mansions!

Location: 901 S. Bonnie Brae Blvd., Denver
Acreage: 1.4
Amenities: Benches, flower beds, drinking fountain, bike/pedestrian path

GETTING THERE:

BY CAR Take S. Colorado Blvd. to E. Exposition Ave. Go west on E. Exposition Ave. Turn left on S. Steele St. Turn right on E. Kentucky Ave. to the park. **BY TRANSIT** Buses 11 and 24 stop nearby. **BY BIKE** Take the Cherry Creek Trail to E. Alameda Ave. Continue south onto S. University Blvd. Turn slight left onto Bonnie Brae Blvd. to the park.

A small, oval-shaped park in the center of the neighborhood, Bonnie Brae is a great place to just take a little break while walking in the Belcaro neighborhood. A short set of stairs in the middle of the park provides access to a small forested grove that makes a perfect place to sit and read a book. Dog walkers come here in the evening to lap the small ellipse of a park and glance at the beautiful Tudor-style cottages along its perimeter.

Belcaro is the official name of the neighborhood, and Bonnie Brae is an area within it. The name Belcaro was the original name of the Phipps Mansion, up the street. Although Denver's residents certainly differentiate between Bonnie Brae and Belcaro, the city doesn't. Regardless, this little two-tiered park is a great jumping off place to enjoy the area.

EXTEND YOUR VISIT

Venture into **Bonnie Brae's alleys.** You'll find awesome mosaic tile artwork in what is, in effect, an outdoor art gallery. Grab an ice cream from **Bonnie Brae Ice Cream**, or head up the hill to the **Phipps Mansion.** The mansion, east of the park on the corner of Belcaro Drive and Madison Street, was built in the 1930s. It is over 33,000 square feet, and it's filled with Chippendale and Queen Anne furnishings.

151 WASHINGTON PARK

Be a local and call it "Wash Park"

Location: 701 S. Franklin St., Denver
Acreage: 157
Amenities: Recreation center, flower beds, picnic shelter, benches, drinking fountain, grills, picnic tables, playground, lake, restroom, tennis court, basketball court, bike/pedestrian path, horseshoe pits, lawn bowling, jogging path, picnic area

GETTING THERE

BY CAR Take I-25 to Washington Ave. Exit east to Buchtel Blvd. S. Turn left on E. Louisiana Ave. Take a left on S. Downing St. to the park entrance on right. **BY TRANSIT** Buses 11 and 24 stop nearby. **BY BIKE** Take Cherry Creek Trail to S. Marion Pkwy. Go south to the park.

Arguably Denver's most used park, Wash Park, as the locals call it, commands the attention of anyone in south Denver. It started as a field in the incorporated town of South Denver. This area was created as a place where citizens could escape the immoral and inappropriate behavior occurring to the north in Denver.

As with most things in Denver, visions and dreams created the spectacular. First, in 1865, John Smith, an eminent businessman and entrepreneur of early Denver, financed a ditch from the South Platte River to supply water to the area, ultimately creating Wash Park's first pond, Smith Lake. At one time, the lake was set aside for kids under fifteen years old to fish and was sponsored by the Izaak Walton League (a conservation organization). Eventually, the ditch became City Ditch and it flowed all the way to City Park.

The ditch started delivering secure water, and during the late 1890s, Mayor McMurray envisioned a new Smith Lake, and a beautiful grand park to go with it. Wash Park was on its way! McMurray hired park creator Reinhard Schuetze, who drew pretty pictures of lush, shady areas with two additional ponds. Since the park had a good water source, it could also have trees. Thus, Wash Park got its first Russian olive trees, which were a favorite of Frederick Law Olmstead Jr., who first planted them at Inspiration Point Park in northwest Denver.

The park's first superintendent, John B. Lang, soon began to manage the 1899 masterpiece. He transplanted trees and shrubs from the mountains, and inspired by the Lake District in England, he named the southern lake in the park Grasmere

E Virginia Ave
Lilly Pond
E Center Ave
E Center Ave
S Ogden St
S Corona St
S Downing St
Smith Lake
E Exposition Ave
Wynken, Blynken and Nod statue
E Exposition Ave
Eugene Field House
gardens
recreation center
E Ohio Ave
E Ohio Ave
S Franklin St
volleyball courts
Washington Park
main entrance
E Kentucky Ave
E Kentucky Ave
volleyball courts
E Tennessee Ave
horseshoe pit
E Tennessee Ave
tennis courts
N
basketball courts
gardens
0   500   1,000 Feet
lawn bowling
E Mississippi Ave
E Mississippi Ave
Grasmere Lake
volleyball courts
S Downing St
S Franklin St
City Ditch
E Arizona Ave
E Arizona Ave
S Gilpin St
tennis courts
E Louisiana Ave
E Louisiana Ave
S Marion Pkwy
bike entrance

Washington Park sometimes offers dramatic skies, as well as lakes, boathouses, and more for the whole family to enjoy.

Lake. Soon, bathers arrived, separated by a rope that delineated the women's side from the men's. J. J. Benedict added the pavilion and boathouse in 1913.

The park's popularity grew with the arrival of the tramway. In 1930, Denver's famous *Titanic* survivor and socialite, the Unsinkable Molly Brown, provided funds to restore the house of Eugene Field. The house was moved from 315 West Colfax to the east side of the park. It has served many purposes over the years, including a library. It is now used as a ranger station. Field is best known for his children's poems, and the statue outside of the building was created to memorialize the characters Wynken, Blynken, and Nod from his poem "Dutch Lullaby."

Two giant flower gardens are in the park. On the west side of the park, you'll find the older one. Built in 1917, it is a Victorian-style perennial garden. It includes an elliptical lawn and symmetrical flower beds with fifteen thousand flower varieties. More informal than the newer one, this flower garden includes fifty-four flower beds. On the southeast side of the park, you'll find the formal Mount Vernon Garden, which replicates the upper gardens of George Washington's home in Virginia.

Bring your mallet so you can play croquet or go mallet-less and lawn bowl near the garden.

Weaving throughout the park is a sophisticated network of trails. Depending on your mobility, there's a lane that will work for you. Skaters, runners, walkers, bikers, amblers, and speedsters all seem to coexist with the help of complicated signage advising movers to pick appropriate lanes. You can easily enjoy over 6 miles of trails within the park, looping around the lakes, gardens, monuments, bridges, and ditches that are nicely landscaped for everyone's enjoyment.

If you'd rather play a sport than smell flowers or bike, this Rockwellian park invites you out for formal games of tennis or informal games of volleyball, Frisbee, lacrosse, or pretty much any other sport you can think of. On weekends and weekday evenings, you'll often find all kinds of tournaments—from horseshoe throwing to lawn bowling—happening in the park. There's never nothing to do in Wash Park. In the winter, the park becomes a winter wonderland. Cross-country skiers and snowshoers leave tracks around families of snow people, dogs and cats included. Tots fall into the snow for their first snow angels, and restless children make snowballs and snowbunnnies in their romp through the evergreens.

Finally, the playgrounds are dreams come true for kids of all sizes. Just opened in the summer of 2018, Wash Park's newest playground took the imaginations of nearby residents and put them into play form. Not wanting a traditional park with traditional equipment, the residents requested out-of-the-box thinking from Denver Parks and Recreation. With log scrambles, tree rings, and log jams, the playground is dotted with ladybugs and butterflies. Kids of all sizes scramble, balance, and giggle among the nature play areas that invite all ages, including parents, to partake in the fun.

EXTEND YOUR VISIT

Several of the buildings within the park are on the National Register of Historic Places. If possible, schedule your time in the park to enjoy the interior of the **Eugene Field house**.

152 DAILEY PARK

Get your news here!

Location: 1 S. Cherokee St., Denver
Acreage: 2.6
Amenities: Picnic tables, playground, basketball court, benches, bike/pedestrian path

Dailey Park is a good place to park with your newspaper while the kids enjoy the playground.

GETTING THERE

BY CAR Take I-25 to W. Alameda Ave. Turn left on S. Cherokee St. to the park. **BY TRANSIT** Buses 0, 1, and 52 stop nearby. **BY BIKE** Take Cherry Creek Trail to S. Broadway. Go south to W. Ellsworth Ave. Turn left to the park.

This park is named after John L. Dailey, who cofounded the *Rocky Mountain News* with William Byers in 1859. S. R. DeBoer designed this park, and this vibrant historic place has welcomed the neighborhood for over one hundred years. In 2010 this park was updated with community input. Now you can cozy up to the shady areas for a nice picnic while your little- to medium-sized kids enjoy the bridges on the playground or the mechanical shovel that digs deep. A double slide encourages racing, while a spring-loaded car offers a fun bounce.

A path squares the perimeter of the park and weaves through a rich stand of shady native trees. In the middle of the park, you'll notice the turn-of-the-century architecture and the brickwork of the maintenance shed. Benches throughout the park offer chances to read the newspaper, something the park's namesake would have loved.

Dailey, active in the community as the city's first chief deputy county clerk, sat on the parks board, raised funds for education, and became Arapahoe County's Treasurer. The *Rocky* competed with the *Denver Post* for years before it ultimately folded in 2009.

EXTEND YOUR VISIT

Dailey Park sits in the historic neighborhood of **Baker**. Be sure to walk around the neighborhood and then grab some lunch on South Broadway, which is just a few blocks to the east of the park.

READ ALL ABOUT IT!

The *Rocky Mountain News*, nicknamed the *Rocky*, was a Denver daily newspaper that ran from April 23, 1859, until February 27, 2009. This Pulitzer Prize-winning paper began before Colorado was a state. When it folded, its circulation was still more than 250,000. Over time, the conservative *Rocky* took positions against the corruption and ill-will of Denver's leadership, often publishing the right article at the right time to effectively expose civic leaders for their misdeeds. It also published America's first advice column, "Dear Mrs. Mayfield." This column paved the way for Ann Landers and others. Its final Pulitzer grab was for Breaking News Photography in 2003 "for its powerful collection of emotional images taken after the student shootings at Columbine High School."

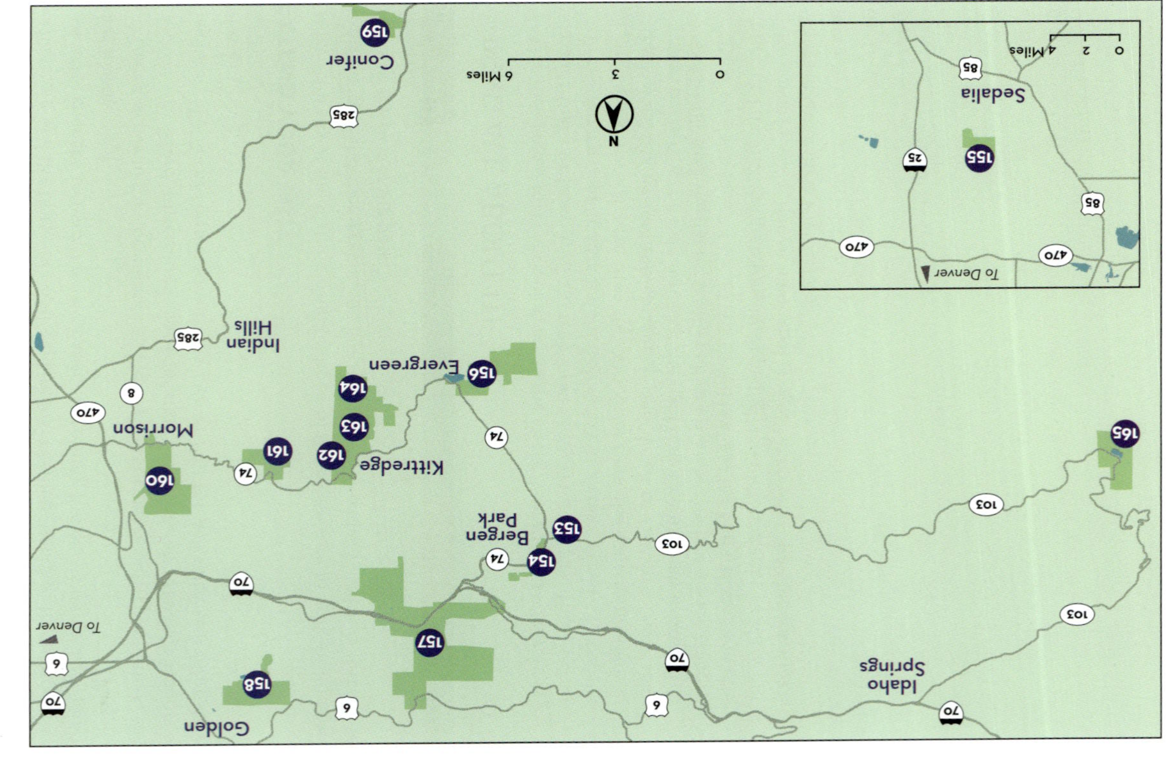

To Denver
70
6
470
8
Morrison
160
285
Golden
70
74
158
161
Indian Hills
162
163
164
285
6
Conifer
159
Kittredge
157
Evergreen
156
74
Bergen Park
74
154
153
6
70
103
N
3
6 Miles
0
Idaho Springs
70
103
103
165
To Denver
470
470
25
85
Sedalia
155
85
2
4 Miles
0

MOUNTAIN PARKS

153 BERGEN PARK

Still a welcoming spot, more than 150 years later

Location: 1450 Old Highway 74, Evergreen
Acreage: 21
Amenities: Picnic shelter, picnic area, tables, grills, restroom, volleyball court, horseshoe pits, trail connections, pioneer trail, Buchanan Park Trail, historic stone well house

GETTING THERE

BY CAR Take I-70 to Evergreen Pkwy. Turn right on Bergen Pkwy. to enter the park. **BY TRANSIT** Buses CX, ES, and EV stop nearby. **BY BIKE** Take South Platte River Trail to Bear Creek Trail to C470 Bikeway to Bear Creek Ave. Turn right on Bergen Pkwy. to enter the park.

In 1859, Thomas Bergen, a one-time territorial commissioner, staked a claim here in the mountains. Soon, his little piece of heaven became a stopping ground for the miners heading to the hills for silver and gold. He built his home and a log cabin to service the miners.

As it was so perfectly situated along the route to Squaw Pass, Frederick Law Olmsted Jr. couldn't resist the land's location or its sweeping views of Evergreen and its beautiful ponderosa pines. Soon after Olmsted eyed the property, in 1915,

The location was once a stop for miners on the way to Squaw Pass; now Bergen Park is a perfect spot for a break or a picnic.

it was donated to the city's Mountain Parks system. J. J. Benedict constructed one of his famous shelters here, this time made of locally sourced white quartz and green mortar. Denverites arrived for cool breezes and shady picnics.

Bergen Park, now squeezed into the middle of a growing area, offers a relaxing spot for locals and travelers alike. Be sure to stop and admire the wonderful stone work at the historic pavilion, or cross Bergen Parkway and see the original marker denoting Bergen's cabin. Hike a mile to reach the back of the park to the south. There you can enter Elk Meadow Park in Jefferson County for an additional 8 miles of trails, or you can go up Bergen Peak for 7 more miles to a heady 9708 feet.

EXTEND YOUR VISIT

Next to the park is the wonderful **Evergreen Center for the Arts**. Be sure to stop in, or head to Bergen's sister park, **Fillius**.

154 FILLIUS PARK

A quick mountainside retreat

Location: 1300 Old Highway 74, Evergreen
Acreage: 109
Amenities: Picnic shelter, picnic tables, grills, restroom, volleyball court, horseshoe pits, historic stone well house

GETTING THERE

BY CAR Take I-70 to Evergreen Pkwy. Turn right on Bergen Pkwy. Take a right to the park. **BY TRANSIT** Buses ES, EV, and EX stop nearby. **BY BIKE** Take South Platte River Trail to Bear Creek Trail to C470 Bikeway to Bear Creek Ave. Turn right on Bergen Pkwy. Take a right to the park.

Fillius Park is named after Jacob Fillius, an early member of the advisory council for Denver's Mountain Parks. This park was once a welcome stop on the drive to Mount Evans. Its wellspring, a spot in the road for people to fill their car's radiators, saved a few vehicles from overheating. From there, Denverites would continue their jaunt through the mountains.

No longer offering radiator refills, Fillius Park now provides soul-refreshing hiking trails.

Nowadays, you may not need radiator water, but your legs will still enjoy a pleasant 4- to 5-mile hike. Fillius Park has several great trails through ponderosa pine forests that take you to some nice views into the town of Evergreen. Like its sister Mountain Parks, the stone hut and outbuildings were designed by J. J. Benedict. The hut at Fillius Park even retains some of its original wooden framing. Built in 1918, this structure features local stones, pine-framed doors, and an indoor fireplace. Once you've explored the shelter, be sure to venture onto the trails outside.

In the winter, pack a lunch and strap on your snowshoes. Hike through the park to several picnic shelters; you may spot mule deer and elk along the way.

EXTEND YOUR VISIT

Just across the street is Fillius Park's sister park, **Bergen Park**. Go check it out and compare the architectural differences between the shelters at the two parks.

155 DANIELS PARK

Bison and views

Location: 8615 N. Daniels Park Rd., Sedalia
Acreage: 984
Amenities: Historic picnic shelter, picnic area, tables, grills, restroom, bison preserve, historic ranch, views

GETTING THERE

By car Take I-25 south to exit 188. Turn right on Castle Pines Dr. Turn right on Monarch Blvd. Turn left on N. Daniels Park Rd. to the park. **BY TRANSIT** No available transit. **BY BIKE** Take the South Platte River Trail south. Keep right to stay on Mary Carter Greenway Trail. Slight left to stay on C470 Bikeway. Take the pedestrian overpass. Turn right toward Plaza Dr. Turn left onto Plaza Dr. Turn right onto Lucent Blvd. Turn right onto S. Broadway. Turn left onto E. Wildcat Reserve Pkwy. Slight right to stay on Dad Clark Trail. Continue straight onto Douglas County East/West Trail. Turn right to stay on N. Daniels Park Rd. to the park.

Locals may remember the iconic Daniels & Fisher department store that anchored downtown shopping in Denver until its destruction in 1971. Its tower remains and provides a landmark to what is now the 16th Street Mall. Daniels Park would not exist were it not for the store's original owners, William and Cicily Daniels. They died suddenly in 1918, leaving the store to two well-to-do friends, Charles MacAllister Willcox, the store's president, and Cecily's good friend, Florence Martin. Martin, an

HEAD TO THE HILLS ON SCENIC BYWAYS

In order to get Denverites to the Mountain Parks, the city had to build roads that would entice the newly mobile public up the mountain. Early automobiles struggled up steep pitches, and these cars of the past needed water to cool radiators. Thus, while Frederick Law Olmsted Jr. envisioned the views, "Cement Bill" Williams built the roads, at first with his own money, crews, and volunteers, and then with help from the city and state. The 40-mile Lariat Loop is a National Scenic Byway that features fifty-six curves and seven hairpin turns. It is actually a combination of two historic routes: the Lariat Trail Scenic Mountain Drive that ascends Lookout Mountain, and the Bear Creek Canyon Scenic Mountain Drive. The Lariat Loop, which is also popular with cyclists out on longer training rides, takes tourists to dozens of open space parks, museums, foothills, canyons, mountain forests, historic dinosaur discoveries, art galleries, and historic buildings and settlements. It connects with the Mount Evans Scenic Byway.

Australian socialite, loved the land, and when she arrived in Denver, she purchased 38 acres along Wildcat Point. To honor her friendship with both Willcox, who sat on the advisory board of Denver Mountain Parks, and William and Cicily, she donated the land to the parks with the stipulation that it be named after the Daniels.

In 1922 development of Daniels Park took off. The city built the rustic stone structure designed by prolific Denver architect J. J. Benedict. The Territorial Daughters of Colorado marked Kit Carson's last campfire. Soon the park became the premier destination up and down the Front Range. Martin donated another 962 acres to the city, which included some of the original ranch properties. In 1977 the city split up the strong bison herd that lived at Genesee Park, and moved twenty bison to Daniels Park.

In the 1970s, Richard Tall Bull, a Cheyenne Indian, requested space in the park for Native Americans to use to celebrate and perform ceremonies. Mayor Wellington Webb agreed and set aside 70 acres for the Tall Bull Memorial Grounds, which were to be used exclusively by the tribe. The grounds commemorate an earlier Tall Bull— the chief of the Cheyenne Dog Soldiers, who was killed in 1869, possibly by Buffalo Bill Cody. This part of the park is open to the public only on Labor Day weekend.

Daniels Park has been updated in other ways over the years. The road through its center recently became curvy to slow speeding drivers and to encourage passive engagement with the park. Daniels Park connects over 12,000 acres of open space and was placed on the National Register of Historic Places in 1995.

Be prepared for 100-mile views up and down the Front Range at about 6500 feet in elevation. You'll see a sandstone mesa that aligns with the first territorial road that moved wagons into Denver along mixed prairie grasslands and Gambel oak and ponderosa pine stands. If it's Labor Day weekend, join the public powwow at the Tall Bull Memorial Grounds. Otherwise, you can spend some time viewing the bison herd that generally hangs out near the shelter at the park's southern end.

Many of trails within the park are undeveloped. You can trek an out-and-back 5-mile route by starting at the shelter house in the south. Walk north along the ridge while admiring the stunning views. Turn left at Grigs Road and pick up Douglas County's East–West Regional Trail at its trailhead on the left. In the winter, Daniels Park is a great location to try out your snowshoes.

For horseback riders, the City of Denver just developed a brand-new, yet-to-be named horse trail that leaves from the southern entrance where trailers can park. From the back of your horse, you may have a better view of the bison herd. The trail connects north to the Douglas County equestrian trail system.

EXTEND YOUR VISIT

Just south of the park is the historic **Cherokee Ranch & Castle**. Be sure to take time to go on a tour in the mansion or sign up to hike to the petrified forest.

156 DEDISSE PARK

Overlooking Evergreen

Location: 29200 Upper Bear Creek Rd., Evergreen
Acreage: 420
Amenities: Historic shelter, picnic area, tables, grills, volleyball court, horseshoe pits, lake, lake house, boat rentals, ice skating, events, trail, golf course, clubhouse, restaurant, nature center, pioneer trail, Dedisse Park Trail

GETTING THERE

BY CAR Take I-70 to Evergreen Pkwy. Take a left on Upper Bear Creek Rd. to the park. **BY TRANSIT** Buses CX, EX, and EV stop nearby. **BY BIKE** Take South Platte River Trail to Bear Creek Trail to C470 Bikeway to Bear Creek Ave. Continue to the park.

Dedisse Park, named after 1860s pioneer Julius C. Dedisse, includes the park, Evergreen Golf Course, and Evergreen Lake. In 1919, as part of its parks program,

Wildlife watching takes on a new meaning at Dedisse Park.

Denver acquired Dedisse Ranch. Soon after, it built the golf course, the historic Keys on the Green clubhouse, and then a dam to control flooding, resulting in Evergreen Lake. The Civilian Conservation Corps moved in and finished creating the park and its shelters. This work was done to National Park Service standards so as to enhance visitor experience and protect the natural conditions.

Throughout Dedisse Park, you'll find old stands of ponderosa pine, open grassy clearings, and shrublands on south-facing slopes. The Evergreen Park and Recreation District (EPRD) built and manages the Evergreen Lake House, where, in the winter, you can rent skates and warm yourself with hot chocolate. The park is also great for snowshoeing and cross-country skiing in season. During the summer, be sure to explore the many quiet trails that run through the park, including a paved trail that leads down to Evergreen Lake. Keep an eye out for elk any time of the year. In addition, there are some great boulder outcroppings here if you want to practice your bouldering or climbing skills! If you're more into horseback riding, enjoy the Dedisse Trail for just under 3 miles round-trip.

EXTEND YOUR VISIT

Head down into the sweet mountain town of **Evergreen** for a great craft beer.

157 GENESEE PARK

Bison overlook park

Location: 26771 Genesee Ln., Golden
Acreage: 2,402
Amenities: Views, bison herd overlook, trails, picnic shelter, picnic tables, softball field, volleyball court, horseshoe pits, grills, restroom, Chief Hosa Lodge, event facility, campgrounds, ropes course

GETTING THERE

BY CAR Take I-70 to the Genesee exit. Drive into the park. **BY TRANSIT** Bus EV stops nearby. **BY BIKE** Take Clear Creek Trail to the park.

In 1918 timber companies threatened to take all the beautiful pine, spruce, and fir on the mountains around Denver. In defense, the city gobbled up the land and preserved Genesee Park under the watchful eye of its designer, Frederick Law Olmsted Jr. Genesee Park is the largest park in all of the Denver Parks and Recreation system, and the granddaddy park of the Mountain Parks. But it is the park's famed bison that attract people to the park now.

If you've driven along Interstate 70 west to the mountains, you've no doubt seen the signs that say "Bison Herd Overlook." That's Genesee Park. The Interstate bisects the park, and a herd of around twenty-five bison often hangs out just north of I-70 near where the overlook directs you. Remember that there is also an elk herd in the park, too! At the overlook, you'll have sweeping views of the Continental Divide. You can also see where the Clear Creek Trail invites bikers and hikers for longer distance adventures. Genesee Mountain, at 8284 feet, crowns the park.

Throughout the park, you'll find historic trails. The first, designed by the Colorado Mountain Club in 1918, attracted Denverites who took the trolley from Golden to the Beaver Brook Trail, which still connects hikers (only) to Lookout Mountain, 8.65 miles away. Those hikers got thirsty and tired. So J. J. Benedict built the Chief Hosa Lodge, named after a southern Arapahoe tribal leader who was given the honorary title Hosa, which means "peaceful and beautiful," by the Ute Tribe. Chief Hosa Lodge is no longer a respite for hikers however; it is now an event space for rent.

"America's first motor-camping area" croped up around Chief Hosa Lodge. This is the campground just to the west of Chief Hosa Lodge at 7700 feet. The best way to ensure you see the bison is to stay overnight in the campground, which gives you two days of bison viewing!

One trail of special interest is the Braille Trail. Designed for the visually impaired, the trail offers a rope system to guide hikers along the path. Braille signs are set up to interpret the way. To get to the 0.7-mile-long Braille Trail, follow the signs in the park to Stapleton Drive (it's a dirt road). Follow it past the bison viewing area to the trailhead parking lot. At the trailhead of Beaver Brook Trail, follow

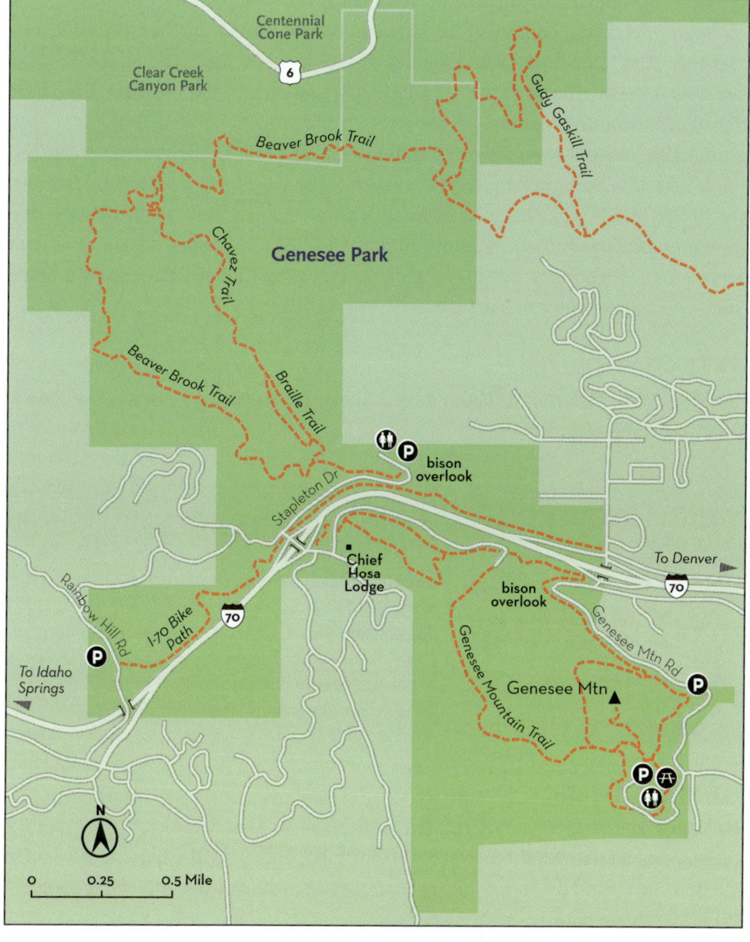

signs for Chávez Trail. You'll find the sign for the Braille Trail about 0.5 mile from the trailhead of Chávez Trail.

Wherever your hiking takes you in Genesee Park, be sure to pause to admire the historic shelters in the park. Designed by J. J. Benedict, these structures use natural stones and timber. Many of them were built by the Civilian Conservation Corps from 1937 to 1941. These classic buildings and the park itself were placed on the National Register of Historic Places in 1990.

As for the bison, the City of Denver acquired the herd in 1918 from Yellowstone National Park in an attempt to save a dying species. The herd succeeded, and the city split it in two, moving the second group of animals to Daniels Park. Each herd has about two dozen healthy beasts.

Finally, in the winter, although there is no downhill skiing here, you can certainly hike with well-gripping shoes, snowshoe, or even cross-country ski. The Beaver Brook Trail is a challenge even when it's warm and sunny, so if you attempt it in winter, be sure you are fit and well-prepared with appropriate gear. For a less strenuous, but certainly still challenging outing, snowshoe the Genesee Mountain Trail for a good chance to see bison.

EXTEND YOUR VISIT

Just down the road from Genesee Park is **Lookout Mountain**. If you're a Buffalo Bill buff, you won't want to miss it.

158 LOOKOUT MOUNTAIN

Buffalo Bill Park

Location: 987 Lookout Mountain Rd., Golden
Acreage: 75
Amenities: Views, Lariat Trail Scenic Mountain Drive, trailhead of Beaver Brook Trail, nature center and preserve, historic spring house, Buffalo Bill grave and museum, Pahaska Tepee, picnic shelter, tables, restroom, grills

GETTING THERE

BY CAR Take I-70 west to exit 256. Go north. Take a right on Lookout Mountain Rd. to the park. **BY TRANSIT** No available transit. **BY BIKE** Take the Clear Creek Trail to Golden. Take a left on Ford St., a right on 19th St., which turns into Lariat Loop Rd. Continue to the park.

It's no surprise to find a buffalo at Lookout Mountain; but, for many, the real attraction is Buffalo Bill's grave.

Atop aptly named Lookout Mountain, you can see Denver to the east, 12 miles away. To the west, you can view the Continental Divide, and to the north you can spy the city of Golden. It's a view that Colonel William Frederick Cody, who is better known as Buffalo Bill, couldn't get enough of. As his last request, he asked to be buried on top of Lookout Mountain. He was interred there in 1917.

Follow the signs up Lookout Mountain to its most popular attraction, Buffalo Bill's grave. There you pay respects to this one-time Pony Express rider and his wife, Louisa Cody. Buffalo Bill is famous for his buffalo wrangling, his acting in and producing of the Buffalo Bill's Wild West show, and his relations with Native Americans. You can find artifacts and information about this American legend in the Buffalo Bill Museum. Next to the museum is the historic 1921 Pahaska Tepee, site of the original Buffalo Bill museum. It was opened by Cody's foster son, Johnny Baker, and it is now a gift shop and tourist destination. Pahaska means "long hair," which is the name the Lakota gave Buffalo Bill.

After absorbing as much Buffalo Bill history as you wish, experience the fabulous trails and views from within the park. Stroll under ponderosa pine and Douglas fir. Like other Mountain Parks, the park features native stone shelters. These were designed by architects W. E. and A. A. Fischer and were built in 1913. On the way up the mountain, you can find the historic entry gate to the Denver Mountain Parks. Just always keep a wary eye out for cyclists ascending the famous Lariat Loop while you're driving in the park.

Beaver Brook Trail is a particularly fun excursion. About 8 miles long, this point-to-point trail meanders across Lookout Mountain along a ridge overlooking Golden. You'll scramble over boulders, cling to the side of a cliff, and amble through pine forests to magnificent views, ultimately arriving at Genesee Park.

In the winter, if the road is open, you can find short hikes throughout this park and its surrounding neighbor parks. High on the mountain, deer and elk might keep you company. The Buffalo Bill Trail leads to Colorow Point Park, the smallest of the Denver Mountain Parks. It is named after the Ute chief who held tribal council there. At an elevation of 7500 feet it provides one of the best views of the Continental Divide within the Denver Mountain Parks.

EXTEND YOUR VISIT

A mosaic of open spaces surrounds Lookout Mountain. Some are managed by Jefferson County, others by Golden, and even more by the Colorado Division of Forestry. It's a jumbled mess that even the best map has trouble capturing, but there's at least one place you'll want to reach: **Boettcher Mansion**. After a tour of the place, you can hike the **Forest Loop Trail** that starts at the Lookout Mountain Nature Center. This short, 0.5-mile trail provides a super interlude through the woods. You'll likely spot deer. It's a great walk for kids or for visiting friends who haven't quite acclimated to the altitude.

159 JAMES Q. NEWTON PARK

Meadows and aspens

Location: 11026 South Highway 285, Conifer
Acreage: 435
Amenities: Special permit picnic area, picnic shelter, picnic tables, grills, fire pits, softball field, volleyball court, horseshoe pits, hiking trails, restroom

GETTING THERE

BY CAR Take I-70 to US 285 south to the park. **BY TRANSIT** Buses CS and EX stop nearby. **BY BIKE** Take the South Platte River Trail to the Mary Carter Greenway. Go to the C470 Bike Trail. Continue left onto Deer Creek Rd. Continue on High Grade Rd. Take Pleasant Park Rd. to Hwy 285 to the park.

With a large pavilion for rent and miles and miles of trails, this Mountain Park near the town of Conifer is well worth a visit. You'll find the ponderosa pine forests you're used to, along with wide meadows filled with potential views of elk and deer. Informal trails lead hither and yon throughout the park; be sure your friends know where you're going before heading out. The park is named after the youngest Denver mayor (elected when he was thirty-five) and the first one born in Denver.

Quigg Newton, who served as mayor from 1947 to 1955, modernized Denver. He removed the patronage system, created a regional planning office, established competitive bidding, and reorganized the police department. Newton went on to become the president of the University of Colorado, growing its enrollment to twice its size. After pursuing other professional opportunities, he semi-retired to practice law at his brother-in-law's firm in Denver.

This park is a great off-the-beaten-path destination in the fall for leaf color viewing and enjoying the meadows. Several aspen grove stands can be seen throughout the park. They generally look their prettiest in the third week of September, but the display varies by up to two weeks depending on when the frost sets in.

EXTEND YOUR VISIT

If you have a summer wedding planned, you might want to make a reservation through Denver Parks and Recreation to use the giant pavilion with outdoor seating. Or, if you're not ready for that sort of commitment, enjoy a quick hike, and then jump over to the tiny town of **Conifer** for a warm cup of coffee.

160 RED ROCKS PARK

View amazing red rocks and hear fantastic music

Location: 16351 County Road 93, Morrison
Acreage: 734
Amenities: Historic amphitheater, trading post (welcome center), visitor center, exhibits, restaurant, geologic overlook, picnic area, picnic shelter, restroom, Trading Post Trail, trail connections to adjacent open space parks

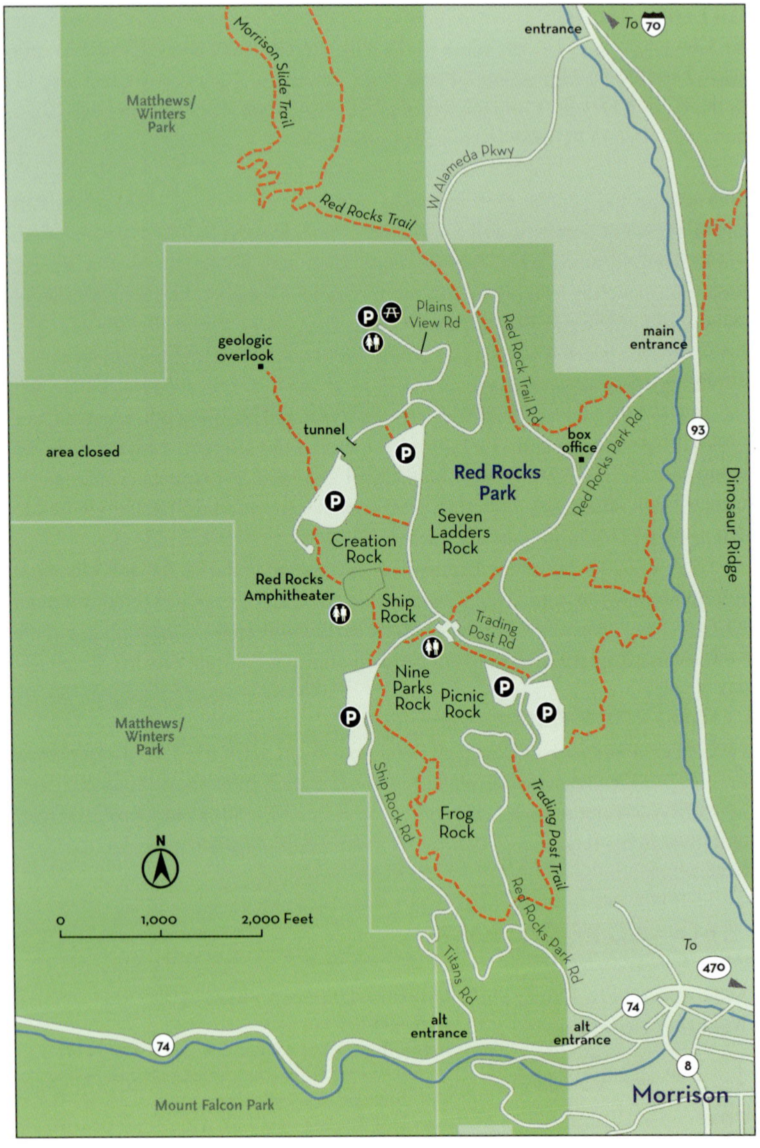

Matthews/Winters Park
Morrison Slide Trail
entrance
To 70
W Alameda Pkwy
Red Rocks Trail
Plains View Rd
geologic overlook
main entrance
Red Rock Trail Rd
93
tunnel
area closed
box office
Red Rocks Park Rd
Red Rocks Park
Seven Ladders Rock
Creation Rock
Red Rocks Amphitheater
Ship Rock
Trading Post Rd
Dinosaur Ridge
Nine Parks Rock
Picnic Rock
Matthews/Winters Park
Ship Rock Rd
Frog Rock
Trading Post Trail
Red Rocks Park Rd
N
0   1,000   2,000 Feet
Titans Rd
To 470
74
alt entrance
alt entrance
74
8
74
Morrison
Mount Falcon Park

GETTING THERE

BY CAR Take I-70 to CO-470. Go south on CO-470. Exit at W. Morrison Rd. Turn right. Exit north on CR-93/Mt. Vernon Ave. Turn left on Red Rocks Park Rd. to the park. **BY TRANSIT** No available transit. **BY BIKE** Take Bear Creek Trail to W. Morrison Rd. Continue to the park.

This park features what may be the world's most famous natural amphitheater, Red Rocks. This red-hued park also has soaring majestic rock structures and a series of short trails that connect the magnificent landmarks. From most anywhere in the park, you'll have close-up views of burgundy, orange, and red rocks; or sweeping vistas of the oddly shaped rust-colored walls in the valley and downtown Denver in the distance. The natural beauty of the park and the man-made architecture of the amphitheater are hard to separate as they blend so nicely together.

The land now known as Red Rocks Park changed hands—and its name—many times. The original owner, Marion Burtz, named it The Garden of Angels in 1872. Leonard H. Eicholtz, its second owner, added trails, ladders, and roads. The next owner, John Brisben Walker, also owned the magazine *Cosmopolitan*; when he acquired the famous set of rocks he changed the area's name to Garden of the Titans to compete with the Garden of the Gods in nearby Colorado Springs.

Walker improved the temporary stage with a wooden one and turned the area into a bona fide tourist destination. Unfortunately for him, the tourist industry was fickle, and Walker had to sell off portions of his holdings to John Ross in order to pay his bills.

Ross wanted to develop the park through his Bear Creek Development Company. At the same time, the city wanted the land for its Mountain Parks system. In the 1920s, lawsuits were filed. After a series of legal maneuvers and a decision by Colorado's Supreme Court, the city prevailed in its bid to purchase land outside of its boundaries. As a result, the city used the eminent domain process against Ross, ultimately acquiring the land for the park and reportedly paying Ross $54,133 for his troubles.

As the city grew its holdings, visionaries stepped in to decide what to do with them. George Cranmer (see Cranmer Park), head of Denver Parks, envisioned a grand amphitheater for Red Rocks. He hired Burnham F. Hoyt to design it. Together they knew the project would take many hands of labor. Fortunately for them, Mayor Benjamin Stapleton supported the idea of Roosevelt's New Deal and its Civilian Conservation Corps. The CCC arrived with dynamite and strong backs. Five years later, on June 15, 1941, Red Rocks officially opened. The premiere

performance featured Helen Jepson from the Metropolitan Opera of New York who sang "Ave Maria."

Since the grand opening, Red Rocks has hosted musical performances that have set records, awed audiences, and garnered awards; the theater itself has been awarded many prestigious recognitions for sound quality and appearance. The theater is set between the two famous red rock formations, Ship Rock (named after the *Titanic*) and Creation Rock. Concert goers have climbed hundreds of steps to the stage's 6450 elevation every season, often gasping for breath and checking their pulse at the pulse stations on the way up to their seats. Famous acts that have performed at Red Rocks include the Beatles, U2, Nat King Cole, Louis Armstrong, Harry Belafonte, Ray Charles, Ella Fitzgerald, the Eagles, Santana, Willie Nelson, Journey, the Grateful Dead, Tears for Fears, Kiss, Bon Jovi, Sting, Stevie Nicks, B. B. King, Nora Jones, Duran Duran, and DeVotchKa, among others.

Nowadays, the concert season goes from spring to fall and includes other events like movies, yoga, and oratories. In August 2015, the park was recognized as a national historic landmark. Shortly after, the historic CCC camp was entered into the National Park System. Throughout the year, though, regardless of the concert season, you'll find highly fit individuals climbing and descending the amphitheater's many steps in order to work up their heartrates and strengthen their quads.

The amphitheater, although famous and definitely visit-worthy, is just one aspect of Red Rocks Park. Hiking in this park might be even better than seeing a show. A series of short trails takes you above the amphitheater, along several ridges, and through the center of the park. The wheelchair-accessible Trading Post Trail, at only 1.5 miles, is packed with the best of Red Rocks Park. It's a moderate trail that out-of-towners and kids will love. The trail passes Frog Rock, Picnic Rock, Nine Parks Rock, Ship Rock, Creation Rock, and Seven Ladders Rock. Along the trail, you can see the geologic history embedded in the rocks. It shows how the plains clashed up against the Rockies, spilling these red-iron monoliths in their path. Dogs are allowed on the trail on leash. As with other trails in the park, watch out for rattlesnakes.

Surrounding Red Rocks Park are various open spaces managed by other entities where the various park's trails lead out of the park. In particular, the Red Rocks Trail leads hikers and bikers out to Matthews/Winters Park and onto its Morrison Slide Trail; it's a great trail for capturing a bird's eye view of the red rock monoliths and downtown Denver. If you're not a hiker or not adjusted to over 6000 feet of altitude, you can drive to the upper level parking lot and walk to the top of

OPPOSITE: *Famous for its musical amphitheater, Red Rocks Park also offers unbeatable hiking.*

the amphitheater to catch similar spectacular views down into downtown Denver. Folks with disabilities can also access these views from the upper level parking lot. Additionally, while at the top of the amphitheater, be sure to enter the Visitors Center to explore the history of Red Rocks, then descend to the Trading Post and visit the Colorado Music Hall of Fame.

Horseback riders can have some fun in the park! Horses are limited to the Red Rocks Trail, but it journeys out of the park to Matthews/Winters Park where riders can stage and park their trailers.

EXTEND YOUR VISIT

Restoration of the Civilian Conservation Corps camp just outside of Red Rocks Park is underway. Workers walked daily from this camp to do their magic at the amphitheater. Denver Parks and Recreation occasionally opens the site to visitors; check their website for more information. In the meantime, head over to the cute town of **Morrison** for a preconcert meal or after-hike ice cream.

161 LITTLE PARK

A little bigger than little

Location: 21700 State Highway 74, Idledale
Acreage: 412
Amenities: Historic stone well house, picnic area, tables, grills, restroom, volleyball court, horseshoe pits, Bear Creek Trail

GETTING THERE

BY CAR Take I-70 to CO-470. Go south. Exit W. Morrison Rd. Turn right. Go west on CO-74. Turn left to the park. **BY TRANSIT** No available transit. **BY BIKE** Take Bear Creek Trail to CO-74. Turn left to the park.

Most people pass right by Little Park, as it's hard to find and there is no signage. If traveling westbound from Denver, look for a small left-hand turn about half a mile before approaching Lair o' the Bear, a Jefferson County open space park. If you are going toward Denver, the right-hand turn is just a few feet past the Idledale sign. The parking lot for Little Park is down a steep road.

Little Park is not little. The original 40 acres of land for this park was donated by C. W. Little, and it grew to its current size through purchases and donations. Intriguing historical artifacts are apparent from the start: Look for an octagonal stone well house along the banks of Bear Creek by the parking lot.

The stone shelter at Little Park was designed by J. J. Benedict.

When driving along the Lariat Loop, cars used to have to stop to refill their radiators. This well house was a place to do that. In 1933, Bear Creek flooded and took out the town of Starbuck (at the present site of Idledale) with a gush of 20-foot high water. It made a shambles of a garage, two grocery stores, two dance halls, two cafés, a popcorn stand, the octagonal structure, and a post office. The Civilian Conservation Corps and the Works Progress Administration saved the day. They restored the shelter, moved and rebuilt the road, and helped the town recover.

Not much of Little Park is developed for hiking, although there are unofficial trails that go up its mountain. You'll find a wonderful developed 6-mile (one-way) trail along Bear Creek that connects Little Park through Lair o' the Bear to Corwina Park, Pence Park, and O'Fallon Park. Lair o' the Bear is a Jefferson County open space park and draws many families with small kids for its short and easy hikes along Bear Creek. Parking can be tight at Lair o' the Bear. If you can tack on just a third of a mile more to your hike, parking in Little Park's parking lot might be a better option. It also offers a composting toilet and trail maps.

In the winter, the Bear Creek Trail offers a perfect platform for excellent snowshoeing or cross-country skiing. Depending on snow depths, you may get away with a good pair of hiking boots that have good tread. Bear Creek draws bears, so be sure to follow proper precautions.

Horseback riders have a 6-mile (one-way) ride on the Bear Creek Trail. They can park their trailers in either Pence Park or Lair o' the Bear and then ride in either direction on the Bear Creek Trail through Corwina Park, Little Park, O'Fallon Park, Lair o' the Bear, and Pence Park.

EXTEND YOUR VISIT

Pull into **Idledale** for a warm cup of coffee, or if you'd like to continue enjoying the outdoors, experience **O'Fallon** and **Corwina Parks** next door.

162 CORWINA PARK

Panoramic gateway

Location: 25280 Highway 74, Kittredge
Acreage: 277
Amenities: Historic shelter, picnic area, tables, grills, restroom, hiking trails, Panorama Point Trail, Bear Creek Trail

GETTING THERE

BY CAR Take I-70 to CO-470. Go south on CO-470. Exit W. Morrison Rd. Turn right. Go west on CO-74. Turn left to the park. **BY TRANSIT** No available transit. **BY BIKE** Take Bear Creek Trail to CO-74. Turn left to the park.

Once again, this is another park that is a part of Frederick Law Olmsted Jr.'s vision and shopping spree (see Bergen Park). The Corwina homestead property was a beautiful tract, and Olmsted wanted it to help complete his vision of the Denver Mountain Parks system.

Hike up to Panorama Point in Corwina Park to get a 360-degree view of Evergreen.

Situated on an oxbow of Bear Creek, this ponderosa pine and Douglas fir–dominated property has the perfect characteristics for a Denver Mountain Park. Its dramatic outcroppings and amazing panoramic view from the high point have captivated Denverites since 1914. In 1918 the city added a shelter, water well, and pedestrian bridge to enhance the experience.

When visiting the park, be sure to hike up Panorama Point Trail to catch some 360-degree views of the Evergreen area; it's 2.4 miles round-trip. You can also jump on the Bear Creek Trail down by the creek, which goes for almost 6 miles one-way. It connects a chain of parks that are also on the National Register of Historic Places. (See Little Park, Pence Park, and O'Fallon Park.)

Horseback riders may enjoy a 6-mile (one-way) ride on the Bear Creek Trail. They can park their trailers in either Pence Park or Lair o' the Bear and then ride in either direction, but only on the Bear Creek Trail.

EXTEND YOUR VISIT

Head over to **O'Fallon Park** to see the historic four-sided chimney.

163 O'FALLON PARK

Fireplace park

Location: 25500 State Highway 74, Evergreen
Acreage: 814
Amenities: Historic fireplace/monument, picnic area, picnic tables, grills, Picnic Loop Trail, West Ridge Trail, Meadow View Trail, Bear Creek Trail

GETTING THERE

BY CAR Take I-70 to CO-470. Go south. Exit W. Morrison Rd. Turn right. Go west on CO-74. Turn left to the park. **BY TRANSIT** No available transit. **BY BIKE** Take Bear Creek Trail to CO-74. Turn left to the park.

Starting his career at his father's radio station, KFEL, and then moving on to law school, Martin O'Fallon represented the less fortunate through his law firm. When the city wanted to finish its vision of creating a large tract of open space that included Corwina and Pence Parks, O'Fallon donated the remaining acres in 1938 to complete the puzzle. His only requirement? The land must be for "the use and pleasure of the people."

At the time, it was common for Denverites to drive the Lariat Loop, finding places along the road to stop and enjoy. Since this chain of parks sits along the riparian Bear Creek, people would pull over, add water to their radiators, and enjoy the park's amenities. They used the tall, four-sided chimney made of local rocks that you can still see today to cook their catch, warm their hands, or enjoy a cup of hot cocoa. Today, hikers find it's a nice place to take a break.

To get to the chimney, a great hike for younger kids, find the picnic area past the park entry. Walk up the road to the north along Bear Creek. The kids will love the ambling creek and scenic views. At the end of the road is a footbridge that takes you to the start of Meadow View Trail. Follow that trail to the left to reach the Stone Chimney Trail, which takes you to the four-sided chimney. Round-trip is less than a mile.

For an additional 6 miles of unpaved trail through O'Fallon Park, you can make several nice loops through high meadows and over rock croppings on the West Ridge Trail and the Meadow View Trail. They loop each other and combine with the

A four-sided chimney and some tall tales await you at O'Fallon Park.

Bear Creek Trail, which you can take either direction for several miles. Both of these trails make a challenging snowshoe hike in the winter; for an easier snowshoe outing that's just as picturesque, stay on the Bear Creek Trail. Horseback riders can park their trailers in either Pence Park or Lair o' the Bear and ride in either direction on the Bear Creek Trail.

You can hike east to Corwina Park or west to Pence Park. All trails in O'Fallon Park are closed to mountain bikes and are hiker-only. The exception is Bear Creek Trail.

164 PENCE PARK

Bear Creek Trail southern terminus

Location: 4400 Parmalee Gulch Rd., Evergreen
Acreage: 304
Amenities: Bear Creek Trail, parking, restroom, picnic tables, grill

GETTING THERE

BY CAR Take I-70 to CO-470. Go south. Exit W. Morrison Rd. Turn right. Go west on CO-74. Turn left on Myers Gulch Rd. Continue to Permalee Gulch Rd. to the park. **BY TRANSIT** No available transit. **BY BIKE** Take Bear Creek Trail to CO-74. Turn left to Myers Gulch Rd. Continue to Permalee Gulch Rd. to the park.

Kingsley A. Pence was an opportunist. He gathered together his real estate friends, members of the Motor Club, and his buddies at the chamber of commerce and collaborated on an idea. They wanted to capture the tourist trade that Colorado Springs had attracted with the Garden of the Gods. To do that, they would find money to convince the city to buy land for the Denver Mountain Parks, an idea hatched by John Brisben Walker (see Red Rocks Park). They were successful. During the city elections in 1912, the Mountain Parks Amendment passed with an eight-thousand-vote majority.

Pence Park, named after Kingsley Pence, is the southern terminus of the Bear Creek Trail and completes the tract that comprises Corwina, O'Fallon, and Pence Parks. In Pence Park, you'll find north-facing slopes covered with dense ponderosa pine forests; at the park's highest point in its southwest corner these transition to rocky outcrops. Cyclists can ride along the 6-mile (one-way) Bear Creek Trail from here all the way to Little Park, and hikers will enjoy hiker-only access to high points along the 2-mile round-trip Independence Mountain Trail.

In the winter, point your snowshoes or well-treaded hiking boots up the Independence Mountain Trail to breathe in clean, fresh, winter air. You might even enjoy picking up a few pine cones and twigs to build small fairy houses at the base of trees.

Horseback riders have a 6-mile (one-way) ride on Bear Creek Trail if they park their trailers in either Pence Park or Lair o' the Bear. The ride can be taken in either direction, on Bear Creek Trail only, through Corwina Park, Little Park, O'Fallon Park, Lair o' the Bear, and Pence Park.

EXTEND YOUR VISIT

Be sure to visit nearby **O'Fallon Park** to see the impressive four-sided chimney.

165 ECHO LAKE PARK

Start here for Mount Evans

Location: 13261 State Highway 103, Idaho Springs
Acreage: 602
Amenities: Echo Lake Lodge, restaurant, historic shelter, picnic area, picnic tables, grills, restroom, fishing, trails and trail connections

GETTING THERE

BY CAR Take I-70 to CO-103. Turn left to the park. **BY TRANSIT** No available transit. **BY BIKE** Take Clear Creek Trail up to Lookout Mountain Rd. Continue to Evergreen Pkwy. Continue to Squaw Pass Rd. to the park.

At 10,600 feet in elevation, Echo Lake Park is the jumping off point to get to Mount Evans, whether it be by car, bike, or foot. But it's also a nice place to come and visit, cast a line, or throw a kayak into the water for some alpine views. You'll find the amenities you usually find in Denver's Mountain Parks, including a lodge built by J. J. Benedict in 1926. The Echo Lake Lodge features a good restaurant and gift shop; it also provides campground information for the Arapahoe National Forest and information about backpacking trails, including the Chicago Lakes Trail and Lincoln Lake Trail, which lead you up Mount Evans.

The short 2-mile trail around Echo Lake is great for visiting family who may not be ready for the Mount Evans's altitude but still want a mountain experience with spectacular views. Echo Lake Park represents the subalpine ecosystem, with surrounding forests of Englemann spruce, subalpine fir, and limber pine. In the winter, the road to Mount Evans closes, but at Echo Lake, you can ice fish, ice

A WINDING ROAD TO THE SKY

The Mount Evans Scenic Byway isn't for the faint of heart. With steep cliffs, unbelievable views, and nary a side rail, you'll need to focus as you drive around hairpin turns and undulating climbs. It's the highest road in North America, and it climbs more than 7000 feet in just 28 miles, reaching an altitude of 14,130 feet. Building it was a feat itself.

At first, the City of Denver thought it would build the road as part of a complicated deal to create a national park out of Echo Lake, Summit Lake, and Mount Evans's summit. Eventually, the Colorado Department of Transportation ended up building the road, but it took much longer than expected due to the inability of the foreman to hire healthy men who could work full days at that altitude.

After paying to access the road to the top, you'll pass through ponderosa pine forests, finally making it above timberline. It's in this strange landscape that you find a singular amalgam of hardy wildflowers, lichens and grasses, furry mammals like pikas and marmots, rock-jumping mountain goats, and alpine lakes. Mount Goliath, managed by Denver Botanic Gardens, features bristlecone pines; it's on your way and it's worth a stop.

You might also see cars in black and white wraps when you're on the top of the mountain. Disguised to hide their brands, these cars are prototypes sent by automakers to this easily accessible high elevation area to test the oxygen and braking systems of future models.

If you decide to drive to the top of Mount Evans on the scenic byway, be super careful to accommodate the cyclists you see, many of whom are training for international-level events. The road is generally open Memorial Day to Labor Day. The exact opening and closing dates are weather dependent. Volatile weather during the summer requires you to be ready for wind, rain, lightning, hail, and even snow.

Many people bypass Echo Lake on the way to summit Mount Evans, but its vistas are worth a visit, especially for out-of-towners adjusting to Colorado's altitude.

skate, snowshoe, and cross-country ski when ice and snow conditions permit. Be sure to bundle up as the winds coming down from Mount Evans can shiver you completely through.

EXTEND YOUR VISIT

Add a drive to the highest paved road in North America, up to the top of **Mount Evans**. Be sure to check weather conditions for road openings and closings.

Acknowledgments

Putting together a book is a team effort. I'd be very remiss if I didn't thank the fabulous and amazing librarians at the Denver Public Library's Western History Collection, the interesting and intriguing rangers at Denver Parks and Recreation, and the wonderful and awesome walking movement leaders and member-owners at Walk2Connect.

In addition, I can't thank the team at Mountaineers Books enough for their editorial direction and copyediting perfection. Thank you to Diane Durrett, Mary Metz, and Kate Rogers.

Special hugs go to strangers who became true friends in our adventure to walk all of Denver's seventy-eight neighborhoods and its trails. To Robbin, Lisa, Debbie, Laura, Melissa, Gail, Shirley, Georgie, Carol, Jane, Janice, Julie, Terry, and Dawn: Thank you, I love you all.

To Mrs. Karen Haas of Skyline Elementary School in Solana Beach, California, for forcing me to diagram sentences; and Mrs. Beth Carson of the Orme School in Mayer, Arizona, for forcing me to write stories every day in my journal; you deserve the biggest hugs of them all.

I must thank Bette D. Peters, Louise Farrah, and Leland H. Peters for their excellent book *Denver's City Park*, which was referenced for the City Park entry.

We must thank Denver's early city pioneers for their long-sighted vision and spirited initiatives. The current Denver leaders would do well to adopt their long views.

And finally, a special shout-out must also go to the hundreds of volunteers and organizations who have friended the park system. They have often given it a voice, an extra hand, and written words of support. Thank you especially to The Park People and the Denver Mountain Parks Foundation for holding grace and inspiration.

OPPOSITE: *The City of Takayama Park includes a small bonsai garden such as you might see in Denver's sister city in Japan.*

Funicular
Trail
To Upper
North Parking Lot
P
YOU MUST
STAY
ON THE TRAIL
No-Off Trail Use
No Climbing

Resources

Of course no one person can know everything about Denver's amazing array of parks, so I drew upon a number of resources in compiling the information found in this book. Here are a few that were particularly helpful.

The Denver Library, specifically in its Western History Genealogy Department and its Digital Collection, offers an incredible array of writings about the region's history. Two that I found especially helpful were:

Colorado Portrait and Biography, edited by Henrietta E. Bromwell:
https://history.denverlibrary.org/sites/history/files/BromwellColoradoPortrait andBiographicalIndex.pdf
Neighborhood History Guides: history.denverlibrary.org/neighborhoods

BOOKS

Dawson, J. Frank *Place Names in Colorado*. Denver: J. F. Dawson Pub. Co., 1954.

Elliott, R. Donald and Doris L. (Salmen) Elliott (ed.) *Place Names of Colorado*. Denver: Colorado Council of Genealogical Societies, 1999.

Goodstein, Phil H. *Denver Streets: Names, Numbers, Locations, Logic*. Denver: New Social Publications, 1994

Hoffecker, John F. *Twenty-Seven Square Miles*. Colorado: US Fish and Wildlife Service, 2001.

Noel, William, William J. Hansen et al. *The Park Hill Neighborhood*. Denver: Historic Denver Guides, 2002.

Peters, Bette D., Louise Farrah and Leland H. Peters. *Denver's City Park*. Denver: University of Colorado at Denver, 1985.

Pyle, Robert Michael. *The Thunder Tree*. Corvallis, OR: Oregon State University Press, 2011.

Skari, David. *High Line Canal: Meandering Through Time: A Historical Trail Guide*. Denver: C&M Press, 2003.

Stone, Wilbur Fiske. *History of Colorado*, Vol. 4. Chicago: S.J. Clarke, 1918.

OPPOSITE: *Denver's Mountain Parks were developed so that Denver residents would have their own place, like Red Rocks Park, to play in the mountains.*

PERIODICALS

The Denver Post
Rocky Mountain News

WEBSITES

Denverite: https://denverite.com
Denver Parks and Recreation: Denvergov.org
Red Rocks Park: www.redrockspark.com/author/tqjohnson
Red Rocks Park and Amphitheatre: www.redrocksonline.com

Index

About the Author

Chris Englert, an avid traveler and country counter, retired early from higher education publishing sales. She hit the trails of the world and hasn't stopped walking since. Her love for connecting while walking has taken her around the globe, through the world's amazing cities, and into the world's unbelievable beauty.

Chris writes and maintains two blogs, at EatWalkLearn.com and DenverByFoot.com. She has authored the top-selling book on urban hiking in Denver, *The Best Urban Hikes: Denver* and the top-selling book on Denver's neighborhoods, *Walking Denver's Neighborhoods*. Chris loves to speak at events, enthusiastically motivating the world to get outdoors for adventure and discovery.

In early 2019, Chris took off on a four-month Latin American adventure as a digital nomad. Her forty-five companions were a combination of Gen Xers and Millennials. Whether playing her first game of ultimate Frisbee in Santiago, Chile, or picking coffee in the Cocora Valley of Colombia, her heart always remains at home with her superman of a husband, their incredibly talented teenager, and an overzealous giant schnauzer, Zeus.

Chris loves to hear from her readers. You can contact her on social media at @DenverbyFoot for all things Denver or @EatWalkLearn for global walking vacations. Be sure to share your next adventure with her.

MOUNTAINEERS BOOKS is a leading publisher of mountaineering literature and guides—including our flagship title, *Mountaineering: The Freedom of the Hills*—as well as adventure narratives, natural history, and general outdoor recreation. Through our two imprints, Skipstone and Braided River, we also publish titles on sustainability and conservation. We are committed to supporting the environmental and educational goals of our organization by providing expert information on human-powered adventure, sustainable practices at home and on the trail, and preservation of wilderness.

The Mountaineers, founded in 1906, is a 501(c)(3) nonprofit outdoor recreation and conservation organization whose mission is to enrich lives and communities by helping people "explore, conserve, learn about and enjoy the lands and waters of the Pacific Northwest and beyond." One of the largest such organizations in the United States, it sponsors classes and year-round outdoor activities throughout the Pacific Northwest, including climbing, hiking, backcountry skiing, snowshoeing, camping, kayaking, sailing, and more. The Mountaineers also supports its mission through its publishing division, Mountaineers Books, and promotes environmental education and citizen engagement. For more information, visit The Mountaineers Program Center, 7700 Sand Point Way NE, Seattle, WA 98115-3996; phone 206-521-6001; www.mountaineers.org; or email info@mountaineers.org.

Our publications are made possible through the generosity of donors and through sales of more than 700 titles on outdoor recreation, sustainable lifestyle, and conservation. To donate, purchase books, or learn more, visit us online:

MOUNTAINEERS BOOKS

1001 SW Klickitat Way, Suite 201 • Seattle, WA 98134

800-553-4453 • mbooks@mountaineersbooks.org • www.mountaineersbooks.org

An independent nonprofit publisher since 1960

Mountaineers Books is proud to support the Leave No Trace Center for Outdoor Ethics, whose mission is to promote and inspire responsible outdoor recreation through education, research, and partnerships. The Leave No Trace program is focused specifically on human-powered (nonmotorized) recreation. For more information, visit www.lnt.org.